Critical accla___ ___
Nobody's Perfect:
Living and Growing with
Children Who Have Special Needs

"Nancy B. Miller has written an important, upbeat guidebook for parents raising a child with a disability. Her insights about the emotional journey these families undertake are right on the mark. And her ideas for building self-esteem, coping in difficult times, and achieving independence make good sense. This is a book worth passing on."

Gilbert M. Gaul
two-time Pulitzer Prize winner for **The Philadelphia Inquirer**
author of **Giant Steps: The Story of One Boy's Struggle to Walk**
parent of a child with spina bifida

"Nancy Miller has a genuine understanding of the unique needs of parents who face the daily challenges of raising a child with special needs. *Nobody's Perfect* provides anecdotes, information and—most importantly—strategies for successful parenting. This book is a 'must' for every parent and professional bookshelf!"

Richard D. Lavoie
Executive Director, Riverview School
Producer, "How Difficult Can This Be? The F.A.T. City Video"

"Nancy and the Moms have cut through to the essence of so many . . . issues. The content . . . is wonderful. I would call it a parents' pocket support group! It is down to earth and practical. . . . The Moms say out loud things that pass through every parent's head . . . and do so with an amazing amount of insight that was indeed learned and can be achieved by other parents in the same situation."

Mary C. Cerreto, Ph.D.
Assistant Commissioner
Department of Mental Retardation
The Massachusetts Office of Health and Human Services

"If [this book] had been around when my daughter was growing up, I would have soaked up its reassurance. Dr. Miller cheers parents on while offering helpful suggestions for making things easier for the family. . . . Every parent who has a child with a disability should keep a copy on the bedside table."

Sandra Kaufman
author of the highly acclaimed book **Retarded Isn't Stupid, Mom!**,
a personal story about raising a child with a disability

"Nancy and the Moms have certainly demonstrated parent–professional collaboration! This book is a lovely mix of strategies for whole families. It contains excellent support and information for parents of all ages [and] terrific insight from which others can learn."

Patricia McGill Smith
Executive Director, National Parent Network on Disabilities

"This bountiful volume provides an amazingly detailed roadmap through the complicated hills and valleys of that 'foreign land' we parents of children with special needs must all explore. . . . This wonderfully helpful book will be the *first* book I will recommend to new parents."

Emily Perl Kingsley
former board member, National Down Syndrome Congress
"Sesame Street" writer
parent of a young adult with Down syndrome

"As an occupational therapist who has worked with physically handicapped children, this book would have been a 'god-send' to many families experiencing life with their special needs child. As an adoptive parent of a medically fragile child, each chapter was devoured, as Dr. Miller put down in words what we have been living the past 2 years! It's wonderful that the stages of adaptation have finally been identified."

Mark and Teri Muir
adoptive parents of a child with complex health care needs
La Habra, California

"I am not aware of a book like this, and I think it fills a need. [It is] valid . . . with good insights and recommendations. . . . The how-to-manage ideas are varied, real, and sometimes funny. . . . The stories about real parents and what they are doing to survive . . . are very supportive. . . . I would definitely buy this book and definitely recommend it."

Barbara C. Cutler, Ed.D.
New Autism Consultants
author of **You, Your Child, and "Special" Education: A Guide to Making the System Work**
parent of a young man with autism

"This is an important contribution to the field of families and disability—and most importantly—to parents, themselves. . . . Dr. Miller's descriptions of the four stages that most parents experience and re-experience as they live and grow with their child are a wonderful blend of research-based knowledge and . . . parents' own stories. . . . By weaving together [this] information, . . . Dr. Miller has written a book that 'rings true' in a way that parents will not only recognize but find reassuring as well."

Betsy Santelli
Coordinator, Parent to Parent National Survey Project
Beach Center on Families and Disability
University of Kansas

Nobody's Perfect

Nobody's Perfect

Living and Growing with Children Who Have Special Needs

by
Nancy B. Miller, Ph.D., M.S.W.
Private Practice
and
Assistant Clinical Professor
UCLA Department of Psychiatry
and Biobehavioral Sciences
Los Angeles, California
with
"The Moms"
Susie Burmester, Diane G. Callahan,
Janet Dieterle, and Stephanie Niedermeyer

Illustrations by J. C. Dieterle

·P A U L·H·
BROOKES
PUBLISHING C^O

Baltimore · London · Toronto · Sydney

Paul H. Brookes Publishing Co.
Post Office Box 10624
Baltimore, Maryland 21285-0624

Typeset by Maple-Vail Composition Services,
Binghamton, New York.
Manufactured in the United States of America by
BookCrafters, Falls Church, Virginia.

Library of Congress Cataloging-in-Publication Data

Miller, Nancy B., 1939–
  Nobody's perfect : living and growing with children who
  have special needs / by Nancy B. Miller with moms
  Susie Burmester . . . [et al.] ; illustrations by J. C. Dieterle.
    p.   cm.
  Includes bibliographical references (p.   ) and index.
  ISBN 1-55766-143-X
  1. Handicapped children—Family relationships. 2. Handi-
capped children—Care. 3. Parents of handicapped children. 4.
Parenting.
  I. Title.
HQ773.6.M54   1994   93-2556
                                                          CIP

British Library Cataloging-in-Publication data are available from
the British Library.

Contents

Foreword

Nobody's Perfect is a remarkably practical and useful book. Breaking down the adjustment process into countless distinct and specific coping strategies, this bountiful volume provides an amazingly detailed roadmap through the complicated hills and valleys of that "foreign land" we parents of children with special needs must all explore. The warmth and consummate reality of the contributions from the "real Moms" make *Nobody's Perfect* readable, understandable, and utterly recognizable by validating feelings and experiences we parents all have shared. This wonderfully helpful book will be the *first* book I will recommend to new parents.

Emily Perl Kingsley

Emily Perl Kingsley is a writer for the popular children's television show "Sesame Street," for which she has received nine Emmy Awards and six Emmy nominations. The mother of a young adult with Down syndrome, Ms. Kingsley is a frequent lecturer on that subject and on mental retardation and disability rights. Her son, Jason, will graduate from high school in June 1994 with a regular full academic diploma.

Preface

In February 1987, I was invited to have dinner with four women who are mothers of children with special needs. We had met 6 years earlier at the UCLA Intervention Program for Handicapped Children when their children enrolled in the infant–toddler program and they joined one of the weekly parent support groups I was leading.

In the beginning, none of the mothers knew anything about "special needs" or how to be the parent of a child who had some. All they knew was that their worlds had been turned upside down, and they needed to find help for their children and a sense of understanding and direction for themselves.

During our reunion dinner, the Moms recounted their adventures with their children since "the beginning." Their stories ranged from heartbreaking to hilarious and were filled with hope, disappointments, successes, and frustration. With all of their stories, my strongest memory of that evening was the collective ability of these women to put their struggles in the broader perspective of their total lives. I was particularly impressed with the bond of friendship among the four of them, especially considering the diversity of their personalities, cultural backgrounds, lifestyles, and goals. Their children, whose special needs were not at all similar, had brought them together by chance; they stayed together because they saw their differences as strengths; and they had developed the kind of friendship that could be the subject of a book in itself.

These four women had changed since "the beginning." They

continued to face challenges in finding services they could count on, and they all experienced daily hassles that sometimes seemed insurmountable. But their basic attitudes were different. They knew they would meet the challenges and handle the hassles somehow, and they knew that having some balance in their family lives was most important.

These four families were adapting and functioning in positive ways. I knew many other families who were also living and growing with children who had special needs—some with fewer challenges and some with many more. Although every family's experience is unique, I wondered if there were enough common feelings and attitudes that families "went through." And I wondered if these feelings and attitudes could be described in a way that might help families to know that what they are going through is "normal."

After our reunion dinner, I invited the Moms to collaborate with me, to talk about their experiences, and to help me write this book; they readily agreed. After 5 years of intense and unforgettable time together, this book was born.

The book begins with brief autobiographies of the Moms up to the time when their children with special needs were born. These are followed by Part I, which describes a model of adaptation. The model, which evolved from my conversations with the Moms, my clinical work with families, and the research and writings of other professionals and parents, consists of four stages—Surviving, Searching, Settling In, and Separating. Each stage is described and applied directly to family living, with my co-authors' reflections about their experiences and feelings woven into the text.

Part II, Strategies for Successful Adaptation, describes specific relationships that are important in the lives of both parents and children with special needs. These include relationships with partners, other children, friends and relatives, professionals, and people you meet in public. Each chapter includes a list of issues that often arise, explains ways parents may react, and suggests ideas to prevent or reduce problems and to build better relationships. Following Part II is an epilogue entitled "The Moms and Their Children Today," which briefly brings the reader up to date as the children are entering their adolescent years and the mothers are facing their own "letting go" issues.

Throughout the text, the pronouns "he" and "she" are used alternately for convenience and readability.

The mothers and I have written this book for you if you have a child who needs something extra for a developmental or medical reason. As you begin to read this book, you may be asking how "children with special needs" are different from "typical children who have special needs sometimes." Children with special needs may require more help more often and for longer periods of time— sometimes for their entire lives. Some of the more familiar problems that result in children having special needs include attention deficit hyperactivity disorder, asthma, autism, cerebral palsy, diabetes, Down syndrome, epilepsy, hearing or visual impairments, learning disabilities, mental retardation, spina bifida, and severe emotional disturbances. In this book, "children with special needs" refers to children who, because of their disabilities, may need any of the following:

- Specialized interventions at home or school or in the community because of delays in language, physical, cognitive, or social development
- Regular medical interventions for health conditions
- Individualized education programs for learning disabilities
- Extra caregiving for daily living skills
- Special aids to enable and enhance communication
- Special therapies for improving physical strength and coordination or for persistent emotional or behavior problems
- Special equipment to increase mobility

In the "old days," there wasn't much help and there wasn't much hope for children who had special needs. There were exceptions, of course (there are usually exceptions to everything), but for the most part, children with disabilities were undereducated, underestimated, and undervalued.

Things are changing. We are increasingly aware in our society that all children have the right to be valued, educated, and challenged. People are learning that "special needs" are simply a matter of degree.

Laws are being enacted to ensure the rights of people with disabilities. Technology is rapidly advancing, medical breakthroughs are occurring more frequently, educational and therapeutic programs are improving, and professionals are enhancing their knowledge and skills. A wider range of services for children and their families is emerging as parents become more empowered advocates. We have a long way to go, but as parents, professionals, politicians, and people with special needs work together, we are already creating a new kind of future.

Nancy B. Miller, Ph.D., M.S.W.

About the Author

Nancy B. Miller, Ph.D., M.S.W., Post Office Box 2046, Los Angeles, California 90049

Nancy B. Miller has a private psychotherapy and consulting practice in Los Angeles, California. She is Assistant Clinical Professor in the UCLA Department of Psychiatry and Biobehavioral Sciences and is a popular guest speaker and workshop leader nationwide.

Dr. Miller has been on the UCLA faculty for more than 20 years. She was Social Work Training Coordinator with the University Affiliated Project, developed courses in developmental disabilities in the School of Social Welfare, was Social Work and

Clinical Research Coordinator for the UCLA Intervention Program for Handicapped Children in the Department of Pediatrics, and has been a consultant for campus Child Care Services for 20 years.

Dr. Miller received her Master of Social Work degree from Michigan State University and her doctorate in anthropology from UCLA. Her decision to study broader cultural issues was an extension of her research of siblings of children with disabilities and her work with Native American families in the Navajo Nation and in Los Angeles. Her current focus is the influence of American cultural values on attitudes about disabilities.

Dr. Miller has numerous professional publications in books and journals, including several pioneering studies of brothers and sisters of children and adults with disabilities. She co-authored the *Therapist's Guidebook for Systematic Parent Training* (1977) with Wm. Hans Miller, Ph.D., and was editor of the *Proceedings of the First Intertribal Symposium on Mental Retardation* (1978). She also edited the *Peer Counseling for Seniors Training Guide* (1986), which won the California Governor's Award in 1989.

Dr. Miller has appeared on national television and radio and was the originator and writer for two UCLA films, *Siblings as Behavior Modifiers* (1973) and *Jamie* (1972). She also writes for children and has published in *Highlights for Children*.

About the Moms
and Their Children

DIANE AND CATHERINE

I'm the fourth oldest of nine. My parents were Mexicans, and we lived in a small farm town in California. We spoke only Spanish at home until we started school and our teachers told us to go home and speak English to our parents.

For several years, we all got up at 4:30 in the morning, put on layers of clothes, and drove to the fields to pick cotton. As the day got hotter, we'd peel off layers of clothes. My mother brought wonderful burritos with her homemade tortillas wrapped in waxed paper; they'd stay warm in the day's heat. We'd find some shade and have our lunch. The best part was the end of the day when they'd let all of us kids jump in the cotton that was piled high in the trucks.

My father wanted a better life for us so we moved to Los Angeles where he could get a better job and buy some property. I don't know how he did it, but he bought a corner lot with two houses. He rented out the bigger one, and we lived in the smaller one. There were my mom and dad and seven kids. We eventually moved into the bigger three-bedroom house, and my parents had two more kids. I remember getting the mattresses out every night and putting them in the living room.

I was 11 years old when we started school here, and I knew we were different. We were the only Mexicans; I never heard other kids talking about getting mattresses out. They all seemed to have their own bedrooms, and they didn't all have to share things. We had only one bathroom. I don't remember it being so bad. We just did it.

After we moved to Los Angeles, both of my parents worked, and the responsibility for the house and babysitting fell to the older kids. But that's part of our heritage, whether the mother worked or not.

After high school, I went to college for a year. Then I realized I didn't want to go to school any more. I got a job as a bookkeeper at a small aircraft business, and that's where I met Ray. He was 25, recently back from Vietnam. He got rid of everything he owned when he was in the service. These were things that he later wished he had kept, but at that point he didn't want any memories of that time. Everybody likes Ray. He always finds time to help other people. That's what attracted me to him. He was such a good person, and I just knew he would be a good husband and father.

Life was nice after we got married. We had a house. We waited 6 years to have children, and then we had Sara. She was 6 weeks premature, but she was healthy and beautiful. We loved her so much. Two years later, we were ready to have another child. My second pregnancy was normal, and the doctor scheduled a repeat C-section. When Catherine was delivered in September 1979, I knew something was not right. The room got very quiet. Then the pediatrician said, "I want to show the mother the baby." He held her up so I could see her and said, "The baby has a problem, and it has to be taken care of right away. Your daughter has a hole in her back, which means the spinal cord has not grown properly."

He turned her around and showed me the opening about the size of a quarter, and said. "This has to be closed to prevent the area from getting infected. There will probably be some paralysis. She's not moving her legs very much at all. I'm going to go out and tell your husband and get this taken care of."

I said, "It's a girl? You're kidding. I thought it would be a boy." That's all that registered at first. She was so pretty, her color was good, and she was a big baby.

And then I started crying; not sobbing, just tears coming. They took Catherine away and took me to the recovery room. No one would tell me how much she weighed or how long she was, although I kept asking. No one told me the "normal" things.

Ray was in and out of my room every 20 minutes, going back and forth from my room to the surgery floor. The surgery to close the opening took 4 hours.

A week later, Catherine developed fluid in the ventricles of her brain and had to have surgery again to put in a shunt. They told us that hydrocephalus goes along with this, and the shunt would drain fluid before it could build up. She had a condition I had never heard of and couldn't even pronounce for a while: myelomeningocele which means opening of the spine. The lay term is *spina bifida*.

The neurosurgeon was very positive. He said children with spina bifida can grow up to lead normal lives. They need braces or crutches or have to use a wheelchair, but that doesn't prevent them from leading full and rewarding lives.

A lot of my relatives and friends said, "Why would that happen to you? It's not fair." I didn't really feel it wasn't fair. I remember lying in my hospital bed and thinking there must be a reason that God gave us Catherine. When they were doing the surgery, I thought, "Okay. You let her be born and she's alive. Don't take her away. You already gave me her." With Sara, I remember that I just loved her so much. That feeling is so euphoric when you have a baby, and I remember being pregnant and thinking I couldn't love another one that much. After Catherine was born, I thought, "You can. You can love another baby as much as the first one. Just don't take her away."

SUSIE AND BETSY

My memories of our wonderful farmhouse in eastern Pennsylvania where we lived with our grandparents go back to when I was 3 years old. While my father worked for the railroad as a tariff clerk, my mother was busy raising my two brothers, my sister, and me. She worked the huge garden with my grandmother, and one of my favorite memories is working beside them in the big kitchen as we canned and preserved all of our fruits and vegetables.

We had a large extended family on my mother's side, and holidays were great fun. Everyone sang in German, including all of the kids, even though we didn't have any clue what the words meant. I still don't, but when I hear the old melodies I can lapse right into the language.

I was an intensely happy child. I can remember waking up happy. I loved to talk and play and did both with endless energy. I was quickly labeled the "noisy" one—a reputation that I have cultivated carefully to this day.

My mother and I are incredibly alike. We look alike and have a similar sense of humor and creativity. We are both tenacious and enthusiastic about everything we do, whether it be work or play. I can remember my mother staying up all night to make incredible dresses for my sister and me for special occasions. She could stretch those pennies while making us look beautiful. Whoever wrote a "a silk purse out of a sow's ear" must have been at her sewing machine during those years.

My grandmother was another major influence in my life. She was a wonderful cook and loved to cook for lots of people. I'm sure I get that from her. Her passion was her garden; she respected and honored the earth and passed that love on to us. When I am in need of a comfort zone, I retreat to my vast treasure of memories of her. My grandmother died when I was 12, the darkest day of my childhood, and I often wonder what further influence she would have had on us if she had lived longer.

After high school and a few years as a dental assistant, I became a flight attendant and flew for 8 years. Four of us shared an apartment in New York. We were smart, ambitious, and single, and we spent every cent we earned on clothes and travel. We had free passes to everywhere.

I met Bruce when I was touring the TV studio where he worked. We dated for a year. I thought he was sweet, shy, and funny, and one of the kindest people I had ever met. I have always loved being married to Bruce. He was so smart, resourceful, full of ideas, and calm. I flew for 5 more years, and my relationship with Bruce was solid and happy. He was producing TV game shows and mastering the computer. We had a sailboat, and we traveled a lot. We bought a house ("charming, in need of work") and formed friendships that have endured to this day. We had Andy, who was bright and gorgeous, a total joy. Andy grew, and we prospered. A year later, we moved to Los Angeles. It was a positive career change for Bruce—a chance he couldn't pass up.

The next 2 years were good for us. We were settling in our new environment, Andy was coming into his own, and we were meeting new people. Then I got pregnant. We were elated.

In November 1979, Betsy Alison Burmester was born. As soon as I saw her, I had some real concerns. Something was wrong. All of the Apgar scores were fine, and the pediatrician said, "Everything seems okay." But I knew Betsy wasn't okay. She wasn't pink and rosy; she was gray and dusky, couldn't suck, and had poor muscle tone. I sneaked into the nursery to read her chart, looking for a clue of what might be wrong.

Two weeks after we brought Betsy home, she stopped breathing. We dashed to the emergency room, and Betsy was admitted to the hospital. After many tests without any conclusive findings, we took her home on an infant monitor—a machine to measure heart rate to tell us if Betsy stopped breathing. We began the long trek of developmental testing, seeing specialists, and watching our lives change dramatically.

STEPHANIE AND EMMA ROSE

I was born and raised in California, the oldest of four children. We often moved, but always lived near college and university campuses while my father was pursuing his graduate degrees and later when he became a college professor. As a family, we were deeply influenced by his interests and became involved in many of the social, political, and human development movements of the '60s. We marched in picket lines, went to rock festivals, and became very involved with the transcendental meditation movement. Despite the fact that we were very poor at times and always seemed to be on the move, my mother managed to create a very loving and stable home environment.

My experiences growing up gave me an early awareness of the social and political issues in our country. My family helped me to cultivate values and principles that are not always popular in our culture but have stood me well, especially in raising my own family. My ambition was always to be a full-time mother, a role I find deeply fulfilling on many levels.

Paul and I met when I was 22. The thing in my life that I'm the most thankful for is that we found each other and got married. We had a strong sense of having been brought together by a destiny that was guiding both of our lives. Paul is a person of great strength, resolution, and resourcefulness, but the quality in him that I most admire and fell in love with is his capacity for loving and nurturing others.

We had been married about 2 years when I got pregnant. We were very happy about it. We wanted to have a home delivery because we felt that a normal pregnancy shouldn't be treated as an illness that necessarily requires hospitalization. We found some books on alternative childbirth and a childbirth center that specialized in home births. Paul participated in the whole process.

On September 30, 1980, Emma Rose was born. After an unexpected breech birth, she was breathing well, but her body was very floppy and she didn't cry. She flunked her Apgar test. I've forgotten the score; I guess that was my first rejection of a test score.

She looked beautiful. She had red hair and a pretty delicate face. Her skin was a wonderful pale pink. Her first sound was a very quiet "waaaa." She wouldn't nurse; instead she stuck her bottom lip out in a gesture that astounded me. She had no instinct to suck or just couldn't do it, and I had the feeling she was really annoyed at being forced to try.

Our pediatrician came to examine Emma and found that she

had a broken collar bone, which is not uncommon in breech births, probable hip dysplasia, and possibly a heart murmur. But he was most concerned about her lack of muscle tone and inability to nurse and told us that she had to be hospitalized immediately.

Suddenly, after the intensity of a home birth and a flurry of activity, everyone was gone. Instead of the three of us being together and bonding, my husband and the baby were at the hospital, and I was totally alone at home and overwhelmed with sadness. At that point, all of our rosy expectations were suddenly irrelevant. Emma had taught us our first and most important lesson—to accept and value her as a unique individual.

She was hospitalized 9 days for observation and extensive testing. They did every test they had available. They couldn't find an explanation for her condition, and some of the specialists shared speculations about possible retardation and neurological trauma. Throughout these difficult days, we felt really positive about her, not in the sense of denying her problems, but because we felt strongly that somehow she would be okay in her own way. After a week, we noticed she was much more lively and responsive when she was out of the incubator, so we asked them to keep her out, which led to an improvement in her feeding ability and resulted in her being discharged.

At 6 weeks, she was diagnosed as having a chromosomal abnormality similar to Prader-Willi syndrome, but no one could say with certainty what her long-term prognosis would be.

JANET AND RYAN

The cultural influences in my life were many. My father's parents were from Greece and Mexico, and my mother's parents came from Puerto Rico. Mom had seven siblings, and Dad had three. We had family get-togethers every weekend; if we weren't with one side, we were with the other. Celebrating almost anything is a big part of my family history, and I still have the attitude that life is for celebrating. We had tons of baptisms, first communions, graduations, birthdays, showers, and weddings. I like to think of it as stocking up great memories for those times when life isn't a party and for times of quiet reflections and reminiscing.

My dad worked for a major communications company—mainly in marketing, but his true love was entertaining. He still dances like Fred Astaire and is one of the warmest and most genuine gentlemen you would ever want to meet.

My mom stayed home to raise five of us—three girls and two boys. She was a fantastic cook, a major reason all of our friends liked to hang out at our house. She and my dad were extraordinary in their drive to provide as much as possible for us. They never discussed financial issues with us, but with five children attending parochial schools and wearing braces, they must have done without a lot for themselves.

I attended a parochial school where, I am embarrassed to admit, I played the part of the Virgin Mary in the Christmas pageant 4 years straight. Although for years I vowed to become a nun, I was assured by Sister Mary Louise that I might indeed become many things, but a nun was probably not one of them.

Art and music have always been a big part of my life. I studied the piano seriously (I even had six students when I was 13) and eventually won a 2-year music scholarship to college. Then my plans changed. I met Chris—an adorable, but semi-reclusive genius who was a year ahead of me in school. At first I thought maybe he was a little too quiet for me, but he says he knew right away I was the girl for him. I love hearing that. When we got married, I worked for a major airline, and we were constantly airborne. At a moment's notice, we would throw a couple of things in a bag and off we'd go. We played hard the first 3 years, and I'm glad we had that time because we sure didn't have any more for a while.

Chris went back to school for a master's in business and landed a job as a financial analyst with a large communication company. We bought a house, and a year later announced our carefully calculated entry into parenthood. Everyone was thrilled. I was the oldest female in our family, and Chris the oldest male in his; our baby would be the first grandchild and first niece or nephew.

I had a perfect pregnancy. We hung wallpaper and tiled the bathroom floor, and I handpainted Walt Disney murals in the nursery. We bought furniture and hung curtains, and I sat in an oversized rocking chair and waited for the miracle of birth.

November 12, 1979; it's a boy! Ryan Christopher Dieterle.

All my dreams had come true. And then, without notice, silence fell on the delivery room. The obstetrician announced that our baby had a few problems: a cleft palate, bilateral club feet, scoliosis, a very small jaw, and a receding chin.

I went into shock. My body began to shake uncontrollably. The nurses covered me with blankets and briskly took Ryan away before I had the chance to even touch his dusky body. My world had come crashing down. Chris and I held each other and cried.

Chris followed the doctors and Ryan around and kept coming back to the room. "Ryan's fine. He's just getting stabilized," they said. I had watched those doctor shows on TV. I knew that if you have to be stabilized, it's not a good sign.

What was going on, and why had this happened?

On the second day, the genetic team came. We were told, "We think he has a rare anomaly called Pierre Robin syndrome. The main thing is to get you in contact with a special team of physicians who will see that he is followed for everything he needs. Right now he's having some trouble breathing because of a small airway, so we put a tube down his throat to help him breathe. His chin should grow a bit, and his tongue will move forward to help him breathe easier. He should be home in a few weeks."

I clung to those words like model airplane glue. I counted the days, hours, and minutes. Things didn't seem any better, but I asked every hour anyway. They finally took the tube out of his throat, but Ryan couldn't tolerate it. His color got bad and a few times they had to slap him back into breathing again. Then they had to re-insert the tube. The roller coaster ride had begun.

I didn't get to hold Ryan until the next day. As the nurses told me to watch this wire and that wire and to be careful of the tubes in the I.V. in his skull, I forced a cheery face, but I knew this wasn't what we learned in Lamaze. As soon as I held him, I knew I loved him. But I was fighting being close to him because I knew the situation was really serious.

I was able to leave the hospital, but I was there 12–15 hours a day. Chris came to the hospital every night after work and spent the whole weekend there with me. Chris had taken the week off for our first week together as a family. But soon, his vacation was over.

I wanted someone to tell me this wasn't happening, that it was just pretend, like when you're a little kid. But I knew this was real, and I could hardly bear it. Chris and I cried a lot during this period. One day, when Ryan was about 2 weeks old, Chris and I were hovering over the incubator. Chris said, "It's so darn hard to concentrate at work. Sometimes I just want to bag it all and come running over here to hold Ryan." Chris's love for Ryan was so intense. I knew they had bonded. Totally and completely. He had bonded with our son in a way I had not. I was so terrified that I was going to lose him, and I know I was trying to protect myself from even more grief.

It was such a stressful time. Most of the time all we could do was sit and watch Ryan struggling for his next breath. We wanted to bounce him on our laps, but we had to hold him very carefully because of all the wires and for only a few minutes at a time.

The days were long and sometimes broken up by visits from friends or relatives. I always saw the positive in Ryan when others were around because they looked so sad and seemed like they didn't know what to say. I needed to assure them that things were getting better even though the real picture was dim. My parents came every day, and they were a real support, taking each day at a time.

I sat for hours by the incubator, holding Ryan's little hand, waiting. I brought him a new outfit to wear every day. Ryan was being fed by gavage, a tube that was passed down his nose or mouth, whichever was easier on any given day. He looked like a fish out of water, begging to be thrown back so he could be comfortable again. His color changed from pale to dusty gray and then back again. I took pictures. I watched the monitors and did most of his care. I was one of the only moms that did that kind of vigil. The nurses told me a lot of moms had a hard time coming in and seeing their babies in that condition. I thought it was unusual to leave your baby like that, but I could understand feeling that way. One of the nurses was really critical of the other moms, and I said, "You know, I don't think it's your place to judge that mom. She's doing what she can do."

A month later, I had left the hospital for a few hours and gone shopping with my mom. It was so good to get out; the hospital air was beginning to stifle me. I felt rejuventated when I went back to feed Ryan.

Three nurses were in the hallway talking. One nurse was in the nursery, feeding a baby across the room. I peeked at Ryan, who was in his incubator. Something was wrong. His body was scrunched up against the head of the incubator. There was a rubbery disk over his mouth, the kind they use to pound kids who have too much mucus in their lungs.

I reached into the incubator. Ryan's tiny body was white and cold and limp. He wasn't breathing. "Ryan's dead!" I screamed. "Where is everyone?"

Nurses came running. One of them led me into a small room. "You must think positively about Ryan. He needs your good thoughts now more than ever. They are working on him, resuscitating him, and you must pray for him." I began to shake uncontrollably. What was happening? Could they save him? I felt myself drifting away.

A nurse appeared in the doorway. "Ryan is breathing. We have him back, thank God." I went into the nursery and picked him up. At that moment, I felt the bond I had resisted for so long. I never wanted to let him go.

The next morning, the doctor and a whole team of professionals met us at the hospital. "We don't have much time. A tracheostomy must be done immediately to save Ryan's life."

We went into the intensive care nursery. There was my tiny baby who had weighed more than 6 pounds a birth and had slipped away to only 5 pounds. He had lost a lot of muscle tone and reflex action; his neck was really flimsy; he always appeared exhausted from his struggle to breathe.

Within 2 hours after the surgery, Ryan looked like a new child. His breathing was quiet, and he seemed ready to sleep but he had a new look of awareness of the world around him. His color was glorious; he had a pink glow. He was flailing his arms and legs, his eyes were wide open, and his face relaxed.

The doctor was really serious and said, "We think he'll have to have the trach in for a year."

"A year? No problem," Chris and I said almost in unison. We were ecstatic; we were thrilled; we had thought he was going to die. We were so elated we called everyone we knew and went out for dinner.

I had so dreaded the tracheostomy, but as soon as I saw the look of peace in Ryan's eyes as he was able to breathe, I wondered, "why did they wait so long?" I finally felt like a mom. Chris and I were on a high; we felt a happiness we didn't think possible. Our worries were over. Little did we know.

Acknowledgments

To all the parents I have been able to know these many years, I would love to put your names in neon lights for all you have taught me. Thank you for encouraging me to write a book and reminding me to finish it.

To my co-authors in particular, thank you for trusting me with your stories, and to Bruce, Ray, Chris, and Paul, thank you for your patience.

The UCLA Intervention Program, Department of Pediatrics, is an oasis for all the young children and their families who enter the swinging doors. Drs. Judy Howard and Arthur Parmelee have been my models in their unwavering belief in the validity of parents' feelings and the potential for growth in every child.

To the staff of the Intervention Program, thank you for the incredible team spirit and support these many years and for consistently demonstrating the power of early intervention. Cheers to: Kit Kehr, Kathy Ceppi, Carole Crooke-Whitlock, Eleanor Baxter, Cindy Bernheimer, Annie Cox, Nancy Thibeault, Elyse Chiat, Colleen Hall, Ruth Rosenfelder, Katie Brown, Elise Andrews, Loretta Staudt, Susan Cherry, Miriam Meyer, Terri Webb, and Sharon Cislo.

The UCLA Child Care Services has, throughout my career at UCLA, provided a caring connection and a forum for the discussion of ever-changing child development and parenting issues. A special thank you to June Solnit Sale and Gay Macdonald.

Victoria Thulman of Brookes Publishing has nurtured this book and this author through each step of the publishing process. Her phenomenal patience and good humor helped me meet almost every deadline. And Kathy Boyd has edited the final product with elegant precision.

Mary Cerreto has given me constructive and candid criticism through each phase of the book and has consistently challenged me when I needed it.

Dale Atkins has been my constant supplier of encouragement and enthusiasm. Throughout the long process of creating this book, she has kept me centered. I cherish our walks on the beach.

Herma Silverstein, my writing mentor, has given me a writing place in her magic garden, and a steady supply of coffee, chocolate, and on-the-spot critiques.

Marsha Sinetar, thank you for writing your books.

Thank you Martha and Aven for loving Gus, and for really understanding both the expansive and reflective aspects of the writing process.

Special love and thanks to my daughter, Kathy Carsten, who has taught me so much about mothering. And very special hugs to Nimai, Anjali, and Veda.

My husband, Wm. Hans Miller, has made it all possible by his belief in me and by supporting me in whatever I needed to make this book a reality. His ideas and suggestions have been major contributions to this book and to my continued growth.

Nancy B. Miller

Dr. Judy Howard: Thank you for always seeing beyond our children's disabilities, and for giving us hope and dreams for their futures.

Dr. Nancy Miller: Thank you for the hours upon hours of bended ear; never judging, never preaching, only helping us reach our own understanding and acceptance of our individual situations at separate times.

UCLA Intervention Program staff: Thank you for your support, your encouragement, and your unending devotion with our children and our families.

Our husbands: Thank you, Bruce, Ray, Chris, and Paul, for your love and support throughout this incredible journey with our children. Without your patience and understanding, this project could never have been accomplished.

Our children: You have enriched our lives in ways we never dreamed. Thank you.

Our families: We thank you for your incredible strength through this journey. Your unconditional love and support have enabled our children and us to gain strength and grow emotionally in ways we never dreamed possible.

Our friends: Thank you for your backbone of strength, good humor, and love and for keeping us focused on the light at the end of every tunnel.

Susie, Diane,
Janet, and Stephanie

To Hans
for helping me turn many obstacles into challenges
and for Millertime, the best of all places to Be.

n.b.m.

To our husbands and children

Love,
Susie, Diane,
Janet, and Stephanie

Nobody's Perfect

I

The Four Stages
of Adaptation

1

Introduction to the Four Stages of Adaptation

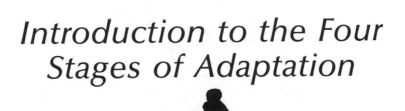

In the discussions that led to this book, the Moms looked back and tried to look forward. They asked many questions of themselves: How were they different from "the beginning"? What had made the changes they experienced easier or harder? Were the changes related to their children's progress, or did they go through a process of growth that was separate from how their children were doing? How did they think their experiences with their families and friends, their interactions with professionals, and their reactions to society's attitudes about disabilities had changed during the years since their children were born?

I had no predefined model for describing the changes they experienced, and it was only after 4 years of observing and participating in their lives, a countless number of hours of discussion with each individual mother and as a group, and many readings of transcripts of our conversations that a specific pattern emerged. Initially, I resisted the concept of "stages," as there were no clearly delineated passages that, once mastered, were integrated and left behind. But, there were distinct changes in all of the mothers' sense of control over their lives, their increased self-confidence and skills in their parenting roles, the balance of their lives, and their attitudes about the future. These women had adapted to their lives as mothers of children with special needs in ways that felt positive and fulfilling. These four mothers were happy with themselves and their lives. They were a long way from the frightened, sad, and confused Moms I had met more than 6 years before.

I struggled with how to "label" the pattern we observed and decided that "stages of adaptation" best described the process these mothers experienced. There appear to be four distinct stages, which I have called Surviving, Searching, Settling In, and Separating. They occur in that general order, although instead of occurring one at a time, one after another, they co-exist as a background framework, with one or more stages activated as a temporary "state" in the foreground at any given time. For example, a parent who is Settled In, with life basically "going on," may have to deal with her child needing an unexpected surgery. A "state" of Searching is reactivated as the parents search for surgeons and second opinions and arrange to take time off from work. They may also re-experience the feelings they had in the beginning when they were in the Surviving stage— worry, fear, confusion, and helplessness. But this time, the feelings are familiar to the child's parents; they know the feelings will pass, how to get relief, where to look for help. They have a support network, in contrast to their feelings of being alone in the beginning. Foreground states come and go. They may be triggered by events or memories related to their child, or they may be activated by the parent feeling tired or ill, or experiencing any passing mood state. Foreground states do not signal the loss of progress, or perma-

nent regression, or pathology. Usually, they are reactions that become resolved by employing a coping strategy or with the passage of time. Sometimes an activated "state" may be the focus for days or weeks (or longer), but it may frequently be in the foreground for only a few moments.

The concept of stages of adaptation not only describes what was and had been occurring in the lives of these four mothers, but it helped me to understand, in a way that worked for me, an adaptive, orderly, optimistic, and normal process that I believe most families experience as they raise children with special needs. As I work with other families, and as I reflect on the families I have been privileged to know during the last 25 years, this model has given me a new understanding of and perspective about the innate strengths that parents utilize in their adaptation.

The four stages are summarized below, and each is described in detail in subsequent chapters.

SURVIVING

Surviving is what you do to keep going when you are feeling completely helpless because something totally out of your control has taken away your child's equal chance at life. Surviving is different for everyone; it may last a week or years. Some of the feelings may linger for a lifetime; some may be triggered by expected events or unexpected memories. Surviving is reacting and coping, and it involves a multitude of uncomfortable feelings that may include fear, confusion, guilt, blame, shame, and anger. You and your partner may experience different feelings at different times; some of them may be unique to only one of you.

There is no right way to get through this stage, but there are some things you can do to make it easier—understand that the feelings you have are normal, take care of yourself during the process, and use your support networks.

You pass through this period of Surviving in your own way and in your own time. Many parents remember specific turning points—when they began to feel a sense of control, of optimism, and of hope. This was when they knew they had survived.

To say, "I have Survived" is to say, "I have endured. I have prevailed. I have overcome." It is to move ahead with life with purpose, energy, and a sense of trust that whatever happens, you will somehow find a way to deal with it.

SEARCHING

The second stage is Searching. You will probably have periods of Searching during your whole life with your child. There are two kinds of Searching—Outer Searching and Inner Searching. Outer Searching begins with your first questions about your child: "What's wrong?" and "Can it be fixed?" Outer Searching begins while you are still Surviving. It consists of looking for a diagnosis and for services.

Inner Searching begins when you ask the first questions of a different nature: "Why?" and "What does this mean for my life, my relationships, and my other children?" Inner Searching is trying to find your identity as the parent of a child with special needs. Like Outer Searching, Inner Searching begins while you are Surviving and may continue a long time afterward. Inner Searching is the quest for understanding. Your life has changed, and you don't feel like you have a lot of control over much of it. You find yourself questioning your own attitudes about "differences," and you find that you are increasingly aware of society's attitudes about people with disabilities. Your priorities begin to shift, and your relationships with friends may change. Your plans to go back to work or to have other children or to move to the country may be put on hold or may need to be changed. What does this mean to you?

Some parents feel incompetent, frightened, and overwhelmed with this new challenge; others feel motivated, energized, needed, and fulfilled. Many feel an exhausting conflict of overlapping emotions. Every parent is different. There is no right way to feel, and many feelings shift and change. How you feel today may change in a few weeks, months, or years. For some parents, the Inner Search does not involve major self-questioning; for others, the process may be long and complex and may result in major changes in life direction and philosophy.

SETTLING IN

Settling In is the third stage in your process of adaptation. At some point your Outer Searching may become less time-consuming. Your child may be settled into a school program; necessary interventions may be in place. When you are Settled In, you choose your battles and balance your child's schedule and your family life. Settling In also involves a change in attitude. Not only has your Outer Searching subsided for a while, but more important, your attitude about it settles down. The frantic pace lets up. You realize that change takes time and that you are dealing with a lifelong process. You realize that your other children need you to be more involved in their lives. You may decide you want to go back to work, to go to school, or to have another child. You may think your marriage needs some freshening up, or you may realize that your energy needs to be dispersed in different ways.

You have also learned new skills. You have more information. You are more confident and assertive, and you know shortcuts. You have a network of people to call to find out about resources.

SEPARATING

At some point, the fourth stage, Separating, comes into focus as the next major life stage. Separating, of course, begins at birth, and is a gradual, normal process that occurs in tiny steps throughout childhood. But when a child has special needs, the process may need to be altered or slowed down. Children with physical or cognitive limitations may not be able to initiate separating experiences on their own; extra parenting is involved to help children become more independent and self-sufficient. It may take longer for children to learn self-help skills; they may need physical assistance or much repetition in learning.

And your part of the Separating process—letting go—also must occur. It is so hard to pull back, to risk having your child make a mistake or falter. If your self-esteem and feelings of self-worth and being needed have become entangled in your child's daily life, it may be even harder to step back. Separating then becomes another period of loss and grieving.

Typical children grow up and leave home—separate. With children who have disabilities, you may have to initiate separation, plan it, find it, and make it happen. Your child may need intermittent or occasional out-of-home programs for weekends, for school weeks, or for vacations. Your child may benefit from a residential school or a group care home. Separating decisions may have to be made at different times than with typical children, and plans may have to change as your child's needs and abilities change.

When your child has special needs, it is possible that you may not have had as many separations as typical families. Your child may not go to play or sleep overnight at friends' homes, or visit relatives as often as some typical children.

Separating re-evokes feelings you had during Surviving—guilt, grieving, and psychological turmoil. It involves more Outer Searching and increased Inner Searching. And when your son or daughter leaves home, leaves for school, or separates in whatever way is appropriate for him or her you may again become Settled In, involved in your child's life in new ways. And life moves on.

While the stages described here are presented as evolving in a linear, developmental sequence, they actually have a circular, dynamic quality—as shown in the schema in Figure 1. The tasks involved in each stage may overlap, and issues you face while Searching may reactivate feelings you had during the Surviving stage. You may be Settled In, but a program closing or a setback in your child's medical condition may thrust you back into Outer and Inner Searching. The renewed Searching may in turn find you again feeling

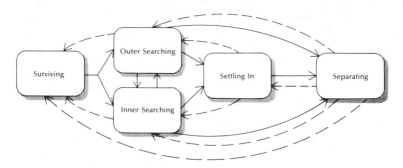

Figure 1.   The schema for the stages of adaptation.

some of those uncomfortable emotions you met while you were struggling to Survive.

Human behavior is, of course, too complex and too individualized to be reduced to simple diagrams and formulas. However, there has been a substantial amount of research in areas such as social work, anthropology, and psychology to support many of the ideas presented in this book related to the lives of children with special needs and their families and to the normal growth and development of both children and adults during the life span.

2

Surviving

Surviving is what you do to keep going when you are feeling completely helpless because something totally out of your control has taken away your child's equal chance at life.

When you first learned that your child was going to need special medical, educational, or therapeutic interventions, you probably felt pretty overwhelmed. You had something new and frightening to deal with, and you had to begin adapting to an uncertain future. The first stage of your adaptation is called *Surviving*. Everyone Survives in different ways.

WHAT IS SURVIVING?

Surviving Is Different for Everyone

You may have learned your child would have special needs even before he was born—through prenatal diagnosis. You may have learned your child was going to have special needs abruptly and traumatically at birth or as the result of an illness or injury. Or you may have learned about your child's special needs gradually, one anxious step at a time as your child showed signs that something was not going right. You may have noticed delays in learning or development, unusual behavior patterns, or repeated medical problems. You may have adopted your child with the knowledge that she would be at risk for or have special needs, or you may have married into a family to become the step-parent or adoptive parent of a child with a disability. You may be a foster parent for children with special needs.

It may not matter if this is your first child, your only child, your natural child, or if you have a boy or a girl. It may not make a difference if you are a young parent, an older parent, a single parent, or if you plan to work or stay at home.

The nature of your child's special needs and their severity don't make them any easier or harder to deal with. Having a specific diagnosis may not make it harder than just knowing your child is "at risk" or is "slow to develop." When and how you learned your child has a problem doesn't make the process of adaptation easier or harder; the attitudes of your extended family, your cultural group, or your religious beliefs may make adaptation easier or harder. There are no "right" ways of getting through this initial stage. You Survive in your own time and your own way.

> *Diane:* They told us she would have some paralysis. But all the professionals were so positive. They said this has happened but things can be done. She may never walk, but she can use a wheelchair. We were trying to be positive. I never thought, "Why me?" I knew we were starting down a long road; we had a lot of questions that couldn't be answered then. All we could do was to take things a day at a time.

Janet: Sometimes I fantasized about running away. Starting over with a false name. In each fantasy I would escape to a different place and imagine living there—
Paris, Tahiti, even Antarctica sounded appealing. No
one would ever find me again. Those thoughts lasted
only moments, but they were coping mechanisms that
somehow got me through.

Stephanie: Having a child made me feel more responsible, and she inspired me. Emma couldn't do anything
but lie there and smile as I sewed clothes for her and
made a quilt and dolls. We had no clue as to her potential, and there was no use worrying about that. I
was her mother one day at a time.

Susie: Those beginning months still terrify me to think of
them because there is so much I don't remember but
raw fear. I was frightened all the time. I remember a
mom saying she wanted to go to the bathroom or go
for a walk or go somewhere where she wouldn't feel
constantly frightened about her child, but there was no
place.

When you become aware that your child has a problem, is developing a problem, or is at risk for a problem,
you begin to deal with this information in two ways—you
cope and you react.

Surviving Is Coping

Coping is doing what you have to do one problem at a time.
Sometimes you may feel like you are trying to empty a
flooding boat one heavy bucket at a time. You may have to
make decisions without feeling very informed or confident. You have to deal with specialists in fields you've never
even heard of who give recommendations you don't understand and with interventions that are said to be necessary.
You may barely cope with all this, or you may handle it

all very well, possibly even better than you would have guessed.

When you are thrown into your new role as the parent of a child with special needs, you usually don't know anything about developmental delays, chromosomal abnormalities, cerebral palsy, seizure disorders, hearing impairments, learning disabilities, openings in the spine, or cleft palate—just to name a few. You might know something about developmental milestones—that your child would sit up at about 6 months and walk at a year or so. You know there will be some problems (after all, nobody is perfect) like sleeping problems, changes in your lifestyle, and increased expenses. Your expectations are to send your child to preschool, to see the pediatrician for regular checkups, and to struggle through toilet training and the "terrible 2s." Little did you know.

In less than a year, the four mothers in this book were collective experts on gavage feeding, suction machines, cleft palates, club feet, gastrostomy tubes, hospital admission procedures, insurance forms, tracheotomies, heart monitors, breast pumps, Pavlik harnesses, chromosomal abnormalities, shunts, orthopedic and neurological surgeries, blood tests, EEGs, and so forth. They had consulted with obstetricians, pediatricians, neurologists, orthopedists, gastroenterologists, cardiologists, nursing specialists, genetics counselors, social workers, nurses, emergency room technicians, lab technicians, physical therapists, occupational therapists, early intervention teachers, and many more professionals.

Coping is dealing with problems and getting by. Coping always feels like you are just keeping up with what you have to do, with little energy for getting ahead of your problems. This is because, while you may be coping with everything, you are using most of your energy to deal with your emotional reactions to your situation.

Surviving Is Reacting

Reacting drains your energy and diminishes your feelings of control over your life. You have no sense of direction over this turn of events in your life. You are trying to figure out what's going on and what to do next. Your reactions may range from confusion to fear to incompetence and may be accompanied by feelings of grief, anger, guilt, and helplessness.

Even if you have no uncomfortable or negative reactions to the fact that your child has special needs, there are many other aspects of this experience that you may not have expected and that may frustrate and disappoint you. You may find that the services your child needs are not readily available, that family members or friends may not initially support you, or that your child's problems are more extensive than you anticipated. Later, as you move beyond Surviving (and you will), you will react in different ways with a greater sense of self-confidence and control. But, in the beginning, you feel more emotionally fragile and vulnerable and you often react with surprise, shock, and sorrow as you begin to realize that nobody is perfect.

THE REACTIONS OF SURVIVING

The reactions described below are normal and often necessary. They are not "bad," "wrong," or "weak." They are the way many people feel upon hearing sad or frightening news. You may have experienced all of them or none of them. But anyone who tells you that you "shouldn't" have any of these reactions has not been where you are. No one has the right to judge how you feel. The reactions are temporary, although some stick around longer than you'd like. Most of the feelings get resolved or fade as you find your-

self ready to move on and as you begin to feel you have
control of your life once again.

Shock

Surviving begins with a state of shock. Shock is numbness,
disbelief, and disorientation. If you are in shock, everything
may seem "unreal." Shock is a normal reaction to a trau-
matic or major loss—be it death, disaster, or diagnosis. It is
a devastating blow to be told that your child may be prevented from growing up with a healthy, working body; an
intelligent, creative mind; and the same hopes and expectations to marry, have children, and be as self-sufficient as
any other member of society.

Shock is a physiological reaction to protect your body
and mind from being overwhelmed. (You can't "decide" not
to feel shock. Your body will feel it anyway.) During a state
of shock, your reaction times are often slowed; you may
think you're losing your memory (or your mind); you may
find yourself experiencing extremes in areas such as eating
and sleeping; and you are at higher risk for accidents and
injury.

Bodily Stress and Symptoms

Fatigue

You may be feeling tired from lack of sleep, restless sleep,
or the worries you are carrying around inside you. You may
want to collapse from unending fatigue—to crawl under the
covers and stay there forever. You go through the motions,
making it until nighttime again, and trying to keep going.
The only thing you look forward to is sleeping.

Physical Symptoms

You may experience headaches, lightheadedness, stomach-
aches, chest pains, loss of appetite, lack of sexual interest,

and other physical symptoms while you are Surviving. Stress can cause physical problems or make them worse. Even if you think they are caused by stress, physical symptoms are real and must be taken seriously.

Feelings of Weakness, Fragility, and Vulnerability

You may feel weak, fragile, and vulnerable with unpredictable emotions and behavior. You may cope well some days and then burst into tears in a grocery line. Not only do you feel helpless about your situation, but you can't even predict and control your own emotions and behavior. You may break a fingernail and dissolve into tears and think that maybe you are really losing it and going over the edge.

> *Susie:* I could evacuate a planeload of people, but I fell apart when Betsy spilled her apple juice.

Grief and Loss

Grief

You may feel grief for the loss of a dream about your child, yourself, your spouse, and your family. Your expectations and fantasies about your child's future are thrown open to doubt, and in their place you have fear and confusion. You grieve for your child who deserves the same chances in life as anyone. You grieve for what your child may never be able to experience.

Feelings of Helplessness and Aloneness

Surviving is an intensely personal journey. You may not be sure what to say to people, and you don't know what they expect from you. If you are fortunate, you can talk about your feelings with your partner, a friend, or a family member. But there is a part of it that is only yours and that you must deal with alone. Sometimes it is hard to know when and how to turn to others for support.

Diane: I kept waiting for the alarm to ring and wake me
up. It was like being in a fog—nothing to grab onto; I
couldn't see where I was going, and I felt so alone,
even though I knew others were out there somewhere
who would help me through this.

No one can totally understand what this is like for you.
Sometimes you may feel like a helpless, incompetent victim. You may feel drained and lifeless, yet that you must
keep going. And when you're at your weakest, you often
have to be strong for others.

Janet: I knew I was strong enough, but I didn't want to
be. When I told my mom this was a tragedy, she said,
"This isn't a tragedy. It's hard, but it will get better."
She told me how proud of me she and my dad were.
She told me how well I was handling this difficult time.
Well, I was tired of handling it.

Sadness

Sadness is a normal emotional reaction to events, thoughts,
stories, or memories that remind you of a loss. You may
feel sad about changes you are having to make in your life
or thoughts about what your child may not be able to do,
or how you will tell the news to your friends and relatives.
Sadness comes and goes and sometimes lingers, and you
may cry at unexpected moments.

Diane: When Catherine was 8 months old, I contacted the
Spina Bifida Association and visited a mom with an 11-
year-old girl. We went to their house, and the girl was
walking around with braces and crutches. She went to
regular school, lived a normal life, and was attractive
and friendly. But all I could see was the crutches. I
really tried to hear about the normal stuff, but I was so
sad that all I could think about was that she couldn't
walk like other kids. The mom said, "You'll get past
this. The hardest part is the surgeries."

Depression

Depression is a chronic mood state that may affect your eating or sleeping (too much or too little). You may have no energy and feel as though you are moving through a cloud of gloom. Some depression is a normal part of grieving and loss; but prolonged depression is a signal to get professional help and get it soon.

When you are sad, you know it will pass; depression feels like it will stay forever. When you are sad, you can usually carry out your daily routine through your tears; when you are depressed, you may not even get out of bed.

> *Janet:* Ryan was 10 months old and I was getting house-bound. If Chris didn't push me to go out, I'd just sit there. If my family hadn't taken us places, I wouldn't have gone. I was so depressed, I avoided doing anything. I knew there was more to life than this, but I was focused on Ryan. Chris didn't say much. He'd fix dinner and I'd say, "I'm not hungry," and he'd say, "Well, you can't not eat forever. You can't be sad forever. Besides, look how cute Ryan is."

Confusion and Fear

Confusion and Chaos

While you are still adjusting and adapting, wishing for things to settle down and for some peace and quiet, you may find your life filled with doctors' appointments, sleepless nights on surgical floors, and sleepless nights at home. And you are always vigilant—watching for signs from your child that the problem really isn't there at all, that it somehow went away during the night. You may feel that you must keep going—you're not sure where, or why, or for how long, but you're afraid to stop.

Uncertainty and Ambiguity

You may experience uncertainty and ambiguity about what is wrong, what to do next, and not having much control over anything. In the beginning, it is frequently hard for professionals to tell you the cause of your child's problem, the extent of disability, and what kind of interventions will be effective. No one can tell you how it's all going to turn out.

> *Janet:*   For about a year, the other Moms called me Miss 409. Everything was so uncertain with Ryan, so keeping a meticulous house became almost an obsession.

Fear

You may experience fear for your child's health, for your child's development, and for how this will affect your family. You are afraid your child will need more from you than you will be able to give. You may be afraid your marriage can't weather this challenge. If you are a single parent, you may be afraid this is too much to handle on your own.

Fears may race through your mind about whether you can afford this, what your insurance will cover, whether you will be able to keep working, and how you will find the right services for your child.

> *Diane:*   My major feeling was fear. Fear for my child and her future. Fear that I couldn't handle this—and I didn't even know what it was I was having to handle.

Preoccupation with Your Child

You may be preoccupied with your child with special needs to the extent that you are unable to take care of anyone else, including your partner, your other children, and yourself. You are so concerned about your child that she comes first, and you resent anyone who might suggest you take a break, go out for dinner, or do something "fun" for yourself.

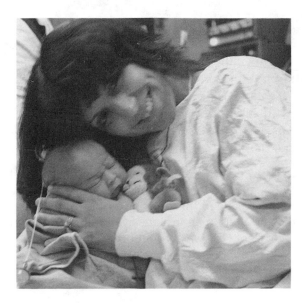

Susie: One day I looked in the mirror. I didn't look so good. Was this the person who used to like to go out in public, who was fairly gregarious at parties? I felt so beaten up. Every time I turned around there was another medical crisis or relatives were coming over and I felt like I had to look strong. My clothes were hanging on me. I didn't look like what I had been. I was a totally different person inside, and it was beginning to show on the outside.

Worrying

You may worry about the future, about what to do next, about doing the wrong thing, or failing to do the right thing. You worry about your partner, your other children, and whether to have more children. You worry about money, insurance, medications and their side effects, and that your child will get sick or won't get well. You can't sleep because of your worrying and that worries you. And you worry that you worry too much, but you can't shut off your brain, and that worries you, too.

Asking Questions that Appear To Have No Answers

Life seemed so simple before. You never asked questions like "Will my child be 'normal'?", "Will he be able to walk (or talk, or think, or see, or hear)?", "Will she be okay if she isn't able to walk (or talk, or think, or see, or hear)?", "What will his life be like as an adult?", "What if something happens to me?", "Am I doing enough?", and a lot of questions that begin with "Why."

> *Janet:* How could God let a totally beautiful act of love result in such tremendous problems for Ryan? After all, we had planned this baby. We purposefully created a life and then in an instant, everything you believed your whole life was brought into question.

Guilt and Self-Doubt

Guilt

Feeling responsible for your child's problem is one way of trying to understand what went wrong. It's taking the blame because if someone can be blamed, at least you'll have an explanation. And for the mother who carried the child, who is more likely to be at fault? You may remember your pregnancy—how you worried if you were doing everything right. What guilty little secrets do you carry that you fear have caught up with you? Skipped your vitamins? Should have stopped working sooner? Was it working at that computer screen? Maybe it was the day you went to your friend's house and they had just sprayed for termites. The "shoulds," "what ifs?", and "if onlys" go on forever.

If guilt is familiar to you, you probably feel guilty about having many of the other feelings described here. Some parents feel guilty about feeling angry and about feeling fragile—and about feeling so guilty.

> *Susie:* The guilt was a whole other thing. I knew I must have done something. I must have taken something,

drunk something, eaten something, breathed something, or exercised too much. What did I do? It had to
be me. I was her mother. There was no doubt in my
mind. I was at fault.

Stephanie: The doctor told us her condition was the result of a chromosomal abnormality, and they had no
idea what caused it. I felt so guilty. I can't believe it,
but I actually asked him if it was the tuna sandwich I
ate while I was pregnant. That stupid tuna sandwich
had haunted me. When he said the problem occurred
right at conception, I felt a surge of release from all
that guilt.

Self-Absorption, Self-Pity, and Self-Doubt

There are so many questions you are trying to answer about
what happened, what you might have done to prevent it,
whether you have the ability to take good enough care of
your child, and what to do next for your child, your family,
and yourself. And you may feel very sorry for yourself—
even if it doesn't last long and even if you never admit it.
Your self-esteem may hit rock bottom for a while.

Janet: Self-esteem? When I heard the word I had to go
look it up.

Shame and Embarrassment

In the history of human societies, the continuity and strength
of a cultural group often depended on its members being
healthy and able to contribute to the everyday economic
needs of the group. Giving birth to a child who might be a
liability to the group—sometimes because of a disability
and sometimes if the child was the wrong sex—brought
shame to the family. In some cultural and religious groups
today, there continue to be feelings of shame and embarrassment when a child is born with a disability. In some
countries today, children with disabilities are hidden away
or institutionalized, with few, if any, services available to
the children or families.

Old traditions and attitudes change slowly, and in some families in our society, feelings of shame persist. A child with a disability is seen as defective, flawed, and a disgrace to the family name and reputation. In some groups, there are traditional cultural or religious beliefs that explain the causes of disabilities, often adding to feelings of guilt and shame in the family.

People you don't know (and sometimes people you do know) may ask you questions or make comments about your child's appearance or behavior that make you uncomfortable or embarrassed. Some discomfort is natural when this is all new to you. You may not yet know how you feel about having a child who looks or behaves like a child who has a disability.

Anger

Anger can take many forms. You may feel a general "Why me?" anger, or it may be more specifically directed at someone—the obstetrician, the delivery team, the hospital staff, the person who gave you the diagnosis, the person who didn't give you the diagnosis, your partner, or your child.

Resentment and Envy

Resentment and envy are forms of anger. Some parents resent their friends or relatives who have "typical" children. They find it hard to be around other parents who compare brands of diapers or complain about teething. They become aware of a shift in priorities and feel out of sync with people they have been close to for years.

> *Susie:* I didn't think I was allowed to get angry.
> *Janet:* I remember thinking life isn't fair. We're brought up to think if we do good, life will repay us. So, therefore, if something like this happens, I must have done

something wrong. And that made me angry because I thought of all the things I did right during my pregnancy, and look what happened to my son.

Diane: I got angry at the doctors because no one told me the normal things like how much Catherine weighed. Their focus was totally on her problem, and no one put it into any perspective for me.

Blaming

Blaming allows some sense of control if you can find someone who made this happen. It gives you someone to be angry at—whether it's your child's other parent, your obstetrician, or the hospital staff. Sometimes specific blame is clear; there are cases of malpractice and negligence. In most situations, however, there is no one to "blame."

Feelings of Betrayal

You entered parenthood with the expectation that life was pretty much fair and that you would have a child who wouldn't be perfect, perhaps, but close to it. You felt as entitled to that as anyone, and it may feel like a promise that has been broken or a trust that has been betrayed.

Janet: I re-read some parts in the pregnancy books to see if I had skipped a chapter. I soon found I hadn't skipped a thing. People don't often write about true sad things that happen unless there is a happy ending or unless the situation is over. For me, it was just beginning, except I didn't know what "it" was.

Denial

Denial is a protective device our minds use when we are not ready to deal with a problem or its implications. The two kinds of denial are chosen denial and unconscious denial.

Chosen Denial

Chosen denial is characterized by "if I ignore it, maybe it will go away" thinking. It may be a creeping feeling that "something is wrong," but since your pediatrician said not to worry, great. You didn't want to believe it anyway, and no one else has mentioned it. You may even have a pretty good idea of what "The Real Truth" is, but you're not in the mood or a state to deal with that right now (thank you very much), and you will deal with it when you have to. You may say, "Today is Tuesday, and I have too much to do to dwell on this problem; so it will not exist until Wednesday."

> Stephanie: It's the Scarlett O'Hara school of thought: "Tomorrow is another day."
>
> Susie: It's appropriate and healthy to screen out the stuff that's hard to deal with. You don't have to vanquish every single challenge.
>
> Janet: And you'll deal with what you have to. What's the rush?
>
> Stephanie: It's easy for someone on the outside to say you're denying—as if you're blocking it all out.
>
> Diane: You always know it's there. Sometimes you just have to take a break from it.

Unconscious Denial

Unconscious denial occurs when you look at the facts and really believe they aren't true or when you call them something else. Sometimes denial is very useful, but it may be harmful to your child if it results in the delay of a needed medical or other intervention.

Some parents deny a little; others deny a lot. It's easier to deny a problem if you can't see it. It's easier to deny if you hang around people who help you deny by minimizing the problem. It's easier to deny if you call it something else.

> Susie: I would say, "She's not mentally retarded; she has a developmental delay." A delay sounded like she

would catch up, and that's what I wanted to believe.
Retarded was permanent, and I wasn't ready to deal
with that yet.

You may see all sorts of signs that your child is not as
bad off as others have reported. Other people, such as friends
and relatives, may unwittingly reinforce your denial by not
saying anything. They may suspect there is a problem but
are afraid to be the first one to say anything and want to
protect your feelings.

EASING THE SURVIVING PROCESS

You may find yourself in this most unpleasant stage of Surviving for weeks or months. The feelings described above
may come and go at expected or unexpected moments; they
may linger; or they may enter your mind and quickly pass
away. You may not experience some of them at all.

Understand that Your Feelings Are Normal

Sometimes you may need to let it all hang out, to weep, to
yell, and to feel very sorry for your child and for yourself.
Knowing that these feelings are a normal part of the process can help you as you meet other parents in your situation. It increases the "honesty factor" when you don't have
to present a facade that you are feeling great and have "it"
all under control.

Remember, everyone is different. Some parents adapt
easily; others carry feelings of anger or sadness for many
years. For many parents, this stage occurs in fits and starts—
a real roller coaster ride with no predictable pattern and no
easy formulas.

Life does go on, and as you are able, you move along
with it. In the meantime, know that the process of Surviving is normal and necessary and that you will pass through

it. If you feel "stuck" with any of the feelings or if they are unbearably intense, you may need some extra help. There are professional therapists and counselors who can be supportive, nonjudgmental listeners and offer suggestions for easing your pain.

Make Time for Yourself

You have been thrown off balance, and of course you are going to feel bewildered, confused, annoyed, and whatever else comes to mind until you regain some sense of control over your life.

As you understand what's going on, you can learn to anticipate when you may be thrown off balance again, plan ways to prevent or lessen some of the discomfort, and find ways to take care of yourself during the process. If you don't take care of yourself, you can't take care of anyone else very well. Some of the ways to take care of yourself may include the following:

- Make time to be alone—to grieve, to heal, to think, and to rest your mind.
- Make time to be with your partner to nurture your couple relationship.
- Make time to be with your other children and keep their lives in balance.
- Make time to be with friends who understand and support you.
- Make time to exercise, to have fun, and to keep your own sense of balance.

Use Your Supports

It's often tempting to shut other people out of your life and to feel that you have to carry your responsibility alone. You may want to close the drapes and stay inside—maybe forever. But try not to reject the people who are reaching out around you. Relatives, friends, neighbors, and coworkers often want to be there for you, but don't know what to do and don't want to impinge on your privacy. This may be an uncomfortable time for others, and they may need you to help them feel comfortable and useful. You may need to tell them what you need, what to do, and how to help.

Consider joining a parent support group. Initially, some parents find it difficult to share their situations with others, and some parents find that listening to other people's problems is too painful. Connecting with other parents who understand (better than anybody else ever will) what you are going through, feeling their support, sharing resources, and problem solving with them can be one of the most important steps you ever take.

TURNING POINTS FROM SURVIVING TO SEARCHING

At some point, you will notice that several things begin to stand out very clearly.

1. You know you need a sense of direction—a focus. You need some goals.
2. You are tired of just coping with each problem that comes up.
3. You know you have to get assertive, get some information, and do some work.
4. You can no longer just react. You have to take action that has purpose.
5. You feel a new energy and sense of purpose.
6. You care about how you look.
7. You realize it could have been worse. The world did not end.
8. You are becoming aware that you have to be your child's advocate.

9. Your priorities about what and who are important in your life may begin to change.
10. Your values about what is important in life may begin to shift in new directions.

How and when do these realizations occur? Sometimes they are gradual, sometimes dramatic. Some people need to hit bottom before they can break free. You may see a turning point in your child's progress; you may be influenced by the words of someone important in your life; or your own convictions may win out over the advice and predictions of professionals.

> *Janet:* One day I sat on the couch all day. I envisioned what it would be like if I went back to work—laughing, talking with friends, bringing home a paycheck, getting things for the house. I saw myself as I was—staying at home, taking Ryan to 550 doctors, cleaning the house, being alone. By the end of that day I knew I had to go back to work. It was the best thing I ever did.
>
> *Susie:* Six weeks after Betsy was born the relatives were visiting. I was serving coffee and cake and holding our daughter up and serving more coffee, and the whole time I was dying a death inside. My aunt, a little teeny woman 80 some years old, came up to me and said, "My dear, this too shall pass." That was one of the most important things ever said to me. At that moment I knew that things may not be okay, but they would be different. And that part I could control.

Turning points signal the end of the Surviving stage. Life does go on. You are no longer a passive victim, able only to react to your situation and to others around you. You are able to find new energy, direction, and purpose and to begin taking action instead of only coping with problems as they occur.

This does not mean that all the feelings disappear and

you are free of them forever. Some will linger and some will re-appear, but you will handle them differently as you know what they are about. This is because in this process, in your continuing growth and development, you will become better acquainted with your strengths and your weak spots, and you will be better able to control how you react to future situations.

When you have regained a sense of control over your emotions (and you will), and have gained a sense of direction (and you will), you will have a new perspective about life and you will have new priorities and challenges. You will know you have Survived.

Being in a state of Surviving doesn't last forever.
It just seems that way at the time.

3

Searching

*Searching is a time of acting, of moving forward
from your reactive stage of Surviving. It is the
awakening of a source of energy, the beginning of
a sense of control over your emotions and your
life, and a time for seeking understanding about
your child, your family, and yourself.*

The second stage of adaptation is Searching—Outer Searching for answers about your child's problems and Inner
Searching for understanding what the problems will mean
in your life. Some searches are long and complex; others
are accomplished with relative ease.

Searching issues may be in the foreground while you
are still struggling through the intense emotions of Surviving. Some Searching issues may dominate your life for a
while; some may never go away.

As you move through the Searching stage, you will find
yourself gaining competence and self-confidence in your
parenting role and a new sensitivity as you find your life

values and priorities beginning to shift. Searching is a time of active growth and expansion and of gaining a new kind of strength as you seek services to meet your child's special needs.

WHAT IS SEARCHING?

Searching Is an Incredible Journey

Searching is an incredible journey of finding resources for your child and of self-discovery. You will soon discover that you have more strength than you ever imagined and you have more potential support than you ever could have dreamed.

Searching Begins While You Are Still Surviving

Searching begins while you are still struggling with the issues of Surviving. Taking care of your child and finding help for your child cannot wait until you have resolved all of the feelings and questions you are dealing with. Searching is a time when the feelings that began as a part of Surviving are scrutinized, expanded upon, and resolved as you gain a sense of mastery and direction.

Searching Follows Two Paths

The two paths of Searching include your Outer Search and your Inner Search. Each path involves asking and answering questions. In Outer Searching, you ask, "What's wrong with my child and can it be fixed?" Inner Searching is a journey toward answers for the question, "What does this mean for my life?"

YOUR OUTER SEARCH

Your Outer Search is the attempt to understand your child's special needs. It is also the pursuit of services to meet those needs.

Outer Searching Gives You Knowledge

Quest for Diagnosis

Your Outer Search is the quest for a diagnosis, interventions, and even a cure. In American society, we are taught to believe that most problems have a solution. And so you, like most parents, have probably embarked on this journey with the assumption that appropriate interventions exist, that help is available, and that your child's problems can be evaluated, treated, and probably even fixed.

> *Janet:* Ryan was a year old. He had been gavage fed at the hospital, but I had a hard time doing it at home. I couldn't get the tube down—you can put it down the nose or mouth—but it would get stuck, or I'd get blood, and I was afraid of getting it into his lungs. I called for help and got nurses who couldn't speak English; a visiting nurse came who had never seen a suction machine. I tried to feed him, but he gagged on formula, and with his cleft palate, it came out his nose. When I took him to the ear, nose, and throat doctors, they were so concerned with his neck and head and ears, they said, "Don't worry. He's just skinny. He's going to be little." They couldn't see the whole child; they couldn't see that he was starving. The circles under my eyes were down to my knees. When you can't feed a child and he's not gaining weight, you feel so desperate, so incompetent.
>
> At 14 months, he weighed 12 pounds and was in the hospital with pneumonia—for the eighth time. Another mom at the hospital saw him and started to cry.

"Oh, my God, your child is dying from malnutrition," she said. I said, "No one will help me." She said, "Stomp your feet. Have a tantrum. Tell them you're not leaving the hospital until they do something. Tell them you won't be responsible; they can have custody if necessary."

I did it. I held my ground and demanded a gastrostomy. He gained 5 pounds in 5 weeks. A month after that, he crawled and walked simultaneously.

You may meet specialists in fields you'd never heard of. You'll hear yourself throwing around terminology that you never could pronounce, and you'll learn enough details about neuromuscular functions, chromosomal structures, diagnostic procedures, surgical techniques, and the side effects of medications to rival any medical degree.

For some parents, Searching is scouring medical journals for definitive answers and exceptions that may apply to their child. For others, Searching is joining organizations and parent groups; attending conferences; reading specialized magazines, newsletters, and books about people with disabilities; and watching television talk shows.

The Search for a Label

Your child has a diagnosis—a label. Is that good news? Or maybe your child doesn't have a diagnosis and therefore doesn't have a clear label. Is that bad news? Or is it the other way around? On the one hand, parents want a label for their child's problem because it feels like once you have a name for something, you can find out what to do about it and how to treat it. Labels can be important for genetic reasons, for funding for certain programs, for learning about research aimed at finding the cause and possibly a cure, and for networking with other parents who have children with the same condition. A label is something to latch onto—to help you know what you are dealing with. You can find books and articles about the condition; you have something to tell other people when they ask, "What's wrong with your child?" Having a label may help you stop Outer Searching because you know what you are dealing with. Having a label may help you *focus* your Outer Search because you have a sense of direction.

On the other hand, a label can also lead to stereotyping—to set expectations about what your child may or may not be able to do. Labels of Down syndrome, cerebral palsy, hearing impairment, autism, and mental retardation all evoke associations about the people who have these conditions. You may meet professionals who have limited expectations based strictly on a label, and the label may affect your own hopes and expectations. Sometimes labels can be limiting and misleading.

When your child does not have a diagnosis, except perhaps for "developmental delay," "learning disability," or "emotional disorder," there is frequently a vague sense of never quite knowing how much further to search or what interventions to pursue. However, without a label, there may be fewer preconceived expectations and, for many parents, the absence of a label has a liberating effect.

Outer Searching Gives You a New Perspective About Disabilities

Contact with Other Families

Your Outer Search leads you to other families who have children with special needs. You will meet and hear about children and families with problems similar to yours and problems that seem greater or less than yours. You will see how other families have struggled and succeeded with the difficult emotions of Surviving and the challenges of Searching.

Families define and deal with the idea of disability in their own way, according to their personal and religious value systems, cultural beliefs, and personalities of individual family members.

New Awareness

Your Outer Search gives you a new awareness of how people with disabilities are viewed and treated in American society. Before your experience with your child, you may not have given much thought about people's attitudes toward disabilities. You will encounter people in your neighborhood, in the grocery store checkout line, and at the park who will say things that will absolutely amaze you with their sensitivity or total lack of it. You will find yourself zeroing in on newcasts and articles about the experiences of people with disabilities and learning how American society meets and fails to meet the special needs of people with disabilities.

> *Diane:* I spent a lot of time cutting out articles from magazines and newspapers about children and adults with disabilities. I still have a lot of them. The other moms are always kidding me. They have yellowed newspaper articles about man landing on the moon and Kennedy's assassination, and I can pull out articles about poster children. I even had relatives and friends sending me things. Every so often I wrote letters to celebrities—the DeBolts, who adopted all those children with disabilities, Mr. Rogers, for his programs that included children with special needs. I didn't always mail them, but my intentions were honorable. I watched everything I could on TV, and I kept a diary for a while. I'm not sure what I got out of all that; maybe it was a way of telling myself that I was not the only one in this situation.

Outer Searching Gives You Strength

Competence and Control

Your Outer Search gives you a sense of competence and control. As you continue your journey and have some successes—no matter how small—you gain confidence from being able to do something to help your child. As you find services and answers (or as you at least learn to ask the right questions), you begin to feel that maybe you are competent and have some control over some parts of your world.

Getting a label, an intervention, or a new medication can often make you feel more centered. You have a focus, something to relieve the anxiety and uncertainty about where this is all going.

> *Janet:*   I hardly even talked to Ryan before we went to
> UCLA when he was 18 months old. Picture a child who
> can't cry out loud, who has a tube in his throat and in
> his tummy, and casts on his feet, and you're so busy
> just trying to help him survive you don't say things
> like, "Ga Ga." I told the occupational therapist, "He
> can't eat. He doesn't understand anything." That first
> hour she taught him four words in sign language. She
> told me, "This kid is smart. Don't let him fool you. He
> understands everything. You start talking to him right
> now."
>
>   I narrated every move I made from that moment
> on. "Now I'm driving the car, shifting into second
> gear, turning the corner." I sang to him. I read to him.
> I talked and talked. I saw him as a child with a disabil-
> ity, rather than just seeing his many disabilities.

As you find out there really is help out there, you don't feel as depressed or helpless. You have a new energy that is purposeful and a sense of challenge and motivation. You feel a growing sense of optimism and hope, and you begin to trust your own instincts.

Empowerment

Your Outer Search can make you feel empowered. As you feel more competent and successful and as you face the frustrations of dealing with bureaucracies and barriers to service, you may find yourself wanting to take on the system, whether it be your local school, the medical establishment, or the entire federal government. And as you meet other parents who have children with special needs and learn there is more strength in numbers, you may discover that using your energy, talents, and time to work on projects that benefit large numbers of people with special needs can play an important role in your personal healing and growth.

Obstacles to Success in Your Outer Search

Some answers are found with relative ease and moderate expense. Other answers are elusive, if they exist at all. Searching for solutions can be a maddening mixture of success and failure, hope and despair, and accomplishment and frustration.

Your Outer Search may have taken a smooth course of finding resources. In a perfect world, your child would have had a competent evaluation followed by easy access to a convenient, affordable program that would provide your child with quality intervention and support services for your family. And your insurance would have paid for everything. You could take a deep breath and relax for a while, knowing you and your child were in good hands. But then again, maybe you are like most other families—stuck in an imperfect world where things just haven't gone that smoothly.

Child-Related Issues

There is always the possibility that your child may not improve as much as you hoped in a particular program. Or maybe she hates going somewhere so much that you decide the activity is not worth the hassle of getting her there. Your child may lack the necessary stamina or skills to participate in some activities or may have unpredictable medical crises that prevent regular involvement in a program. Sometimes programs don't work out because your child's behavior is too disruptive or aggressive. And sometimes the best-intentioned "special" help makes your child feel worse.

> *Diane:* Catherine was enrolled in adaptive physical education at her school. She didn't like being pulled out of

class. She thought the activities were boring. Sometimes the teacher wouldn't even show up. So I went to the office and asked, "Where do I sign the papers to get her out of this?" Being with the rest of her class, even if she couldn't participate in everything, was much more important for her life.

Parent-Related Issues

- *Searching can make you feel powerless* as you try to buck systems with inflexible rules and have to spend countless hours on hold and waiting for people to call back.
- *Searching can make you feel frustrated and angry* if funds are cut back or your child doesn't qualify for something you think he needs.
- *Searching can lead to feelings of incompetence and confusion* as one professional tells you to "act now" and another says "wait and see."
- *Searching can make you exhausted.* You may spend hours on the freeway, in waiting rooms, juggling all your responsibilities, and not sleeping because you know you have to do it all again tomorrow.
- *Searching can feel like a distraction*—that you're really not dealing with unfinished Surviving feelings or that you're pushing some important issues under the surface.

Sometimes you just get tired of calling for appointments, starting in new programs, and getting connected to new people, and then having to move on and do it all again. Maybe you just want to stay home for a change. Maybe the money is tight, or you feel like someone else in the family needs to have a turn at an activity.

Maybe you feel unsure about how to call and get information or whom to talk to. If you are shy, if asking for help is new to you, or if you have difficulty speaking or reading English, you may not even know what services to ask about.

Or perhaps your child is enrolled in a program, but you aren't sure the program is really helping her. So you don't get her there on a regular basis; you tend to arrive late; or you miss appointments.

And sometimes you can't take advantage of a program because of some lingering Surviving feelings, such as uncertainty and discomfort in your new role as the parent of a child with special needs:

> *Susie:* When a lot of mothers were signing up their kids for horseback riding, I didn't even bother to check it out for Betsy. She might have loved it, but I knew that her retardation would really stand out in that kind of situation, and I couldn't deal with that at that point.

If you are dealing with some other personal problems—ongoing depression, trouble in your marriage, or an addictive behavior pattern—that are interfering with your getting help for your child, you may want to consider seeking professional counseling. It may help to have an objective, supportive person to listen to your concerns and to get some new ideas about how to move forward.

Program-Related Issues: Confusing Choices, Tough Decisions

Needed services may be unavailable or too expensive. You may meet professionals who don't have answers to your questions or who misdiagnose. You may hear of promising interventions that have worked for a child "just like yours"— medications, acupuncture, homeopathy, experimental surgeries, growth hormones, nutrition supplements, patterning, facilitated communication, and so forth. There are swimming programs, horseback riding, gymnastics, scouting programs, camps, Special Olympics, physical therapy, sensory integration therapy, speech-language therapy, computers, and communication boards (to name a few). What works? What doesn't?

Stephanie: We took Emma to an orthopedist because she
had had a little dysplasia in one hip when she was
born. When he X-rayed her, there was no dysplasia but
he wanted to put her in a Pavlik harness for 10 weeks
to be sure. Okay, fine. Doctors know.

The harness suspended her legs to develop the
joints, and she wasn't supposed to ever be out of it—
meaning only sponge baths. One thing we had noticed
right away, though, was that when she got in water,
she moved. She splashed. She adored it. So we said
forget the sponge baths and gave her a bath every day.
We were so naive about doctors; we thought we had
to do what he said or she'd end up with some terrible
problem later.

After 10 weeks we went in and he said, "Leave it
on another 5 weeks to be sure." And we did. Five
weeks later, he said, "I think another 5 weeks would
be good." I think he had Emma mixed up with his
5,000 other babies. I went home, took off the harness,
and tossed it. I've never allowed anything like that to
happen again.

Balancing Your Child's Life: How Much Help Is Enough?

You hear conflicting philosophies, and they all make sense.
You may find yourself seeking and using a multitude of interventions because you don't know what *not* to do for your
child. And no one can tell you the exact number or combination of interventions that will work best for your child.

How much "help" is too much? Some children are so
overprogrammed that the benefits have to be weighed against
the costs to both the child and the family. One of the major
problems in trying to cut back is deciding which interventions are the most important. It may be hard to look at the
"big picture" of a child's schedule, to see how much time
is left for play—for nonstructure. How do you let one of
the therapies go when it may be the very one that will make
the critical difference in your child's progress?

This is where your role as parent makes you the professional. You are the person who sees your child as a whole individual, not just a "small bundle of special needs." If you have concerns about the nature or number of interventions your child is receiving, talk to some of the other professionals who know your child and your situation. You may want to try a modified plan for a while and see how things go. You need to rely on your own intuitive expertise to make the choices you feel will benefit your child—while honoring her right to experience the simple joys of childhood.

YOUR OUTER SEARCH:
YOU GOTTA DO WHAT YOU GOTTA DO

Searching is an individual, deeply personal journey for answers, for cures, for remediation of your child's disability. There is no right or wrong way to conduct your search. Many people will give you a great deal of conflicting advice. Some will say you're doing too much (maybe you are); some will say you're not doing enough (maybe you aren't). You are the only one who can decide how far, how wide, how long to search. You have to try everything you have to try in your search for what your child needs. You may do too much, too little, or the right thing at the wrong time, the wrong thing for too long, or the right thing for not long enough. There are no perfect programs, infallible interventions, or quick cures. However, you will make some wonderful choices, and your child will benefit from the caring skills of many terrific professionals. You will have your own series of adventures, filled with triumphs and mishaps. Nobody's Perfect.

YOUR INNER SEARCH

Your Inner Search is a journey of self-discovery that begins with the realization that life is going to be different than you had planned. It is looking for a new identity that includes being the parent of a child with special needs. It is the struggle to understand your own attitudes and values about human imperfections, and it is a re-evaluation of your life's goals and priorities beyond your parenting role.

> *Susie:* One morning I looked around me. Betsy was on the kitchen counter in her infant seat, staring straight ahead, busy being not normal. The house was in shambles and the sun wasn't shining. I looked in the mirror and nothing terrific stared back. I knew something had to happen and fast. But I didn't know what to do.
>
> I needed to be at home for Betsy, but I needed to begin living again. I wanted things to be different and realized I would have to make them different.
>
> Coincidentally, I was talking to one of the moms in my son's carpool a few days later. She had invited 65 people for a fundraising dinner in her home and desperately needed help. I agreed to do it. I put together a buffet. It was a huge success and launched my catering business.
>
> The business became all consuming. It allowed me to complain about a cake not turning out or a job too difficult to contemplate, not a child who stopped breathing or wasn't developing muscle tone. I knew I was exchanging one set of problems for another—but these I had control over, and Betsy's I did not.

Old assumptions, expectations, plans, and dreams must be examined and new priorities must be established. For some parents, a major part of the Inner Search involves changing their expectations about their child and the family life.

Like other parents, you had some expectations: Your child would be more or less "normal," healthy, well-behaved, and happy and would grow up to be independent, possibly get married, have children, and so forth. You probably assumed he would have *some* problems—after all, no child is perfect. Maybe your child would have problems with math, be clumsy on the soccer field, or be obstinate, but there wouldn't be anything you couldn't handle.

Inner Searching Involves Asking Life Questions

Much of your Inner Searching time is spent asking yourself questions that have no immediate answers. They are Life Questions that most parents struggle with. Even parents of children without specific special needs must redefine their values, life goals, and priorities at different times in their childrearing because all children create some degree of concern for their parents sooner or later. The difference for you is that many concerns are abruptly brought into the foreground because of a specific, possibly serious, problem with an unknown outcome.

> *Stephanie:* Inner Searching is forced self-development. You work at finding answers to questions that parents of typical children may never have to spend much time on. I have to say that having a child with special needs is a good experience to have gone through even though it's devastating at the beginning.

The questions below are normal ones that you will ask yourself. You may feel anxious, depressed, and incompetent because you can't answer them (and no one else can answer them for you). The answers evolve over time. Some you won't know until life takes you to them, and by then your questions will probably have changed. For example, the question, "How will my child's disability affect my other children?" has many answers. Each of your other children may be affected in a lot of different ways on different days, according to what else is going on in their lives and in your life.

Right now, especially if your Inner Search is in the foreground, it may feel like your child's disability is and will always be the central, controlling theme. But, life goes on and things change. Your child's disability may always be there, but the emotional urgency and intensity around it lessens, and the meaning of the disability changes for you. What you saw in the beginning as the single most important factor in determining your child's future happiness and success was your child's diagnosis or disability. What happens through your Inner Search is that you see your child as a total person who needs a strong sense of self-esteem, persistence, optimism, and support to deal with some limitations related to her disability. And in this process of your Inner Search, you ask yourself a lot of questions—and you find a lot of answers about yourself in your personal growth.

1. Can I be a good enough parent to meet all of my child's needs?
2. How will my child's disability affect my partner, and how will our relationship change?
3. How will my child's special needs affect my other children?
4. How will our circumstances affect my desire or ability to have more children?
5. How will our circumstances affect my job, my education, and my other interests?
6. How will our circumstances affect our friendships and our relationships with relatives?
7. Who can understand what I'm going through?
8. What if my child grows up and cannot be independent, get married, or have children?

9. Will my child be able to go to school and have friends?
10. Will my child be normal, healthy, and happy?
11. Who will take care of my child if something happens to me?
12. Will I ever stop worrying about all this?

> *Susie:* I thought of being in my family, with all my siblings who have kids who are all talented, bright, and gorgeous. They're never sick; their friends are gorgeous; they all read 50 years above their grade level; and they paint, play instruments, and can do it all with their toes. And I wondered, where do I fit in my family now?

You may learn many surprising things about yourself during your Inner Search. You may find strengths you never imagined you had and some weaknesses you wish you never had to face. Your Inner Search may also stir up some of the feelings you had while you were Surviving. These may be feelings that you pushed away but never really finished dealing with.

Inner Searching Involves Self-Questions

Self-Questions are specific, practical questions that relate to improving your daily life and attitudes while you are waiting for answers to your Life Questions to unfold. Self-Questions help you know what you can do today to understand yourself better, to identify your own strengths and limitations, and to find new ways to grow.

Self-Defeating Thoughts in Your Inner Search

A major step in your personal growth is to recognize what you can control, focus on those things, and work to change them so that you have a positive sense of inner strength and direction. It is learning to take the things you cannot control and let them go or work around them. You can begin with recognizing how you think about the world around you. Maybe you can't control your situation, but you can usually control how you react to it. Sometimes we are our own worst enemies, and we carry negative, pessimistic, self-defeating thoughts around that can be obstacles to our own growth. We usually learn these thoughts in childhood, and we frequently aren't even aware of how negative and self-defeating they are. Here are some of the most common negative thoughts that can lower your self-esteem and feelings of competence:

- Believing you are a victim and that you are helpless to make any changes in your situation
- Holding on to unrealistic hopes and expectations and allowing yourself to be disappointed over and over again
- Focusing on disappointments, obstacles, failures, and defeats
- Waiting for someone to rescue you and make your life better
- Expecting other people to feel sorry for you
- Feeling that you are entitled to more in life and remaining bitter and angry
- Believing that you don't have a right to be happy when your child has such a serious problem

---

SOME THINGS YOU MAY BECOME
AWARE OF DURING YOUR INNER SEARCH

- Life is not fair.
- Nobody cares about your problem as much as you do, and no one else can ever really understand what it's like for you.

- No one is going to rescue you and make it all okay.
- If you devote all of your time, energy, and thoughts to your child, someone will pay the price, and that someone may be your child.
- Being realistic about your child's abilities and limitations does not mean giving up hope.
- Even if your child does not progress in ways important to you, it does not mean you are a failure.
- Your child and your child's disability have nothing to do with your self-esteem.
- How your child feels about his abilities and limitations is more important than what he can or cannot do.
- Things will change. Some will become harder and some will become easier, but they become different. How you deal with them is what matters.
- You are not the same person you would have been if your child did not have special needs. You can see that as a disappointment, a challenge, or a blessing.
- Somewhere along the way you are going to make mistakes. Nobody else is perfect, so why should you expect it of yourself?

WHEN OUTER AND INNER SEARCHING JOIN AND TAKE A NEW PATH TOGETHER

Many parents, as a result of both their Outer and Inner Searching, become actively involved in specific areas related to children with special needs. They identify an area of their own competence or develop new skills they use in developing programs, fundraising, advocacy, volunteer work, or returning to school to develop expertise in a field related to special needs. Many parents become attorneys; social workers; speech-language, occupational and physical therapists; teachers; teacher's aides; tutors; or recreation assistants. Many programs your child may benefit from would not even exist without the direct and indirect efforts of parents. Many of the advances in education, public policy decisions, and legislative changes have been enacted because of the energy and commitment of the families and friends of children with special needs.

TURNING POINTS FROM SEARCHING TO SETTLING IN

1. You realize there aren't any quick cures or easy solutions—that most children with special needs require a variety of programs and professionals for a long time and that change may be almost unbearably slow at times. You know the services you have now won't last forever, but at least for a while you can shift into cruise control and enjoy the scenery.
2. You realize that some of your questions don't have answers and that you need to get used to living with ambiguity and uncertainty. This isn't easy, but sometimes it seems like the only thing you can count on to be predictable is unpredictability.
3. You realize that most of your concerns about the long-term future can't be answered in your child's early years because so many things can influence the future. Progress may be smooth and uneventful, but there may be medical complications, unforeseen learning problems, or other factors. You realize that all children develop differently anyway and that some things cannot be predicted, and you hear all kinds of stories about other kids who have defied all of the predictions and proved the professionals wrong.
4. You become aware that there are continuous breakthroughs in areas that may improve your child's life or may provide technology, medications, surgery, or edu-

cation programs that will help her to be more independent, socially active, and personally fulfilled. You stay hooked into those programs and with those people and organizations that will be your link to new information and assistance.

Searching never really ends, but is part of a vital, expanding life. You will always have periods of Outer Searching—sometimes by choice, at other times by necessity. Your Inner Searching, once it begins, generates its own energy. You will find that you just keep growing. You are adapting to your new life, integrating your child's special needs into your identity, and fitting your identity into your total life. Because of the challenges you have met—and will continue to meet—with your child, you have acquired new dimensions of living that affect every area of your life. You will need to make some big decisions and many small ones. You cannot know today what you will want for your child or yourself a year or 10 years from now. You move through the future a day at a time, making each day the best it can be.

4

Settling In

*Today, well lived, makes every yesterday a dream
of happiness, and every tomorrow a vision of hope.*
— Anonymous

*Settling In is seeing the world for what it is and
seeing yourself for who you are. It is moving beyond the intense emotions of Surviving, feeling
less of the sense of urgency of Searching, and
gaining a greater sense of control and balance in
your daily life.*

Settling In is the third stage in your adaptation process. It
is a time of more predictable, settled-in living—even if you
are still busy with Searching issues and have occasional and
sometimes extended visits from those old Surviving feelings. Settling In is a time of integrating your child's special
needs into the rest of your life and working to establish a
new sense of stability and harmony for yourself and your
entire family.

Susie: Every year at Girl Scout cookie time when the little
Brownies would come to the door, I immediately went
into a depression because I knew Betsy couldn't do
that. Now I know what's going to happen, so I prepare
for it. I've even gotten to the point where I no longer
buy 200 boxes of cookies.

WHAT IS SETTLING IN?

During Surviving, most of your energy was spent on coping. You were reacting, without much reflection or ability
to anticipate and plan ahead. You persevered, managed, and
did what you had to do. You may still experience some
Surviving feelings. Some just linger around for a longer time
than you'd like; some get triggered unexpectedly by events
or memories or your mood of the day, but these feelings
tend to stay around for less time and you feel a greater sense
of control over them.

As Searching issues moved into the foreground, you
spent time and energy getting information to understand
and meet your child's needs and trying to sort out your
own feelings about your new life direction. Sometimes your
Searching may have taken on an urgent (maybe even des-
perate) quality based on a fear that you had to hurry to
find every intervention available or your child would never
improve. Searching can be exhausting, especially when you
may never know which combination of interventions at
which time will produce the best results—or fail to create
changes you hope for.

The emotions you felt in your Outer Searching move
into the background as you feel Settled In. You may still be
engaged in Searching *behaviors*—such as looking for programs and seeing professionals—but your attitudes are different.

Your Inner Search may move into the background, but

for many parents, their Inner Search can stay in the foreground with Settling In. Your Inner Search may shift from the more abstract, reflective, and often unanswerable Life Questions to more specific, active, and immediate Self-Questions. As you find you have energy and vitality freed up from the earlier periods of Surviving and Searching, you become better able to tend to the quality of your daily life and self-care.

The ABCs of Settling In: Attitude, Balance, and Control

Settling In Is a Shift in Attitude

A shift in your attitudes becomes apparent. It may not hit you like a lightning bolt, and you may not be able to pinpoint how or when changes occur. It may come at different times for different issues, and it may be affected by your mood or how your child is doing on a particular day.

- *Your definition of "normal" changes.* You know your situation isn't "normal" as you used to define it, but you develop a new normalcy that describes your family. Your "new normal" may include a lot of time keeping appointments, daily management of medications or equipment, endless insurance forms to complete, and special programs to call about, but it also includes the full range of joys, losses, challenges, daily fun, and daily hassles.
- *You don't feel as much of a sense of urgency.* The sense of urgency you felt while you were Searching begins to lessen. You realize that interventions take time, that you aren't going to see instant results, and that your child may go through plateaus of not seeming to be learning anything new—or may even regress for a while. You realize you don't have to spend every available minute "teaching" your child and that more isn't always better.

- *You find yourself letting go of unrealistic expectations.* As your definition of "normal" changes, you begin to let go of unrealistic expectations you'd been clinging to. You realize that you won't put all of your Surviving emotions behind you forever. You will have your own "private blend" of feelings that may pop up on a bad day or when it's time to face another surgery or a change in your child's school program. You are able to see these feelings as okay and do not expect never to feel sad, guilty, or frightened again. And you know that Searching will be reactivated from time to time, even if your child is enrolled in a program that you expect (and hope!) will continue for a long time.

  Letting go of unrealistic expectations also includes coming to terms with "what is." Sometimes "what is" is not as positive or optimistic as you had hoped. A promising surgery may have failed, a new medication may not have been effective, or a school program may not have worked out as you had anticipated.

- *You don't worry as much.* You probably still worry, but you are learning that worrying wastes a lot of energy, makes you upset, and generally drags you down. You realize that worrying doesn't change the outcome of anything—even if it does help you feel like you're sort of in control of things when you worry about them.

  Janet: We build up so many things—like, "What if he had to go to a new school?" or "What am I gonna do about puberty?" But then when they come, you just go through them. You need to get information and be practical, but worrying sure won't make it any easier.

- *Settling In is a time of shifting perspective about your child's needs.* It is the shift, for instance, from seeing a wheelchair as "giving up hope" that your child will never walk to seeing it as an opportunity for your child to be mobile and independent. Instead of thinking of your child as "confined to a wheelchair," you see him as "liberated by a wheelchair." Your focus was on your child's "loss," on what he couldn't do. You are shifting into finding ways for her to do it anyway, or any part of it that can be made possible. Mobility enhancers, sign language, communication boards, braces and crutches, helmets, adaptive equipment—initially these are resisted by many parents as symbols of disability, of giving up the search for a cure. But as you change your perspective, you see that these are all aids toward more independent functioning and increased social interactions for your child.

Settling In Is a Shift in Balance

Your early emphasis was on remediation—correcting your child's specific disabilities. As your child grows and as you adapt, you are better able to see your total child and to work around the disability. You increasingly recognize the need to teach your child to compensate—to develop strengths in other areas—and to build a strong sense of self-esteem.

- *You establish some new priorities for your life and your child's life.* You know you can't "do it all," and your child can't participate in every possible therapy or program. You realize that you may have to let something go for a while and you may have to take breaks in certain areas. You know some services are not worth the effort you have to put into getting them. You are better able to select what's important now, what can wait, and what you have to let go of. And you are feeling okay about it, too.

  Diane: In the beginning, we fight for anything we can get, but there comes a point when you say, "I'm going to lose this battle and it's okay," or "the battle isn't worth it."

Stephanie: Emma was turned down for speech-language
      therapy. We could have appealed it, but it wasn't
      worth the effort. You have to stir up a lot of stuff on
      the bottom of the pond and let yourself get upset and
      angry. If you cry and yell loud enough, you'll get it.
      Sometimes that's worth it, but you have to weigh the
      cost. What she gets in an artificial surrounding 30 min-

utes a week won't necessarily make that much difference. Maybe someday it will be worth driving a half
hour each way, but not now. And I don't feel guilty
about that.

- *Your child's total needs have become your focus.* The
disability takes less of your energy and attention, and
your child's total needs become your focus. You no longer
spend most of your energy, time, attention, thoughts,
conversations, and private thoughts on your child's
problems. You deal with them, but you don't dwell on
them. You think about whether your child is having fun
instead of whether "this helps her learn." You can play
with your child without wondering if it is stimulating
or structured enough.

Stephanie: Settling In is a form of benign neglect—I'm
stopping all the lessons; this is how it is now. I'm
going to let her just be who she is. It's letting her take
more risks, make more mistakes, and figure out how
she wants to spend some of her time.

- *You are getting on with the rest of your life.* Your child's
special needs must be taken care of, but so must the
needs of everyone else in your family—and that includes you. You become a master of time management.
You learn to juggle daily requirements as you deal with
everyone's schedule and try to make some time for
yourself.

Your daily life may be more predictable. There may
be fewer medical crises, and your child may be enrolled
in a program you can count on for a while. You may
only be in the "eye of the storm," but you know a
breather when you see one and you know to appreciate
it when it's there.

> *Diane:* We weren't given a choice, and we're dealing with it the best way we know how. Other people say, "I couldn't do what you're doing." How do they know that?

- *You learn that the balance changes as some things get easier, some things get harder, and a lot of things just get different.*

> *Diane:* The new wheelchair is great. It's a sports chair and very light, so I can put it in the car without straining my back. We don't have to wait for Catherine at malls or sit and rest a lot because she's tired. She can keep up now, and she likes to play around with it. We have to remind her to not run into people.
> *Susie:* I didn't mind childproofing the house when Betsy was 2. But now she's 8, and I still have to make sure things are out of reach. I get tired of it.

As your child grows bigger, he may be harder to lift, move, dress, bathe, and assist into and out of a wheelchair or carseat; it may be harder to control his behavior problems in public; and it may be harder to explain his "immature" and inappropriate behaviors. As the gaps get wider your child may draw more negative attention.

Your child's problems frequently improve with age and intervention, and your skills for dealing with the problem areas also improve. Your reactions get better—you learn ways to prevent or sidestep many uncomfortable feelings and when those feelings do break through (and they may from time to time), they don't last as long.

> *Susie:* Whenever we're in a good place, the kids are doing well, and we're on a plateau, there's a part of us that's just waiting for something to happen. We just aren't trusting that life will go on like this. And you know what? We are really right to have those thoughts. It's a level of preparedness, a form of defense, because

we shouldn't ever trust ourselves to live in the little
summer house with all the flowers always blooming.
That's not saying that something will happen. And it's
not pessimistic. But it's better to be prepared and to
say, "Well I know something is coming, and I can handle it. And when that's over, I know I can handle the
next one."

Janet: Doesn't that keep you from enjoying the moment?
Susie: You have to work with both—find a place for both.
You keep a level of vigilance, but you don't sit and
wait for something to happen.

Settling In Is a Shift in Control

There are some things in life over which you have no control—even if you do everything right. No longer do you feel
helpless, incompetent, frightened, and confused (at least not
as often). No longer do you only react because something
"out there" seems to be controlling your life, your feelings,
and your future.

Susie: I think the jury's still out. I'm doing okay this year,
but what about next year? And what about tomorrow?
We have an IEP [individualized education program]
meeting tomorrow morning. Am I going to handle it
well? I'll need to be assertive in order to get what's
best for Betsy, and I want to work with the system in a
productive way.

- *You have a lot more information than you did when
you learned your child had special needs.* Not only do
you have much more information than you did when
you were Surviving and then Searching, but you also
know how to find the information you don't have. You
know more about your child, your rights, what is available, and what should be available. You may have some
answers about your child's disability. Perhaps you have
a diagnosis, a sense of direction for the immediate fu-

ture, a stable course of medication, or some increased understanding about what you are dealing with.

- *You have new skills for Searching.* You have developed new Searching skills. You don't waste as much time waiting for people to call back or waiting in doctors' offices. You are more assertive and more knowledgeable, and the professionals you deal with recognize this.

    Janet: When I take care of Ryan's medical needs, I feel more like a practitioner. I try to prevent as many extra hands on him as possible. I take on a different role; I get clinical and objective and try to think of the alternatives.

- *You are moving forward with a sense of vitality and purpose.* You feel vitality and purpose as you move forward. You are working on making your life and your family's life as stable and cohesive as possible. You are no longer feeling defensive and uncomfortable about your situation, and you are spending less time looking back and second-guessing whether you should have tried this intervention or followed through on that recommendation.

    Diane: You can't go back. "If only . . . or, what if we hadn't had that operation, would things have been better?"

    Stephanie: You can say that, but why live like that?

- *You are finding out what works for you.* As you learn what works for you, you start to feel control over how you deal with your situation. And when you feel like you have some control over your life, you are better able to make choices about how you will live your life. It's being able to be positive, neutral, or angry as you choose; to fight the battles that are important and let the others go; and to know that you can't always control what happens to you, but you do have a choice about how you will react to it.

- *You have a network of people.* You have developed a network of other parents and professionals and, as you establish more of these connections, you and your child can benefit by including people with special needs in your network. Through contacts with adolescents and adults who have similar disabilities, your child can gain many insights about living in society as a person with a disability, learn practical skills for daily living, and have role models for maintaining positive self-esteem and handling frustrations and challenges.

  You and your network know about resources, and each of you knows other people who know resources. You have people to call when you need to find help or when you need a shoulder to lean on. Networks also have more power than individuals because they can work together as advocates to see a barrier removed, an elevator installed, or a policy changed.

- *You are a lot more flexible than you used to be.* As you gain a greater sense of control over your emotions and increased feelings of self-confidence as a parent, you are able to relax and be more flexible about the daily ups and downs of life. You have more trust that things are basically moving forward and that most daily hassles will work out in some way. You realize that you don't have control over a lot of things, and you are able to not care as much and to not take as many things personally. (When the children are whining and arguing, it doesn't automatically mean you're a bad, incompetent parent.)

  Feeling in control allows you to be more flexible. And when you are able to really "let go" of a lot of control issues, an interesting thing happens—you have even more control over your life. How? Because you are *choosing* what will and won't bother you. *Being able to choose* how you react to events around you is not only greater control it is also greater freedom.

Obstacles to Settling In

Some families are not able to enjoy the normality of feeling Settled In, or this stage of adaptation may be delayed. Here are some obstacles families may experience on their way to Settling In.

1. If a child has continued medical crises or aggressive or self-destructive behaviors or if the physical or mental health of any family member is at risk, there must be a continuing search for solutions. The search may be for temporary answers or perhaps long-term solutions. Every family has different needs, and every community has different resources.

2. Although we are moving toward higher quality, more varied services in American society, families without personal financial resources or excellent insurance policies may have limited access to services. Many public programs and policies are not yet responsive, creative, and flexible in dealing with the unique needs of each child and family.

3. Some children have such severe medical, learning, emotional, or behavior problems that their families are not able to meet their needs in the home. Some children may need, for varying periods of time, 24-hour supervision for severely disruptive behavior problems; others may need tightly organized structures for all of their daily routines in order to improve their socialization and self-help skills. The decision to have a child live outside the home is never easy. Some families—despite their efforts and the very best community supports—are unable to withstand the strains placed on the family unit.

4. You may learn that your marriage or couple relationship can't weather this new direction your family life has taken. You may change, your partner may change,

or one of you may be unable to change to adapt to the special needs your child may have. Perhaps there were some shaky areas before this happened, and they became larger issues that couldn't be resolved.

5. You may be a single parent by choice or circumstance, having to juggle all of the Searching responsibilities alone with no one to help find and evaluate programs and then to take your child there and home again and no one "built-in" to tell you what a great job you're doing. And so one more Searching responsibility you have is to find someone to provide emotional support for you and to share some of the tasks that may be required for your child's daily care. Support groups are especially valuable in your situation—even though it's one more place to have to go and one more evening away from your child and family.

6. Those old Surviving and Searching feelings may come into the foreground again. You realize that Settling In may come and go; life may really be normal with routine ups and downs and may go on that way for years, months, a week, or maybe a whole day. (If you've had a long period of steady crises, even a day or two of relief can seem like a new life!) You learn what can trigger a rekindling of old Surviving feelings and find ways to cut them short or avoid them altogether.

> *Susie:* If it does become too oppressive, you must change your environment. Whatever that means to you. Go to a friend's house, to a museum. Something to short-circuit it.

> *Diane:* We're all doing better than we used to. The difficult times are shorter. It used to last a week, and now it's moments.

Searching issues certainly come and go. They may be imposed if, for example, a program changes or your child needs additional interventions. Your family may move to a new community (or even across town), and you may find you have to look for new schools, programs, and professionals. Or your insurance may be cancelled.

By now, you are probably aware that although you're pretty Settled In, many feelings of Searching and Surviving can occur together. Just when you think you're done with anger, your child's wheelchair breaks again. Just when you think you're finished with guilt, you find out that the clinic you almost called 2 years ago really did have an intervention that would have helped.

> *Janet:* The medical side is always hanging there with Ryan.
> I consider him a well child right now. If his scoliosis
> doesn't get worse, his feet don't deteriorate, and I
> never have to get his cleft palate repaired again, he'll
> be okay. They're always after me to get checkups for
> his ears, eyes, and feet every 6 months, and for his
> back every 4 months. Medical intervention is not all
> good, and it's not always for the best. You may gain
> something, but you often get something else taken
> away. We're trying to make decisions about that.

THE ISSUE OF "ACCEPTANCE"

There's a lot of talk among both parents and professionals about the term "acceptance." Parents often refer to "acceptance" as a nirvana-like goal they should have already reached. They aren't really sure what acceptance is, but frequently feel embarrassed even to bring it up because they feel they are failing somehow by not having achieved "it." And some professionals make it worse by holding up "acceptance" as a measure of parental adjustment and considering it a goal they should help parents reach. Have you ever gotten the feeling that acceptance means "admitting it" or "giving in to it"? Sometimes "acceptance" has the connotation that you are supposed to "just accept the truth and try not to fight it," like some incurable illness. This was, in fact, probably the standard, acceptable attitude in times past when people with disabilities were shut away and no other "interventions" were thought possible. So, the view of acceptance as giving up has some historical and cultural interest and also helps us to appreciate how far we have come in our understanding and work with people with special needs.

"Accepting" your situation in the sense of sitting back and not seeking or expecting help or improvement for your child takes away all of your control and confidence—and is simply not an acceptable way to view acceptance today.

What is "acceptance," anyway? One definition is, "to take willingly and without protest; to regard as proper and suitable."

Do any parents "accept" a disability for their child willingly and without protest? Are the special needs of an infant or young child ever "accepted" as proper and suitable? Why should parents accept something that everyone else in our society views as unacceptable?

But there is a second meaning of acceptance—"to concede the existence of a situation, to digest it, to put up with it, and to make the best of it." And isn't that what you do? By the first definition, you are supposed to accept your child (but not her disability) willingly. With the second definition, you acknowledge that your child has special needs, take it in ("digest it"), put up with the disability, and make the best of it. In other words you say, "Okay, I get it. The problem is here and it's not going away. How do we understand it, integrate it into our lives, and make it the best it can be for our child and our family?"

Study, Understanding, and Mastery—The SUM of Acceptance

Acceptance is acknowledging that a problem exists— Studying the problem, Understanding the meaning of the problem in your life, and gaining Mastery as you integrate your child's special needs into your total life.

> *Stephanie:*   Acceptance is the result of your Inner Search—of the work you did to accept your child and the situation into which her presence has thrust you and your family. It starts with that initial feeling of, "This is my kid, and I don't care what is wrong with her. I love her for who she is." This acceptance and reverence for our child's individuality is something that should occur in all parent–child relationships but is sometimes actually easier in the case of a child with special needs when we are forced by the circumstances of her disability to let go of our expectations and realize that what is important is not whether she someday becomes President of the United States, but that she realizes her potential (however limited that might be). To recognize, appreciate, and honor her individuality is one of the greatest gifts we can, as parents, give to *any* child.

TURNING POINTS FROM SETTLING IN TO SEPARATING

Your Settling In may last for years, or you may have only had brief glimpses of respite from intense caregiving. Most families are able to make Settling In work for extended, enriched periods of time. Somewhere in the midst of your Settling In you realize that you must start thinking of Separating. You know it's coming in the next few years in some form or another, and you start to wonder what you need to do to get your child—and the rest of the family—ready.

The fact that you are now asking questions indicates

that the fourth stage of adaptation, Separating, is moving into the foreground. You start asking questions like:

1. What about *management issues* for my child's disability? What kind of adaptive equipment, special aids for daily living, or communication devices should we be looking for?
2. What *other people* do we need to start including on our support team? Special aides for physical care, tutors for academic work, extra caregivers for weekend activities, . . . ?
3. What *social programs* would help my child to improve community social skills? Summer camp, recreation programs, scouting, . . . ? How can my child be included in regular social programs and to what extent should we look for specialized programs? For example, should we look for peer groups of children with similar disabilities (e.g., hearing impairments, cerebral palsy)?
4. What kind of *alternative living situations* are out there? What will my child need? What choices should we consider?
5. How is *our family* going to deal with issues of Separation—whatever form it takes? How will our other children fit into the future plans for our child with special needs?

You may not foresee your child leaving home before a certain age, if ever, but preparation for both emotional and physical Separating must begin early. For example, if you believe your child will require a supervised living situation as an adult, the more self-sufficient your child becomes may determine the range of facilities and programs available. And so, you focus your energy on the search for community programs that will enhance social development, physical confidence, and educational achievements to prepare your child for the very best quality of adult life possible.

TWENTY GOALS TO GROW WITH

Goals are ideals. They are destination points in our lives that help us to stretch our limits and grow to new definitions of ourselves. These goals reflect the philosophy of this book and may help you to define goals that are uniquely yours.

1. I have a realistic view of my child's abilities and limitations and clearly value my child as a total person.
2. I do not allow myself to live with unrealistic expectations—and therefore repeated disappointments—about what my child cannot do or may never do.
3. I plan what I can for the future, but live a day at a time with a sense of trust that I will handle what happens tomorrow, next year, or in 10 years.
4. I have the knowledge and skills to seek out information and resources in assertive, creative ways.
5. I have hope without expecting miracles.
6. My self-esteem is intact. I do not measure my worth by my child's abilities or limitations.
7. I try to see the world from my child's point of view.
8. I am able to empathize with others, to be sensitive to other viewpoints, while maintaining my own sense of priorities.
9. I have freed myself from unproductive feelings of guilt, anger, shame, blame, and self-criticism.
10. I generally see the glass as half-full instead of half-empty and am able to live each moment to the fullest.
11. I have a sense of perspective about my life, my problems, and my daily hassles.
12. I have a sense of humor and can laugh at myself.
13. I have an understanding of and an appreciation of individual differences.

14. I have maintained a support network of family and friends.
15. I do the best I can within the context of my total family's needs.
16. I realize that I will not be able to do everything, and I will not feel guilty about that.
17. I will not spend every moment trying to teach, stimulate, and cure my child. I will have times with her that are totally for fun.
18. I will not blame myself for any areas in which my child is unable to make progress.
19. I do not need to explain myself and/or my child to everyone.
20. I cannot control what other people think.

5

Separating

Separating is a normal, necessary process in development, which occurs in tiny steps throughout childhood. Each step of separation is a step toward independence as your child grows up and away from you and as you let go— one safe step at a time.

Separating is the fourth stage of adaptation. The process of Separating includes both *emotional* separateness between you and your child, and *physical* separation, which may occur earlier or later than "normal" when a child has special needs. From the time your child is born, tiny steps of separating are taken throughout childhood as your child becomes more independent and as you allow it—by letting go.

WHAT IS SEPARATING?

For many families, Separating issues move into the foreground around the time of puberty, when questions parents had about the future take on a new immediacy as they recognize the need to prepare their children for adult living in as normalized a lifestyle as possible.

When Separating issues move into the foreground, there is an increased emphasis on teaching your child skills for community living and on preparing yourself to let go. During the Separating stage, old, unfinished Surviving emotions may be re-awakened. Also, Searching issues certainly need to be addressed as you try to find resources to help your child gain greater independence and as you again reach inside to ask yourself what Separating from your child will mean for your life. When you have a child with special needs, Separating doesn't happen as naturally as with typical children. You often have to take the initiative, and Separation can take many forms.

In some families, Separating issues are forced into the foreground while parents are primarily struggling with Surviving emotions. Questions about placement or prolonged hospitalization may need to be addressed. Major issues of Outer and Inner Searching also move into the foreground.

Even with physical Separation from your child (when or if that occurs), there will never be an emotional Separation, and you may always be involved, to some degree, in your child's adult life. But in the natural order of things, parents and children do Separate, and there is a time for parents to expand in new directions. Separating is one more step in your personal growth.

The Tiny Steps of Separating

Separating begins at birth. Each nudge toward growth is a step toward independence and separation. As parents, you know that separating from a child is part of the natural order of things. Parents of typical children assume that, over time, their children will learn to function independently, make decisions and deal with their consequences, become economically self-sufficient, and live independently and establish homes of their own.

How do children separate? By crawling away, playing peekaboo, going to nursery school, spending the night at Grandma's, being left with a sitter, crossing the street alone, riding a bike without training wheels, climbing a tree, testing rules and limits, saying "No" and "I don't have to," going to kindergarten, putting on a shirt even if it's backwards, saying "Look, I can do it myself!", buying a toy at a store with their own money, sleeping at a friend's house, setting the table, going to the mall or movies with a friend, going to camp, going out on a date, and so forth.

RAISING A CHILD WITH SPECIAL NEEDS

Once upon a time . . . There was a mother bird and her baby birds. All of the babies but one were able to fly away. The last baby was weak and would peer over the rim of the nest and then withdraw in fear. The mother bird nudged and nudged until she pushed the baby out of the nest. The baby bird tried to spread its wings, but they were too fragile, and the baby began falling. Suddenly, the mother bird swooped beneath the baby, caught it in her wing, and lifted it back into the nest. The mother bird said to the baby, "I know it is hard for you to fly on your own, and it will take you longer to learn, but you must try every day. As long as you need me, I will be there to catch you if you fall."

Susie: Betsy's not responsible for her future. We are. Other kids are responsible for their futures. My worries are future ones. I futurize. We're doing what we can now about teaching her self-help skills. That's in motion and you can't rush it. It takes her a thousand times to learn something so you just keep practicing.

SEPARATING ISSUES FOR CHILDREN WITH SPECIAL NEEDS

The daily, small experiences children need in order to practice being independent in a safe, protected way may not happen easily for your child. Separation for children with special needs often has to be initiated, planned, or supervised by the parents. This is not part of the natural order of things, as children and parents typically are both actively engaged in Separating activities. But if your child has limited physical mobility, sensory impairments, or delayed communication or social skills, you must often make a special effort for your child to have experiences that allow for feelings of independence and growth. Your child may need extra time or intensive training to acquire the knowledge and learn the skills that will increase her future choices of living, working, and socializing in the community.

> *Diane:*   She has new braces and it's a real breakthrough. She's standing better and can walk better, but they've taken away some of her independence because she needs me to help her put them on and take them off. I told the physical therapist, "There must be another kid who can do it. Find someone who can do it who can show Catherine how to put these braces on and off." And she found someone, and Catherine learned how to do it, and she's so proud of herself.
>
> *Susie:*   Sitting in at that IEP, they said, "She's rolling a ball 80% toward a target." That is meaningless. You can't have a person gainfully doing anything with such small goals. You have to throw the books out with a lot of these children and get practical. I said the operative word for this IEP is *function.* I want Betsy to learn to

function. We're getting down to the wire. I don't know how much longer she'll be learning, and I'm getting scared. Let's forget about rolling a ball and teach her to put on her socks.

What Your Child Needs To Separate from You Successfully

Self-Esteem, Persistence, and a Sense of Humor

Your child needs a strong sense of self-esteem, persistence, and a sense of humor. These will be your child's greatest allies in his growing independence. These qualities are learned best by the ways he is treated by others—including family, teachers, peers, and the professionals who provide interventions.

> *Stephanie:* There is something about Emma I really honor and is a real inspiration to me. She's always known who she is and accepted herself for who she is. She's always worked so hard to try and do whatever it is she needs to do to learn. That shows someone who is a successful person.

Daily Living Skills

Your child may have to learn daily living skills in small steps with a lot of structure. Typical children may learn more quickly than children with disabilities. Typical children also may be able to do more on their own without physical assistance. You want your child to learn as much as possible, so that if she eventually lives in a group home or a semi-independent living arrangement, or if she lives independently, there will be more options available and she will be better able to participate in life in the community.

Pride in Physical Appearance

Your child must take pride in his physical appearance. It is important that your child take pride in areas such as grooming, dressing, and weight. The fact is that if your child has any limitation in functioning or any behaviors that draw negative attention, he may at some point be the subject of negative or hesitant attitudes. If your child's grooming and general physical appearance show a lack of pride and care, it will be a double strike against him.

Living Skills Practice

Your child must have opportunities to practice the living skills that are important in the community. Social greet-

ings and public behavior on buses and in stores are just a few of the living skills your child should have the opportunity to practice. Your child needs to spend time in the community, where she can learn with guidance the many subtle social rules that cannot be taught in a classroom. Appropriate social behaviors are necessary for successful community living, and your child needs opportunities to practice these skills with instruction and support.

> *Susie:* Betsy can get away with more now because of her size. I can't control her, so we have to limit where we go. But I deal only with her now; I don't deal with anyone else around. I care about what she's getting out of the experience. Everything is training now. Everything is a mechanism to keep her included in society. She's 11, and we're starting to think about what kind of environment she needs and where she can feel safe.

Self-Discipline

Your child needs self-discipline. Your child may need more self-discipline than typical kids. You cannot always be your child's lifeguard and rescue squad. Your child needs to know his strengths and weaknesses and know the importance of self-regulation. He needs to learn how to handle frustration, express feelings constructively, and recognize when he is overstressed and know how to calm himself.

> *Janet:* I give Ryan an inch, and he walks all over me. He knows what's hard and he complains, "I can't do it all; it's too hard," and I say, "I know it's difficult, but you still have to do it."

Understanding and Living with a Disability

Your child must understand her disability and learn how to fight her own challenges. Your child must know how to take care of her physical needs, including those related to her disability. Your child must also know how to answer the questions and comments of others.

As your child Separates from your family, she needs to develop her own support network, ideally including other people who have disabilities. Through supportive contacts with others who face the same daily struggles and challenges, your child will find understanding, learn new techniques for more independent living, and experience a new level of feeling empowered and valuable.

Learning To Meet Challenges

Your child must be challenged, not coddled. Your child needs you to let go of his hand and see your confidence that you know he can try. He may not succeed at first, but he needs to know you are cheering because he tried. The very things you are trying to accomplish—independence and confidence—are undermined every time you hang on a little too long or coddle him. If you hesitate, he may hold back. If you are afraid, he may assume there is something to be afraid of. If your child is going to learn from his mistakes, he must have the chance to make them—and the safest place to make mistakes is with you.

Letting Go: Your Role in the Separating Process

When do you start allowing your child to make decisions to move forward—or to give up on something? How do you know when your child is secure enough to judge what she can and can't do? New experiences are hard for some kids, but a child can't always make rational decisions about whether to try.

With a child who is challenged in any way, there is a greater tendency for parents to hang on and to protect. You know the world is going to give her some hard knocks, and you want to postpone her frustrations as long as possible. It's hard to push when you know how hard your child has to work to reach a goal.

Letting Go Means Getting "Tough"

What is tough? When do you start? How tough do you have to get? There are certain things you have to get tough about at certain points, and that is the way it is. Tough means you make some decisions and stick to them. You are probably already "tough" about such things as wearing seatbelts, not running into the street, and not playing with matches.

> *Janet:*   Part of our growing up as parents is getting "tough." There's no time to be sad anymore. This is the world we're living in, and we have to get our kids ready to deal with it the very best they can.
>
> *Diane:*   Sometimes she uses her disability to manipulate, but not a lot. Like putting her laundry away. She'll say, "I can't do it." And I say, "If you have to do it one at a time, then that's how you'll do it." Her sister can pick up an armful and get it done fast. And Catherine will cry and get mad. She has to get one thing at a time, take it to her room, and then get another. That's tough. But that's life for her. I know that she exerts more energy in an afternoon than we use in 2 days, but the reality is that she has to work harder. It took me a long time to get to that.

Letting Go Is Gaining Something

Letting go is an affirmation of your efforts. It is pride in seeing your child achieve the goals you have all been striving for. Letting go is a sense of freedom from parenting, even though your child may never be totally, safely independent.

Letting Go Means Giving Up Some Control

Letting go means allowing others to share in caregiving. It may mean allowing others to share in caregiving and teaching. You suspect that someone else won't do as good a job as you do in caring for your child, but that's part of letting go. You won't always be there; your child needs to be able to work with and learn from other people.

Letting Go Is Admitting You Can't Make Your Child's Disability Go Away

Letting go can feel like you have lost your last chance to make things okay. You now must face some probabilities of things your child may not do as an adult—go to college, have children, marry, walk, dance, drive a car. There are different things some adults with special needs may never be able to do. Accepting what your child *cannot* do is an important step in letting go.

Letting Go Feels Like You Are Losing Something, and You Are

If you are successful, your child won't be as dependent on you. You won't be needed as much, and that is going to leave an empty space in your life that you may not quite know what to do with. You may look forward to that with glee or with a little apprehension or both. If caring for your child has been a major focus of your time and energy for a long time, letting go can be a major loss—and it may trigger some of those old Surviving feelings.

> *Diane:* The hardest part in letting go is not being able to shield her from criticism and hurt, but that's part of growing up for everybody.

Letting Go Means Reactivating
Some Surviving and Searching Issues

When you begin to contemplate decisions about Separating, you are likely to re-experience a lot of those old Surviving feelings that you thought were gone forever. Reactions like guilt ("Have we done everything we could at home?") and fear for how well your child can live somewhere else (and maybe fear for how you will live your life with your child gone). You may feel a new sense of loss. Separations are hard, even if it seems like the best decision for everyone and all plans are looking good.

If letting go for you means placing your child outside your home before the "typical time" that children leave, you may have some very strong reactions that make you think you've regressed back to Surviving. Feelings of guilt, incompetence, fear, grief, and anxiety are quite normal. Many parents also report feeling a sense of failure in the eyes of their friends and family, feelings of shame and embarrassment that they were not "strong enough" to care for their own child, and feelings that they have betrayed their child by "giving up on him."

No matter how much easier daily life may be there is a "hole in the family." Placement is a difficult decision but, for some families, it is necessary. Families who are forced to make such a decision never do so easily.

Some Searching issues will be back, too. There will probably be an active Outer Search if you are deciding what kind of living situation your child will need, finding one, and then figuring out who's going to pay for it. And your Inner Search will no doubt continue—What does this mean for your life? Where do you go from here? How will your relationship with your child evolve when you are not involved as her primary caregiver?

Obstacles to Separating

In spite of all your child's efforts and desires to become independent and your best efforts to let go, there may be other forces that complicate or slow your best-laid plans. Your child may have some persistent problem areas that prevent moving forward, or you may be trying to handle other stresses in your life (e.g., marital, health, or financial problems) that interfere with your best intentions.

There also may be obstacles in the community—a lack of resources or resistant attitudes that make your child's transition into the world outside the parental home a difficult and frustrating experience.

Child-Related Obstacles

If your child has special communication needs, he may need to learn alternative ways to express himself and make his needs known. If your child has developmental delays, he may not know age-appropriate social skills. Separations that would be typical for his age may need to be delayed or modified. If your child doesn't feel secure physically, he may be afraid to try new things. If your child is impulsive or has inappropriate social behaviors, he may run off or be unable to judge his safety in the community.

Parent-Related Obstacles

If you are confused about how much to protect and how much to pull back, you may have inconsistent expectations. If you and your child's other parent disagree about any of these issues, your child may get mixed messages that can delay her developing independence or get you all off track with behavior problems. Your child may not have as many Separating experiences as your other children simply because it may be too difficult to arrange these types of experiences. And sometimes you know she will probably be the target of some social discomfort or rejection and that may be too painful for you.

Many children with special needs are capable of more independent, appropriate, and mature behavior than they exhibit at home. It is not unusual to hear of children who show more competence away from home—at school, at camp, with other relatives, or in other settings. What frequently occurs is a relationship battle between a parent and child that may stem from several sources—the parent may have unrealistic expectations (too low or too high), or inconsistent expectations (e.g., mother versus father, mother on a good day versus mother on a bad day). Sometimes it's hard to find the right balance between what you feel you "should" do for your child and what you and your family can realistically handle. If you want your child to take part in extra activities and you don't have the time or the patience to arrange them yourself, perhaps you could add another member to your support team—a high school or college student, neighbor, fellow church member, or relative.

Community Obstacles

There may be a lack of resources for your child to take part in social activities, after-school and weekend programs, or sports and recreation. Services may exist but may be unaffordable, or there may be a lack of transportation or scheduling problems.

Negative or hesitant attitudes in your community toward people with special needs may make you feel more protective about your child. Some community programs may be "open to everyone," but you need to make sure that staff can be sensitive to your child's special needs and also provide a social environment that will be constructive and positive for your child. Your natural parental goal is for your child to find a supportive world to live in without fear of bias or prejudice. Attitudes are improving, and people with disabilities are gaining greater access to daily life in the community—but we do not live in a perfect world.

YOUR CHILD'S FUTURE—AND YOURS

As your child with special needs grows older, your fears and hopes for the future become the present. Many parents of young children plead, "What will he be able to do when he's 21?", "Will he outgrow his disability?", "If he is 2 years behind at 4, does that mean he will always be 2 years behind?", "Will he be able to be a parent?", or, "Will he be able to read?"

Sometimes professionals can make educated guesses based on experiences with other children or on probabilities. Each child is unique. Some children amaze the experts by excelling beyond any expectation, while others, for a variety of reasons, do not progress to the degree predicted. No one wants to make false promises; no one wants to take away hope.

The Different Ways Parents and Children Separate

At some point, your child is probably going to leave home. That may happen sooner than it would in a typical family, or it may happen later. You may be totally responsible for deciding and planning your child's leaving, your child may leave before you think she's ready, or (ideally) the decision may be made and carried out jointly.

Some families—for a variety of reasons and with all of the best community supports available—cannot maintain their child at home. This kind of decision must be respected and supported without judgment. Sometimes the best and sometimes the only solution for all concerned—the child or adolescent, parents, and brothers and sisters—is for the child who has special needs to live in an environment that is specifically designed to care for the specific needs that prevent continued living in the family home.

Some families simply burn out. Some children have such aggressive, self-destructive, or unmanageable behaviors that safety can be a major issue; the extent of behavioral interventions required for improvement may be too rigorous for any family environment. There need to be short-term individual and group homes with trained, caring personnel that enable children to go home on weekends or to live at home and go there on weekends, or whatever arrangement is needed. There need to be 1-day, 1-week, 1-month, and summer respite programs. There need to be more babysitters for evenings and weekdays. There need to be more weekend activity programs and social programs for adolescents and for adults. Families need more supports and options to prevent burnout and to handle burnout if it occurs. This requires professionals to educate parents, parents to support each other, and funding for both preventive and intervention programs

If you foresee your child living with family members for an extended period of time as an adult, he deserves and needs to function as independently as possible even within the family setting. There is often a tendency to continue "caregiving" an adult who is living at home (with or without "special needs"), which robs the individual of feelings of self-esteem and competence and, in the long run, restricts the lives of the caregivers as well.

Some children or adolescents can do best in residential schools and therapeutic settings that can facilitate social-emotional development in a group setting with peers who also have special needs. These settings may lead to the development of your child's own friendship and support network. Some children go to residential schools or treatment facilities for brief, intensive programs, while others profit from long-term settings. Another option may be for your child or adolescent to live with a caregiver/companion in the guest house in your backyard, 3 blocks away, or in another city.

Wherever your child lives that is away from you, for however long, and for whatever reason, you have made a major shift in your family life. You and your child have Separated.

After Separating

Separating from your adult child does not finish your parenting. Almost all parents and their children who leave home maintain relationships, but in those families (and you with your other children), everyone expects the adult child to be independent financially, have her own support networks, social groups, and work and leisure lives that are separate from the parents.

Your adult child may continue to have some special needs. Depending on the extent of her independent living skills and the community resources available, you may have to continue to be involved and responsible for finding or providing for some of her care.

Some children with special needs:

- Do not become adults with special needs. Their special needs of childhood are resolved through surgeries, medication, and interventions and they are so fully included in society that their disabilities "disappear."
- Integrate into society with specific aids that make their special needs more of an inconvenience than a disability. They may use wheelchairs or braces and crutches; hearing aids; guide dogs and hearing dogs for persons with visual or hearing impairments; medications to control seizures, hyperactivity, or other disorders that may in-

terfere with daily living; specially equipped cars for driving; or personal assistants for increased mobility and community involvement.

- Are limited in their ability to be included in a full range of activities in the community. In some cases, mental retardation, physical disabilities, and some kinds of behavior or emotional problems may limit work, living, and social opportunities. People with extensive disabilities may require personal assistance with daily living skills and may have major equipment or medical needs that restrict their mobility.
- Will always need ongoing supervision and protection because of chronic medical needs, extreme cognitive limitations, or dangerous or self-injurious behaviors.

Susie: The ideal for Betsy? To be placed in a situation with as much self-expression as possible allowing for her autism. A loving group home with four or five others, not an institution. But we don't know what's out there, and we aren't ready to even start looking at it yet.

Your Child as a Member of Society

For many reasons—including the 1990 enactment of PL 101-336, the Americans with Disabilities Act, the increasing empowerment of people with disabilities, and the advocacy of parents and professionals for people with special needs—disabilities are definitely coming out of the proverbial closet. Children with special needs are beginning to be included in programs with their typical peers in their home schools and communities, and there is a growing awareness and acceptance of people with disabilities through books, magazines, films, and television.

There are no absolutes for the kind of living situations that should be mandated for children, adolescents, or adults with special needs. There are always, of course, strong

opinions and varying schools of thought regarding placement decisions by families. The general operating principle
today is that children with special needs should be able to
live with their families and that communities should offer
the supports necessary for children to live at home, attend
the schools of their choice, and participate in a full range
of community activities.

Residential options, respite programs, and social and
recreational activities must be developed to meet the growing number of growing children with special needs whose
families desire and expect that they will be able to live their
adult lives in the community. Programs that are affordable,
culturally sensitive, and responsive to the unique needs of
single and working parents must be developed and made
available in order for all people with special needs to have
equal opportunities.

Children, adolescents, and adults with special needs
must be able to take advantage of social and recreational
programs that already exist in the community. But until
and unless there are leaders and staff who are able to successfully orchestrate this inclusion, there will be a need for
specialized programs in which people with all kinds of special needs can feel accepted and successful.

What will be the ideal living situation for your child's
adolescent and adult years? What resources will actually be
available?

Institutional living and institutional thinking belong to
American history. Placement out of the home used to be
an all-or-nothing decision, and institutional placement was
the only option for many years. We have moved far beyond
that, as we have learned that institutional care, no matter
how competent, does not meet current concerns regarding
the rights of individuals with special needs to be included
in the community with dignity and equality.

Because of the social advances being made, the opportunities for regular, integrated, mainstreamed, inclusive community living are expanding. We have a long way to go. Quality community living arrangements take time, money, and trained personnel to develop and maintain. Programs develop as a response to demand and need, and as parents become increasingly knowledgeable about the range of possibilities for fulfilled living, they will undoubtedly continue to provide major impetus for program development.

As the parent of a child with special needs, you want your child to meet the future with as much self-confidence and competence as possible. You have the right to have your child treated with the same dignity as every other individual in our society.

II

Strategies for
Successful Adaptation

6

Raising a Child
with Special Needs

Stephanie: Kids have it so much more together than
adults do. They accept things and work with things,
and they bring none of the baggage that we do. I can
remember being in a body cast for months as a teenager and everyone said, "You poor thing," and I
thought, "What's the big deal? I'm in it. What am I
supposed to do?"

You want your child to have the best possible chance for
successful inclusion in society and for feeling connected to
other people. You want him to have vitality and a feeling
of self-worth. You want your child to have control over decisions about his life, to live as self-sufficiently as possible,
and to be able to pursue goals for his personal fulfillment.

THE FOUR BASIC NEED GROUPS

As all children grow from infancy to adulthood, they share some basic needs. Your child may have some unique, extra needs because of limitations related to a physical disability, a chronic illness, mental retardation, or a major sensory or attention deficit.

The Need for Physical Safety

Children begin life totally dependent on others for keeping them alive and for protecting them from harm. This is a child's first and most basic need. It provides the foundation for the child's ability to trust and connect with others. All children have the following basic needs for physical safety:

1. *Children need to feel that someone will protect them* from getting lost, hurt, abandoned, or deprived of food and shelter. They need to feel comforted through hugging, feeding, holding, rocking, or being covered with a soft blanket.

2. *Children need to know they can rely on someone to rescue them* when they are cold, hungry, wet, in pain, or feel unsafe.

3. *Children need caregivers who will look out for the things the children don't see as irritating or dangerous*—a hot stove, electric sockets, a steep flight of stairs, or a car in the street. And children need to trust that their caregivers will not physically abuse or neglect them.

Your child may have some special needs for physical safety:

1. *Your child may experience irritations differently from a typical child.* Uncontrollable crying may be related to neurological immaturity or physical distress, or your child may have difficulty being comforted. Your child's signals for help may be misread or not read at all, which may cre-

ate increased anxiety about physical safety. Your child may need special skills for enlisting help, particularly if she has a problem with communication or mobility, or if she has a major sensory impairment. And you must learn to interpret your child's signals and cues.

2. *Your child's environment may need to be modified and customized* with special furniture, adaptive equipment, and creative arrangement of toys, clothes, and toothbrushes for easy access. You may need to build ramps, install an elevator, or widen doorways. If your child has allergies, irritants, such as carpeting and drapes, may need to be removed. Hazards in the home may need to be corrected and monitored—for example, locks may need to be placed on cabinet and closet doors.

3. *If your child has a severe visual impairment, he must be able to rely on the predictability of his environment*, and on his senses of touch, hearing, and smell to protect himself from physical danger. Toys or other objects left lying around can be dangerous. Your child may not see hazards, such as another child on a bicycle, a tree limb, or a hole in the sidewalk.

4. *If your child has balance problems or unpredictable movements, she must learn to live with the inconveniences these can cause* and you must live with the knowledge that she may knock over cups, spill food, or trip. You must allow for mishaps, supporting your child's efforts no matter how messy the process may be.

Your child may be motivated to walk, but if her legs and feet aren't ready to hold her, she will fall. If your child wants to climb, but doesn't have good enough balance, she may fall. You don't want to squelch your child's motivation for independence, but you must keep her safe. A typical toddler may more easily integrate all the parts until she can master the skill, but your child may need many more tries than a typical child. Your child may also need much more patience—from both you and herself—than a typical child.

5. *Your child may need to have extraordinary irritations imposed on him,* such as medications, braces, surgeries, and casts. He may need assistance with bathing and toileting, making it more difficult for him to have a sense of control over the privacy of his body. You must be able to ensure that all procedures are carried out with dignity and respect for the private parts of his body.

6. *Your child may trust others too much, wander off, or have no appropriate reserve with strangers.* As your child gets older, she may be vulnerable to personal danger because of poor judgment in initiating contacts with strangers. If your child "makes friends with everyone," and seems to have little sense of proper social limits for talking to others, she needs specific instructions, much practice (often with "decoys" for practice), and a lot of supervision. When you are out in public, you may need to be constantly vigilant to prevent wandering off.

7. *Your child may have medical issues or unpredictable interruptions in daily living,* such as seizures, asthmatic attacks, broken appliances, or lost (or forgotten) medication. Unpredictable crises that can endanger your child's physical safety require that you make sure there are backup plans and people for the even the simplest and most routine events.

The Need for Emotional Security

It is difficult to separate physical safety from emotional security because from a child's point of view, you can't have one without the other. All of our needs are affected by each other, and they build on each other. Each time you hold your child with love, you are meeting his need for physical comfort and emotional security, and he is learning how to be social and to feel good about himself. Like the need for physical safety, there are some basic needs for emotional security that all children have:

1. *Children need to feel loved and well taken care of.* They need to feel accepted as they are—with no strings attached. They need to hear you say, "I'm so lucky to have you as my child." They need to feel that they are loved and valued just because they exist, and they need to feel understood and know that they are being listened to. A child needs to know, "I will be loved no matter what I achieve or what I fail; I will be loved no matter what I can or cannot do." Your child needs to believe that the best she can do is all she needs to do. She needs to feel secure that there is someone who makes her feel okay and someone with whom she will not be criticized or humiliated because of her limitations, appearance, or behavior.

2. *Children need you to hold on and they need you to let go.* They need to move away at their own pace, knowing you will be there when they want to come back and that you will rescue them if they go too far too soon. They need you to encourage their independence and sense of control over themselves and their environments as they learn to dress and feed themselves, make choices, and begin to test your limits.

Children need to pull away and detach themselves from you as they are ready. They need to know that emotional protection and physical safety are always available in the background so that they can take risks and grow.

3. *Children need to experience and experiment with their environments, their bodies, and their minds.* They need to play—to learn about their world, master their fears, create, practice their skills, pretend, and be in control of a little part of their lives.

Children need to laugh, and they need you to laugh

with them, but never laugh at them. They need to see the world in silly ways and to play with words and sounds. Children need to hear their parents laugh and to know that humor is a regular and important part of daily living. Children need to be touched—tickled, cuddled, hugged, kissed, and carried upside down. Touching conveys connection, affection, safety, and calm.

In addition to these needs all children have, your child may have special needs for emotional security:

1. *If your child can't physically move away from you*—"run and hide" or find private space—he needs to have other ways to separate. Perhaps he needs a divider to hide behind or large pieces of fabric or scarves to "disappear" behind. Peekaboo may have to be assisted. If you have other children, they can be amazingly creative for finding ways to modify games.

2. *If your child has problems with communication*, it may take longer to listen to her than to other people in your life. It may mean developing a greater level of attention, sitting still, and tolerating more than you have had to before. If your child cannot communicate verbally, you may need to find other ways, such as sign language or communication boards, to help her express her needs, ideas, questions, and feelings.

3. *If your child is unable to hold or manipulate toys*, he may need to find other ways to play. He may need assisted play equipment—someone to interact with him, to hold objects, or to move pieces on a game board. He may need adapted play—toys that are a larger size, a Velcro board so pieces won't fall, or computer games with a variety of touch and signal boards.

The Need for Socialization and Relating

A child begins to learn about relationships in her primary bond with her parents. As she becomes more physically and

emotionally independent, she discovers that there are more people to relate to and many rules she must learn for getting along with everyone. Like the other basic needs, all children have needs for socialization and relating:

1. *Children need to learn how to live successfully in the world today.* They begin by learning how to live in the family—learning the family rules, routines, and rituals; learning to share and cooperate with others; learning boundaries of personal space, privacy, and private thoughts;

Mom a great respecter of privacy

learning values of right and wrong; learning to communicate feelings, fantasies, dreams, and desires; and learning to handle frustrations, failures, joys, and losses.

2.   *Children must learn thousands of rules for daily living.* Many rules are so taken for granted that we don't even think of them as rules—table manners, toileting and grooming habits, bedtime rituals, eating behaviors, and compliance. Becoming a member of society is a major task for all children. Children do not naturally self-regulate. For example, children learn table manners by what they are told to do and told not to do, by watching how other people behave at the dinner table and imitating them, and by experimenting with what they are told to do and testing the limits ("Dad said I can't throw food across the room, but what if I just drop some peas off the edge of the table? What will happen if I put some in my milk?"). Children learn by finding out what pleases and displeases other people—especially the important people in their world.

3.   *As children expand to the world outside, they need to learn the rules of the community*—the rules and rituals of playing and working with others, safety, and how to behave around teachers and coaches and in stores and in church. They learn about talking to strangers, crossing the street, and checking out library books. They discover that different places have different rules for how loud you can talk and how long you must sit, and they'll probably learn about bigger kids and bullies.

Your child may have special needs for socialization and relating:

1.   *If your child has trouble learning new rules or social cues* or easily forgets, you may have to repeat rules over and over and over again. If your child has a problem when there is a break in routine, he may need a great deal of structure and very clear consequences for his behavior. He may also need to have his daily life organized to a greater

degree than your other family members (including you!). Children with learning or remembering problems may need extra structure and consistency in their environments.

2. *If your child has a sensory impairment,* she may not be able to learn the many rules of daily living in the typical ways other children learn. If your child has a visual impairment, for instance, she may not be able to distinguish looks of pleasure, disappointment, or anger in other people. If your child has a hearing impairment, she won't naturally pick up the many verbal cues that pass among your family members unless she is looking at the speaker. So your child may need you to find new ways to communicate the hundreds of daily interactions that you and your other family members take for granted.

3. *You may need to make socialization experiences happen* if your child does not develop a natural network of friends. You may, for example, need to make a special effort to arrange get-togethers with other children. Your child may be excluded because other parents may be uncomfortable or fearful about your child's special needs, and so you have to take some initiative. It may be hard for you to watch your child with other children if he has a hard time keeping up or if he is less agile or makes more mistakes than others. Sometimes the only (or the easiest) alternative is to just not go, but you may need to evaluate other possibilities. Your child may be more successful playing with just one or two other children or with children who are slightly younger than he. Sometimes you can find a family member, neighbor, or college student who can help your child practice outdoor skills, such as throwing, catching, or climbing.

Some activities may have to be modified. Outings may have to be planned, taking into account a short attention span or limited stamina. You may have to take equipment or an aide. If your child is physically restricted, much of the world must be brought to him—or your child may have to be taken to things.

4. *Your child must learn how her pace of living affects people around her.* She may take more time than her brothers and sisters or her friends to dress, to get from one place to another, to eat, or to express herself. She must be able to handle her own stress and frustration and be sensitive to the reactions of others.

5. *Your child needs to know how to work with other people and for other people.* If he will be entering the job market, a work training program, or college, he must develop skills for organizing work and understanding time and how to work within schedules. He must learn to handle money and to shop and the many other skills for living successfully in the community.

The Need for Self-Esteem

How does a child develop self esteem? From feeling safe in her physical world, and secure in her emotional world, from learning how to live among other people, and from her own interpretation of her abilities and limitations.

All children develop self-esteem in four areas: physical, cognitive, social, and psychological.

Physical Self-Esteem: How Do I Feel About My Body?

No body is perfect, and physical self-esteem develops from our attitudes about how we look and how we move.

1. *Children need to have a positive body image* and confidence in their bodies, and to feel comfortable with how their bodies move through space. As children grow, they need to learn about their sexual development, to have information appropriate to their age and understanding, and to understand the pleasure and responsibilities connected to sexual feelings and behavior.

2. *Children need to have pride in their physical ap-pearance* and give importance to self-care and grooming. As they grow up and move more independently into the world, they need to understand that their social and working lives may be influenced by their standards of personal cleanli-ness, including their bodies, hair, teeth, and clothing, and the way they handle their personal environments.

3. *Children need to have pride in and take care of their health and stamina.* They must be taught the impor-tance of nutrition, rest, and exercise in maintaining their bodies and have knowledge of the destructive effects of al-cohol, tobacco, and other drugs. Children who need medi-cation or special diets need to understand how these work and how to participate in making these necessities a posi-tive aspect of their self-care.

Cognitive Self-Esteem: How Good Am I at Problem-Solving?

If we think we are good problem-solvers, learn that we can't know everything and that we may have to ask for help and we'll sometimes make mistakes, we can have good cogni-tive self-esteem.

1. *Children need to have a positive image of them-selves as learners* and confidence in their ability to learn. They need to be able to problem-solve by seeing alterna-tives, anticipating possible outcomes, and weighing choices. Children need to be able to ask questions without feeling stupid or degraded and to make mistakes and see their er-rors as normal and as challenges to try again. They also need to know that they are not failures because they make mistakes.

2. *Children need to recognize and have pride in their strengths* and take appropriate risks to expand and stretch their lives. They need to understand their limitations and develop ways to compensate for those limitations, by

knowing when to ask for help and how to accept help when it is needed.

3. *Children need to have common sense and good judgment;* to show curiosity, imagination, creativity, and spontaneity; and to develop talents and interests. Children need to see alternatives and that most things in life are relative—not all or nothing, black or white, success or failure, and good or bad.

Social Self-Esteem: How Do I Get Along with Others?

A sense of social self-esteem comes from believing in our social and cultural worth, and by respecting the worth and dignity of others.

1. *Children need to feel confident in social interactions with friends* through school, in play, and in activities. They need to feel that others do and will like them, but recognize that not everyone does or will like them. They should be able to enter social situations without undue fear or anxiety and have interest in others and good listening and negotiating skills. Children need to know appropriate social behaviors for a variety of situations, including basic standards for greetings, topics to talk about, and taboos of social behavior (e.g., swear words, name-calling).

2. *Children need to care about other people.* Children must know how to show sympathy for those in pain, develop empathy and know that other people have a point of view, and convey compassion and respect for the dignity of all other people. Children need to know and honor family and cultural traditions for holidays, rites of passage, worship, celebrations, and losses. Children need a sense of moral values in relation to standards of right and wrong, honesty, the worth of individuals, different cultural groups, concern for and care of the environment, and thoughtfulness in their personal relationships.

3. *Children need to understand and respect other*

people's personal boundaries—and they need to know that they have boundaries worthy of respect, too. They need to be assured that they are entitled to a private life, that people know when they like to be cuddled and know when they prefer to be alone and when they prefer to be with others. They need to respect the personal space and belongings of others, understand the right to privacy, and learn whom to talk to and trust. Children need to learn to trust other people, and be capable of attachments to important people outside the family—teachers, therapists, and friends.

Psychological Self-Esteem: How Do I Like Myself as a Person?

You will like yourself if you believe that you are likeable, that you have value, that you are unique, and that your differences are not defeats.

1. *Children need a realistic view of themselves* with all of their abilities and limitations; they need to accept limitations in themselves and in others, to know that nobody's perfect, but no one is expected to be.

2. *Children need to see problems as challenges*, not obstacles. They need to take risks and to fail, focus on their goals, and develop the persistence and patience to work toward them.

3. *Children need to have a stable sense of self*, with a range of feelings, including joy, excitement, fear, anger, and frustration.

4. *Children need to have vitality, enthusiasm, and a zest for life.* They need to be able to be alone, to entertain themselves, to have a sense of humor, to show spontaneity and flexibility, and to generate creativity from within.

Self-Esteem and Special Needs

Your child needs to know what his disability is, how to take care of it, and what to say to others about it. He needs to know how his disability might affect his life and how it doesn't have to affect his life. If your child's major means of mobility is going to be a wheelchair, he must learn to handle a wheelchair and learn to deal with his differentness, and he needs your clear message of your belief in him. You may have to get "tough" and enforce some rules if your child needs to wear a hearing aid, a helmet, a back brace, special shoes, an orthodontic retainer, or a prosthesis.

As your child becomes an adolescent and young adult, he will probably have sexual curiosity and interests not unlike typical children the same age. This can be a complicated, nervous time for parents depending on their child's social, emotional, or cognitive limitations, which may confuse the course of typical sexual development and experimentation. Children with delayed social skills or communication difficulties may be especially vulnerable to sexual exploitation. As a parent, you must balance your own anxieties and responsibilities with your child's needs, rights, and responsibilities for being a sexual person.

Your child must know how society views disabilities and what control he has and does not have over other people's attitudes. He must understand and accept his own pace for movement, play, and learning without feeling inferior, inadequate, or bad. Your child must have a realistic view of his abilities, his limitations, and how he is like and different from others. He needs to know that everyone is different and that different is not "better" or "worse." He needs to know that there is no such thing as perfect.

Your child needs to know that having a disability means that some things take longer to do, have to be done in different ways, or can't be done at all. Your child needs to understand that other people have limitations, too, for all kinds of reasons and that a disability is an inconvenience sometimes; it means you need some extra help. And there's nothing wrong with that.

As your child gets older, he will become more aware of his differences. From time to time, he may express feelings of depression and anger as he understands what his abilities and limitations are and what they mean for his life. These feelings are normal, and talking about them is normal and healthy. Talking about uncomfortable feelings makes them easier to let go of and move beyond. His feelings should be respected and listened to because they are part of his own adaptation process.

Your child must develop confidence in his abilities and skills for expanding his talents and interests. He needs optimism, spontaneity, creativity, playfulness, and a sense of humor. He needs the freedom and the encouragement to express curiosity, seek knowledge, ask questions, and voice opinions.

Your child needs to really like himself and be able to laugh at himself, and he needs to develop patience and a great tolerance for frustration. And he needs to know that his self-acceptance and pride will be his greatest demonstration of who he is. He must learn to reject prejudice and discrimination, and be able to respond to questions and negative comments in ways that maintain a sense of integrity and self-respect. He must learn to ignore thoughtless comments and learn which battles to fight for self-respect. — *Edna helped so much here.*

Your child has special needs. All children have needs that are unique and special to them, but "special needs" is a euphemism some people use to say your child is significantly different in a negative way. You can argue with this, and you may not agree with it, but children with exceptional musical talent and children with intellectual gifts are not included in this category in the same way. So what your child has to learn at some point is: "The fact is you're different, and some people may give you a hard time about that because they don't understand." And parents need to ask, "How can I help you deal with that and know that you're okay?" Your task as a parent is to understand the reality of the world your child will grow up in and to know that there are extra things your child needs to succeed in that world.

Because we do not live in a perfect world, the reality is that your child is a member of a minority group that often faces discrimination and prejudice. And because of that reality, your child needs to learn to withstand with dignity the prejudices and limitations that may challenge him in the community.

THE IMPORTANCE
OF PLAY IN
YOUR CHILD'S DEVELOPMENT

Play is the way your child practices life—imitating relationships, getting mastery over others and the environment, practicing skills, and expressing emotions including fears, frustrations, and confusions. Play is creative and expansive. It is the trying out of new ideas, the putting together of old ideas in new forms, and experimentation with rules. Play expands minds and bodies. It is stretching boundaries and feeling textures and sensations. Play is practicing gross motor skills—jumping, climbing, dancing, and twirling; it is practicing fine motor skills—building block towers, coloring and taking apart a radio; it is defining and refining ideas and plans—drawing pirate ships, treasure maps, dinosaurs, or princesses. It is making yourself feel big in a world where you feel very small; it is giving out orders to the smaller kids in the room when you're usually on the receiving end.

Special Play Needs
Your Child May Have

If your child has been subjected to many medical procedures and surgeries, she may often play "doctor" and hospital as a way of reliving and gaining control over her feelings of helplessness. Your child can usually work out her feelings at her own pace.

If your child has an overly structured life, with therapies, riding in the car, and needing to be cared for, she needs unstructured time both alone and with a parent to just "see what happens." Let her take the initiative, make all of the decisions, and have some sense of control over her time. She may want to just sit and watch the fish swimming in the tank. Your child needs space and time to do nothing, to create his own direction, and to develop his own entertainment skills. To do this, your child needs, to the extent that is possible, his own space and privacy, and assurance of protection of his belongings.

Doing nothing is time that allows new ideas to be generated. It is a time to feel relaxed and to rest your body and your mind. It can be a time to make plans for tomorrow, to sit and remember what a good time you had at the beach yesterday, or to just look around your room at your things.

If your child doesn't have much control over her life or feels weak and powerless, she may like to change the rules of games or make up special rules. You may wonder if that isn't "cheating." Didn't you ever wish you could change some of the traffic rules while you were driving to work so you could get there a little faster? Until about age 7 or 8, most children are creative with rules, but there's usually a turning point when they become very concerned about fairness.

If your child feels stressed, tired, or ill or has been working really hard to master a skill, you may see her play in a way that makes you wonder if she is regressing. This isn't abnormal; it's a way children have of "catching their breath"—stepping back to a place of comfort and safety for a little while.

Special Challenges for Parents

Your attitudes about play were largely shaped by your own experiences and memories about playing as a child and by your ability to be playful as an adult. Some parents see play as unimportant, a "childish" time filler. If your own parents (or other adults) were not playful with you when you were a child, it may be hard for you to play "Candyland" a thousand times and be excited about getting the candy cane card each time, to make up silly rhymes, or to sing with your children. Therefore, unstructured play time may make you uncomfortable. It may feel like time is "being wasted" for your child who could be "learning" something, and it may seem to you like "nothing is happening."

Some parents get impatient and bored with time that isn't busy. You may be tired from so much extra parenting that you want time away from your child, rather than time "just playing." You may feel you should be stimulating and teaching your child all the time, and you may feel compelled to improve on your child's play, correct a drawing, or put an extra block in the tower so it won't fall. It's important to have play time where you don't criticize, don't correct, don't judge, and don't improve unless you're asked. And even then involve your child in deciding what to add or change. Ask questions. Explore your child s fantasy stories and expand on them. Get excited with your child about her creations by trying to see the world from her point of view.

COMMON THINGS YOU MAY FORGET TO REMEMBER ABOUT YOUR KIDS

1. Kids need free time that is all their own to do whatever they want with it.

2. Kids will have bad days, grumpy days, sad days, tired days, and not hungry days—just like grownups. Days that look like regressing or "slipping back" are often just resting spots.

3. Kids will show bursts of learning. Suddenly, they may do many new things, and you may think it's going to go on forever like that.

4. Kids pass through plateaus. When you think they've stopped learning, you may start to feel afraid they'll never make progress again.

5. Kids need to know that they don't always get everything they want, that there are rules they don't like, and that sometimes they will feel frustrated, disappointed, and even angry. But life is like that sometimes.

6. Kids need to test limits in order to grow. Stubbornness in toilet training, eating problems, and bedtime problems are surefire limit testers.

7. Kids have lots of different kinds of feelings and need to know that feelings are okay. They need to find appropriate ways to express them, and sometimes adults have to help them do that.

8. Kids are often messy, sloppy, and clumsy. They spill things, forget things, and lose things. They whine, argue, and complain. They get angry, scared, and sad.

9. Kids feel small and vulnerable much of the time, and their feelings are hurt very easily. They need to hear and see us treat them with respect, fairness, and pride and joy.

10. Kids are a lot of fun, and that's got nothing whatsoever to do with having a disability.

7

Taking Care of You

*Why is it so hard to take care of yourself when
you're so good at taking care of everybody else?*

When you feel like you don't have much control over your
life and you feel overwhelmed with responsibilities, it can
be very hard to make time to take care of yourself. You
may ask yourself, "If anything happened to me, what would
happen to my child and my family?" There are three issues
that will be influenced by where you are in the adaptation
process:

1. *Parenthood and self-esteem*   Being the parent of a child
   with special needs may have challenged your feelings
   of competence and adequacy, but your self-esteem has
   probably also been enhanced in some ways you may
   not have considered.
2. *Parenthood and stress*   Stress is part of the job descrip-
   tion for parenthood, but it can wear you down, harm
   your health, and definitely make you hard to live with.

Everyone gets stressed out by different things at different times. Part of taking care of yourself is recognizing stress, learning how to reduce it, and knowing how to prevent it.

3. *Parenthood and personal growth*   Being a parent, especially when a child requires extra time, attention, and concern, can use up your time and energy. Thinking about expanding your own life may seem trivial and unimportant at times.

PARENTHOOD AND SELF-ESTEEM

Self-esteem: The ability to get things done, feel competent and in control of at least some things in your life, and establish some priorities for what you value and how you will spend your time.

Raising a child with special needs has probably challenged your self-esteem more than once. And there are ways your self-esteem has probably been enhanced.

Self-Esteem Challengers

When all of this was new to you and you were just beginning to get some clues that your child might have some problems, you probably tried even harder to do everything perfectly, to erase the concerns that you—or some professionals—were having about your child's development. You kept trying because you weren't really sure what else to do, but the concerns remained. A typical reaction of many parents in the beginning is to feel confused and incompetent. Fortunately, these feelings tend to decrease as you move forward and as time passes. But, while you're in the midst of them, your self-esteem can really be challenged; for example:

1. No matter how hard you tried to nurse or feed your child, she couldn't take nourishment from you.
2. No matter how much you stroked, rocked, and enfolded your child in your arms, you couldn't soothe his prolonged, irritable cry.
3. No matter how much you encouraged, cooed, smiled and tickled, your child didn't reach for toys, sit up, or babble those first sounds.
4. No matter how much you tried to do the right thing, there were medical problems that required hours in doctors' offices or emergency rooms, hospitalizations and surgeries, invasive procedures, and vague or unhelpful responses from professionals.
5. No matter what you knew to be the facts and no matter what anyone said to support you, somewhere deep down inside, you wondered if you did something wrong.
6. No matter how much you tried to think positive and how much your friends and family did to cheer you up, you still found yourself crying a lot; parenthood just wasn't the joyful time you anticipated, and you felt guilty for not being happier.
7. No matter how supportive other people were, you pulled back from friends and family because you didn't want people to notice you were feeling anxious, and you didn't want anyone looking too closely at you or your child.
8. No matter how much you hovered over your child, trying to feel awe and joy, all you could feel were confusion and fear.
9. No matter how many parenting books you read, how many techniques you tried, and how well you were doing with your other children, your child was slow to learn, and you felt incompetent.
10. No matter how many of your old coping skills you tried, they just didn't work anymore. You were used

to being effective and solving problems, and this one had you beat.

Self-Esteem Enhancers

As you move forward, past the intense emotions you felt in the beginning, you realize that you have not only survived, but you have grown more competent, and self-confident, and that your self-esteem has not only met many of its challenges, but has been enhanced.

1. You survived the first shock of your situation and have experienced a lot of pretty sad and confusing feelings, but you have come through them a stronger person.
2. You were challenged by your child's problems and the changes you had to make in your life and you rose to the occasion.
3. You found out you are more competent than you would have believed.
4. You have more patience than you ever imagined would be possible.
5. You see your child's disability as incidental to your child as a person.
6. You see all disabilities and imperfections in a new way, and you are realizing how naive you used to be.
7. You have organized your life and your family's life better than you would have predicted, even though you have a lot more to do now than you ever did.
8. You are learning a whole new world of information about special needs that you never even knew existed.
9. You are finding a positive shift in values and commitments to other people as you have had to re-arrange your priorities.
10. You have persisted in finding help for your child in spite of discouraging views you may have heard from

professionals and your own self-doubts—and you are
getting a payoff.

11. You have discovered new aspects of your personality—new strengths, talents, and skills you never knew
you had.

12. You are finding you have something to offer other
people—other parents who are having a difficult time,
other children with and without special needs, people
you know and people you don't know who need to be
educated about disabilities.

PARENTHOOD AND STRESS

*Stress: When you've got more to do than you feel
you can do.*

Stress is about responsibility and control. When your responsibilities and your feeling of control over them are about
equal, you can say your life is in balance. You may have a
lot to do, but you manage to do it all, or you do what you
can and let the rest go until later. You may have a lot of
responsibilities, but you may also feel like you've got them
under control most of the time. You may be very busy, but
you may be feeling a "good" stress—the kind that moti-
vates you to get all those things done. You may feel tense
and pushed, but it's a productive energy.

When you feel like you have too many responsibilities
and not enough control over them, your stress level rises.
You may have many—or only a few—responsibilities, but
if your emotional state is fragile, you are over-tired, you
need help and don't have it, or you feel like you don't have
things under control, you feel stressed. That kind of stress
is bad for you.

And then there is the feeling you might recall, of hav-

I loved Florida vacations

ing *lots* of control over what you have to do and very few responsibilities. That's called a vacation.

Recognizing Stress in Your Daily Life

> *Maybe you can't change your responsibilities, but
> you can get a sense of control over them by
> changing your attitude about them.*

Here are some typical responsibilities that can result in high stress if you let them:

- Daily hassles of running the household and family
- Constantly dealing with unexpected crises
- Too many things that need to be done at the same time
- Unresolved problems that just go on and on
- The amount of care your child needs
- Managing the money
- Having to do everything without enough help or support

And here are some attitudes that can make you feel out of control:

- Feeling overwhelmed by the number of things that have to be done
- Fear that things are just going to fall apart
- Fear that you're going to fall apart
- Pessimism about how things are going to turn out
- Blaming yourself when things go wrong
- Believing you can't take time to relax or exercise
- Resenting people for not helping you more
- Concern about how others are judging you
- Worrying about problems all the time
- Feeling sorry for yourself

Stress is something you can actually feel in your body, and you can learn to detect your stress level rising and falling. After you learn to recognize it, you can learn to control it. To find your tension level, you can use the Subjective Assessment of Discomfort (SAD) Scale.

The SAD Scale
(Subjective Assessment of Discomfort)

Begin by asking yourself, "How anxious and worried am I right now?" Rate yourself between 1 and 5 using the scale below. You may use half numbers (e.g., 3.5).

1 = You are totally relaxed and calm; no pressure; no tension.
2 = There is some awareness of tension, but it comes and goes and doesn't distract you. You can work, read, or be involved in a project with a pleasurable state of mind.
3 = You are feeling some tension and responsibility, but it is helping you to focus. You feel some pressure, but it is motivating and positive.
4 = You are feeling uncomfortable tension that is interfering with your work or ability to focus. You are able to keep going, but feel anxious and afraid that it might get worse.
5 = You are about to have a panic attack or collapse from the tension you feel. You cannot keep going and feel like you are going to lose control.

Read the scale and become familiar with the numbers. For about 1 week, stop in your tracks four or five times every day and say, "How anxious and worried am I right now?" Rate yourself using the 1–5 scale. See if you can identify what things are affecting your SAD score. If you have a score of 4 or 5 very often, you can learn to lower your stress level by using some of the techniques that follow.

Reducing Stress in Your Daily Life

Reducing your stress level will not solve your problems. It helps you reduce your tension and anxiety so that you can clear your mind and focus energy on solving your problems. Being overstressed lowers your ability to think, plan, work, and relax. There are really people who say, "I'm too stressed out to relax." You may even know some of them.

There are many techniques for reducing stress; different ones work for different people. A few techniques are presented here that you may find helpful. If they are not enough, check your library or bookstore, or you may want to consult a professional to find a technique that works for you.

One important point to remember: You have to really *want* to reduce your stress level and you *have* to practice. It isn't always easy in the beginning because many people feel guilty for devoting any time and thought to themselves, and others feel the exercises are silly and they feel embarrassed or uncomfortable.

It's often hard to overcome habits of thinking we need to "keep going," no matter how tired, overwhelmed, or cranky we feel. Slowing down and setting some limits for ourselves often feels like we are "weak" and are failing. These are old beliefs based on outdated information about physical and mental health and strength. So, get to work on reducing and preventing stress!

STRESS Buster

S   *Sit*—in a quiet place by yourself. Get very comfortable.
T   *Turn off the world.* Think of your life as a radio. Find the on/off button and turn it off.
R   *Rest your face.* Close your eyes. Squinch them together really tightly. Then relax. Feel the contrast between tension and relaxation in your eyes.
      Clench your jaw really tightly. Relax. Feel the contrast between tension and relaxation. When you relax your jaw, your neck, shoulders, upper back, and arms will feel relaxed.
E   *Exhale.* In order to exhale properly, you first have to inhale properly. Take a long, slow, deep breath, filling your lungs. Hold it for 5 seconds. Now, very s-l-o-w-l-y exhale. Then breathe gently and quietly.
S   *Sit still for 5 minutes.* Savor your solitude.
S   *Stretch slowly*—from your head down to your toes.

Learning the Relaxed Feeling

Sit quietly and take two deep breaths. Spend a moment listening to the sound of your normal breathing.
Focus on your feet and legs and count backward from 10 to 0 — one breath out per count. As you breathe out, think: "My legs and feet are heavy, warm, and relaxed."
Now focus on your stomach. Again, count backward from 10 to 0, one breath out per count. As you breathe out, think, "My stomach is heavy, warm, and relaxed."
Repeat the counting and breathing for your shoulders and arms, thinking, "My shoulders and arms are heavy, warm, and relaxed."

Repeat the counting and breathing, with special attention to your jaw and shoulders, "My jaw is heavy and sinking down; my shoulders are heavy and sinking down." Let your mouth hang slightly open and your shoulders be heavy and slumped. Say to yourself, "This is what I need, *I can make this happen.* There is plenty to do and think about, but I will take this time to relax." Try to memorize this feeling.

Every time you feel any sense of reduced tension and noticeable relaxing, think, "This is what I need. *I can make this happen.* There is plenty to do and think about, but I will take this time to relax."

Relaxing just keeps getting easier. After you have memorized The Relaxed Feeling, you can regain it with the 5-Second Pause. You can use the 5-second pause as many times as you want every day to take a mental break, relax, and gain a sense of calmness and control.

The 5-Second Pause

Breathe in. Breathe in. Hold it. Now, breathe out slowly. Tense and then relax your jaw and shoulders. Recall the relaxed, heavy feeling.

To be able to relax when you need it you must know the feeling that you're seeking. The 5-Second Pause can help, and it can be enhanced by some experience with deep relaxation—whether from recalling a great vacation moment, picturing clouds on a perfect day, getting a massage, meditating, or using the relaxation techniques described previously.

Develop your own personal stress breakers to reduce stress in your daily life. When you're feeling stressed out but you have to keep going, at least give yourself a little break. As kids, we called it recess. It always helps to be aware of where you are on the SAD Scale, to do the Stress Buster, and get The Relaxed Feeling. Sometimes though, you need to do something different to distract yourself for a while. You may like escaping into a novel, riding a bike, or working in a garden. Listed below are a few other suggestions for interrupting a stressful day.

1. *Do the STRESS Buster.*
2. *Use the 5-Second Pause.*
3. *Take time out.* Your kids may think you are really weird for *wanting* time out, but you can let them know that timeout is good for everybody now and then. Take 10 minutes to stop your world and step outside the action to settle your mind. Sit in a cozy chair or on the front porch. Don't think about problems or what you have to do tomorrow. Don't think at all. Let your overworked brain have a break from taking in or putting out. You may want to visualize a calm, relaxing scene or just look at a tree in your yard. Your problems won't go away during your timeout, but they (probably) won't get any worse, and they can feel a lot less overwhelming when you get back to them.
4. *Take a nap.* What a luxury. Sometimes it's hard to arrange a nap around the family schedule, but if you can ever see an hour or two up ahead, go ahead and indulge.
5. *Take a soak or a shower.* Turn off the light and light a candle. Close your eyes and hum a tune.
6. *Take a hike* or even a walk around the block. Stretch your body—walk fast, walk slow, or walk the dog. Breathe in, look up at the sky, and take in the colors around you.
7. *Take a ride* on a bicycle or in your car. Go to a scenic overlook and enjoy the view. Drive to a park and sit

on a bench. Drive down a pretty road and sing with the radio.

8. *Take an action break.* Shoot some hoops, hit some tennis balls, swim some laps, jog around the track or through the park, or play loud music and dance.

Preventing Stress in Your Daily Life

Now you know how to recognize and reduce your stress level. You can also prevent stress by deciding what you are going to worry about, what you will think about, what you will get angry about, and what you will ignore.

The Art of Worrying

Worrying is a cycle of negative thoughts that usually include doomsday thinking. We seem to believe that if we worry about something long and hard enough, it will go away, be resolved, or work out. We worry about things we are anxious about—and worrying usually makes us more anxious. We worry about things we often have no control over, but when we worry we think we have some control. Sometimes we believe that if we worry hard enough about something bad that might happen, it won't happen.

We worry about the mistakes we think we may have made in the past—the "what ifs" and "if onlys" of life (the "shoulda, coulda, woulda" school of thought—guaranteed to keep your guilt going strong).

We worry about the future and think of all the possible negative outcomes. It's as if we are shielding ourselves from bad surprises—if we can anticipate every possible outcome, we won't be so shocked and overwhelmed if it happens.

Worrying is something we think shows we are responsible. "Good parents worry about their children"; if we worry a lot, we feel more involved and caring. If we say, "I'm not worried about that problem," we are often afraid it sounds like we don't care.

Worrying is a habit. It's automatic for most people, and it's mostly unpleasant. Worrying makes you feel tense, anxious, afraid, frustrated, insecure, and out of control.

A little bit of worrying is good. It makes you alert to what is bothering you. But before it gets out of control, turn your worrying into problem-solving. Identify what is bothering you and think of any alternatives for something you can do about it. If there are things you can do, make a plan for when and what to do. If there are things you can't do anything about, try not thinking about them. If it's hard to give yourself permission to not worry, you might consider a Worry Box. Imagine a box that sits on a shelf only you can see. Next, imagine putting your worries in the box, closing it, and putting it on the shelf. Know that your worries are safe, that they are not going anywhere, and that you can take any of them out whenever you choose for as long as you like. The purpose of the Worry Box is to give *you* control over your worries instead of your worries controlling you.

If some things seem so important to worry about that you absolutely cannot put them out of your mind or into the Worry Box, schedule some Worry Time. If you are going to worry, do it efficiently and well. Decide on a time (a half hour is usually enough). Set everything else aside, find a quiet spot, and worry very hard. Then put the problem out of your mind. Don't let it seep into your every thought all day long. You have better things to think about. Or you will, once you have some mental space and give yourself permission to not worry so much.

Most of all, don't be so hard on yourself. All parents make mistakes with their partners, their children, and others. Everyone has bad days, makes bad decisions, and bad choices. It is important to develop a sense of trust in your overall judgment and to move on, learning what you can from your mistakes. Nobody's perfect; we can only strive to grow.

Getting Rid of Pesky Thoughts

No matter how good your intentions are, you will be like everybody else and find that sometimes things you don't want to think about fly into your head like pesky little gnats. These thoughts are up to no good; they can make you anxious, depressed, frightened, and incompetent because you can't keep them away. These negative, awful thoughts (NATs) are everywhere, and they are so fast and so tiny you usually can't see them coming—although you do tend to learn the conditions that breed them.

Imagine a fly swatter in your mind that serves the sole purpose of swatting NATs away. Whenever they appear, abolish them on sight. This can work especially well at night, when unwelcome thoughts try to keep you awake.

Standing Up for You: Saying "No" and Being Assertive

Are you doing more than you can do? Most people who do too much don't think they have any choice about that. There are just a lot of things that have to get done, and what's one more little project or errand or telephone call especially if it will help somebody out or save time for that other person. You may feel like you have to do everything anybody asks you—that if you say "no" it will upset other people or make their lives harder or that they will think you are selfish or uncaring.

No one is going to call you up and say, "I think you're doing too much; let me do some of it for you." Here are some thoughts about setting limits for yourself.

1. If you never say, "No," people will just keep asking. "If you want something done, ask a busy person,"—or so the saying goes.

2. You have the right to say, "No." One mother posted a reminder note by her telephone: "If someone says, Would you. . . ? or Could you. . . ? I will say to myself, the answer is no. What's the question?"

3. You have the right to say, "Maybe." So often we are asked to do something, and we're not sure we want to, can, should. But we feel obligated to give an answer right away, and if we hesitate at all, we usually end up saying "Yes." So, make a rule: Respond by saying, "The answer is, 'Maybe.' " You can say, "I'll think about it," "I'll sleep on it," or "I need to talk to my spouse about it." This is known as "buying time," as it gives you the chance to think about what you really want to do.

4. You don't have to answer the telephone every time it rings. If you want some time to yourself or are busy with one of those things you couldn't say "No" to, you can take the telephone off the hook, turn on your answering machine, or just let it ring.

5. You don't have to give everyone a reason for everything. We often agree to things because we don't have a good reason not to agree. Guess what—you don't need a reason. Sometimes the reason is you just don't want to do it. Sometimes it's okay to not do something because you just don't want to.

6. Use the "broken record" technique. People who are determined to get you to say "Yes" will usually want a reason. Then when you give a reason, they'll tell you why that reason isn't good enough. So you come up with another reason. Plan at the beginning that you will give one answer, "It's not possible for me to do that right now." When they respond, "Why not?", you can say, "It's just not possible for me right now." "But why?", they may say, and you can respond, "Because it just isn't possible." (It does sound like an old phonograph record—stuck on the same phrase.) It's hard to do at first because if you are the kind of person who has

trouble setting limits for yourself you'll feel like you're being abrupt and rude. You really do have some rights in choosing when you want to say, "Yes."

7. It's okay to ask for help. Sometimes it seems like it's easier to do it yourself than to get someone else involved, or it's just hard for you to ask for help. If you've committed to doing something and it turns out to be more work than you thought, you may feel like a failure if you say you can't do it all.

8. Have a "Today is 'No' Day." Say "No" to anything new that comes your way. If that's too drastic say, "I don't think so, but I'll think about it" or "I'll do part of it if you can get someone else to do the rest." After you start taking control of your time and setting limits on what you want to do, you will find out that nothing terrible happens. And, in fact, some wonderful things can happen as you feel more in control of your life and have more time to choose the things *you* want to do.

PARENTHOOD AND PERSONAL GROWTH

We all have many aspects of our lives. When we are under stress, heavily involved in something like raising a child who may require extra time and effort for her physical care, or are going through some emotional turmoil, there are usually parts of ourselves that get neglected. It can be helpful to look at each part to see where you are really taking care of yourself and which aspects of your life might benefit from a little extra attention.

If you are not used to physical exercise or taking time for creative activities or being alone, some of these suggestions may feel awkward and uncomfortable and just not "you." The suggestions are intended as ideas to build from. The five major categories should be the focus. Think about how you express yourself in each area and how you may want to expand your life experiences.

Your Physical Self: Getting Fit and Keeping Fit

The word is out: Healthy food and exercise will help you feel better and live longer. Old habits are hard to break, but you can do it—one meal and one day at a time.

Your Health

Get regular physical checkups and enough rest. If you have any physical symptoms that concern you (or that should concern you), see a physician.

Exercise

Find some regular exercise that's fun, and do it at least twice a week to start. Exercise with a videotape on TV, walk the dog, or hike through a shopping mall. Take a friend if it helps. Stretch your muscles, get that blood flowing, and take long, deep breaths. Hike. Play golf or softball. Swim. Dance.

Your Diet

Watch what you eat. The main cause of being overweight is overeating. If you want a diet, there are enough diet books and programs for everyone to find one that works. Eat less fat and sugar and more fish, fruits, vegetables, and grains. Drink a lot of water.

Your Appearance

How do you like what you see in the mirror? Look nice for yourself and for the people around you. Sometimes when you're not feeling terrific inside, it's hard to care how you look on the outside. On those days, put a little extra effort into your grooming and what you are wearing. Raise your head and pull back your shoulders to stand a little taller and give your self-confidence a lift.

Your Creative Self: Expanding Your Boundaries

When we're feeling low, insecure, tired, or overwhelmed, we must be in a *protective* mode to conserve whatever energy we have. We all have days of needing to pull in and feel safe. But vitality, energy, curiosity, and enthusiasm can burst out when you can begin to reach out, stretch your mind and body, learn something new, or have some fun. If you've always tended to live in a protective mode, you may feel a little awkward (and even silly) trying some expansive, creative activities. Try one of the suggestions below or create one of your own!

Once a Year

Celebrate your own birthday. Even though this only happens once a year, you can spend months planning it. Buy or make yourself a present that will make you feel special—a set of paints, a portable radio, a new hat, gold clubs, or a new book. Send yourself a card. Have cake and ice cream with your favorite flavors (it's *your* birthday). Invite others to celebrate with you, or give yourself the gift of time alone.

Once a Month

At least once a month, do something new and different that's good for you. Get a haircut. Take a long lunch hour. Go to an art museum, a movie, or a botanical garden. Go horseback riding or drive through the countryside. Take a friend or go alone. Go away overnight. Don't have the time? Of course you don't. You have to make it happen.

Twice a Month

Treat yourself at least twice a month. Buy yourself a magazine, a bouquet of flowers, or a new compact disc. Lock yourself in the bathroom and soak in the bathtub for an hour. Go out on the town with friends or go to bed early. It has to be something you wouldn't dream of doing more often because it's just too self-indulgent. It doesn't have to cost any money or take much time. It just has to feel like a real treat.

Every Day

Laugh every day. Watch old reruns on TV, rent funny movies, go to a stationery store and read greeting cards, or read funny books. And most of all, learn to laugh at yourself. Laugh with your partner and laugh with your children. It's one of the greatest gifts you can give to them and yourself. Make up silly words and stories and tell riddles. Walk backward and skip.

Anytime

Start a business or get a part-time job. Do some volunteer work. Buy some new computer software and learn how to use it. Take a class for credit or for fun.

Start—or restart—a hobby or project that's fun for you. Needlework, astronomy, wood carving, sewing, sanding floors, gardening, rollerblading, cleaning out the attic, ceramics, playing bridge, or square dancing. You might choose one that gets you out of the house at a regular time or one you can set up at home and make time to work on.

Get a library card or use the one you already have. Enter the world of fantasy, romance, mystery, science fiction, history, biography, literary epics, decorating, travel, or photography. Take home a pile and browse a bit every day.

Escape when the going gets rough or expand your mind when things calm down.

Learn something really new. Like how to change the oil in your car, hang wallpaper, grow vegetables in containers, or dance flamenco.

Your Social Self: Connecting with Others

Sometimes you don't want to think about doing things with or for other people—you might have a hard enough time just getting *yourself* through the day. Or maybe you are shy, just don't know many people, or feel like you don't have any social skills. Well, there are a lot of other people like you. Start small, set a goal for yourself to reach out and make contact with someone, and go one step at a time.

Call a Friend

Is there an old friend or a relative you've been thinking about but haven't seen or talked to in a long while? Maybe now is the time to think about making contact. Call long distance during off-peak times and you can have a good long chat for only a couple of dollars. Is there someone you miss from your old neighborhood, school, or workplace?

Volunteer

Give a few hours a week to reading to or writing letters for someone who is ill. Shop for someone who finds it hard to get out or babysit for a neighbor's children. Check your local newspaper for volunteer opportunities or call an organization that serves a group you would like to give some time to.

Do Something Fun with Your Kids

Do something both you and your kids will enjoy—not shopping or going to therapy or a doctor's appointment. Don't think about it being educational, therapeutic, stimulating, or purposeful. Just make sure it's *fun*. Take a picnic to the park, go to a playground, take a nature walk, sit by the beach, watch the sunset, or bake cookies.

Do Something Fun with Your Partner

Spend some fun time with your partner. See a movie, go bowling, or play miniature golf. Go for a walk and don't talk about the kids, the bills, or stresses at work. Deal with those another time. Meet for lunch, go to a museum, work on a charity project together. Sit in the park and hold hands.

Join a Group or Club

Join an organization of some kind. A craft club, a church group, a book review group, a political group, or a profes- sional association.

Give a Bit of Yourself Away to Others

Take a stack of magazines and books to a nursing home or send "thinking of you" cards to people you never have time to write to or call. Bake something and take it to a neigh- bor. Pick up a batch of postcards from the drugstore, stamp them, and send them off to say "Hi" to people who cross your thoughts but you don't have time to write long letters or call. Give a thank-you card to your mail carrier or send one to the pediatrician or any of the people who have been kind or helpful to you recently. The nicest things you can give to others are thank yous and smiles.

Your Reflective Self:
Finding Inner Peace and Solitude

Take care of the reflective, spiritual side of your life in whatever way works for you. Going to church or temple, meditating, listening to music, or reading can help you put your life in perspective, lighten your load, or help remind you to be thankful for the positive aspects of your life.

Some time alone with yourself—selected solitude—is essential for letting go of your stresses for a while. Solitude allows you to free your mind from planning your day's chores or worrying about your child or family. Being alone, with no distractions, provides some time for you to find out what you really think and how you really feel about your life. It is a time to consider choices, review decisions, and listen to no one's opinions but your own.

Solitude is often an acquired taste. The idea of being alone makes some people anxious and bores others. Well, yes, it may be boring at first but that's sort of the point. It is a time to rejuvenate and bask in silence or sounds of nature. Being alone with yourself in a peaceful setting helps put some balance into your life. Our daily stresses can become so all-consuming that we forget there is more to life than dealing with hassles and struggles and being busy.

Being alone is about not being busy. It is about being still, quiet, and calm. It is a time to pull in, shut down and find inner peace. It is self-protection time. These times are critical for resting your brain and your body and gaining some inner calm so you can restore your energy and your mental sharpness.

You can design your solitude time however works best for you. An hour a day or even 10 minutes to start, or 2 hours on Sunday or one weekend every few months. This is not time out to recover from stress, but time to just *be* and expand your sense of yourself. Your beginning goal may be in knowing that each week you will create time for yourself to be alone somewhere. It is knowing that you have the right to give yourself that time and that you must be the one to create it and make it happen.

Your Harmonizing Self:
Balancing Your Inner and Outer Worlds

When you learned your child was going to have special needs, there was an interruption in the harmony of your world. All of your efforts to find services for your child and to re-arrange your inner expectations have been directed toward re-establishing a balance between your inner and outer worlds.

Harmony is adaptation. It is about making a better fit between you and your environment. Sometimes harmony is easy to achieve; sometimes it seems forever out of reach. Harmony, in all aspects of our lives, involves compromise. When we reach a state of harmony, we feel like our lives are in balance, in order, and there is a feeling of satisfaction.

Harmony in Your Relationships

When you and your partner have your extra-parenting responsibilities defined and when you are feeling connected, you are in harmony. You feel a sense of balance and support and know that you can rely on each other.

When your other children are getting along in their lives and when your extended family understands and supports you, you feel a sense of harmony.

Sometimes there is a clash of wills, a breakdown in communication, or a mismatch of temperaments. Your harmonizing self goes into action to re-establish your connections to each other.

Are you bothered by the way everyone rushes through dinner? Plan a leisurely family dinner at least once a week—maybe in the dining room with the good dishes. Let your kids help put together a centerpiece for the table or create a casserole. Play soft music, light some candles, and pretend you're eating out at a very fancy restaurant. Think of a special occasion you could be celebrating—someone's report card, Mom's new client, Dad's first painting from art class, or someone getting new braces.

Respect your family rituals and establish some new ones. Most families have special things they eat, special songs they sing, or special gifts they give for birthdays, Christmas, Hanukkah, or Thanksgiving. Rituals are important for children in creating memories and traditions, and they bring a family back around the cycles and seasons of each year. Parents and children learn to anticipate the coming of certain holidays and special celebrations because they know certain things will happen just like the year before. Rituals provide continuity for families and a sense of worth and belonging.

Most of us seem to know when we're in harmony with our environment and when we're feeling that something is off center. And we often have a sense of what to do to increase a feeling of order. You may find there is too much clutter around you and find yourself needing to clean out your kitchen drawers. Maybe you need to get rid of some of that "stuff" in the garage or clean out your car.

You may want to enhance a sense of harmony and well-being in your home by putting some flowers in a vase, buying a new shower curtain to brighten the bathroom, or painting your bedroom a different color.

Have some contact with nature every day. Step outside and look at the stars at night or take a walk around the block during a full moon. Sit in the back yard and listen to the birds or watch a butterfly.

Your Personal Sense of Well-Being

Your harmonizing self is the part of you that continually strives for balance, symmetry, and order in all aspects of your life. The result of paying attention to each aspect of yourself—your physical self, your creative self, your social self, and your reflective self—is that you gain access to a sense of vitality and to a heightened appreciation of all of your senses. You have greater balance in both your inner and outer worlds, with a better use of your ability to focus, work, and gain a better sense of self-direction. It is devel-

oping an image of yourself living out your ideals—whether it be in a career, in your garden, making quilts, or getting a degree in special education. By taking care of the little things, creating harmony in your daily life, and establishing routines and rituals with your family members that gives a sense of being grounded and connected, you develop an overall sense of who you are and where you want to go.

8

Parents as Partners

Many things in life will test your couple relationship—financial hardships, in-laws, family member's illness, remodeling the kitchen, and the arrival of children. When one of your children has special needs, your couple relationship requires a kind of parenting partnership that goes beyond the traditional roles most of us are familiar with. Your relationship may not change much at all. It may suffer because of the way either or both of you react to having a child with special needs or for reasons that really have nothing to do with your child's needs. Or your relationship may grow stronger because of a shared focus and challenge. One thing is for sure—some problems just don't seem as important as they used to. Your reactions to these issues will be influenced by where you are in the adaptation process.

1. Your couple relationship will be influenced by where each of you are in the adaptation process. You may be

in different stages at a given time, or a specific event may trigger conflicting states for each of you.

2. Raising a child with special needs involves extra parenting—different and more things to do and worry about than with a typical child.

3. To have an effective parenting partnership, you need to decide how to share the extra responsibilities, and you need to keep communication and negotiations open.

4. Single parents, divided families, and step-families often have even more complicated issues related to adaptation and extra parenting.

5. Aside from your parenting roles, you need to make extra efforts to take care of your couple relationship and keep it growing.

STAGES OF ADAPTATION AND YOUR RELATIONSHIP

When the emotions of Surviving are in the foreground, one or both parents may be focused on "doing what you have to do to keep going." You may have been drawn closer together or one or both of you may have needed to withdraw at least for a while. You may go through each adaptation stage in different ways or at different times, and you may feel confused about whether your relationship will be able to handle the stress. If either or both of you are preoccupied with Searching issues—finding services or examining your own values and priorities—these too may affect your relationship. One of you may be proactive, wanting to seek specific programs, while the other may want to "wait and see" before making any major commitment of money or time.

By the time you are Settled In, if you have not been communicating well, you may discover that your parenting roles may have become unbalanced, and you may have built up resentment or misunderstandings about each other. When you are struggling with Separating issues—how much independence to encourage or making long-term plans for your child and family—your relationship may feel the impact of the directions each of you wants to go. Knowing that many issues and feelings change, that they will get resolved and you will move on, and that you are both capable of reverting back to old feelings can help you both be there for each other. At some point in all of this you are bound to be in different places at the same time.

NORMAL REACTIONS THAT COULD BE POTENTIAL PROBLEMS

Being Strong But Falling Apart

Perhaps you are being strong for each other, but falling apart inside. This may be especially true when you are both Surviving. Dealing with your child's problems may be the first real crisis you have gone through as a couple. You may not be sure how your partner would react if you "broke down," or expressed your feelings of guilt or fear. You may assume that he or she needs you to be able to handle it or would be angry or rejecting if you showed any "weakness." You may also be thinking that if your partner is already upset about your child and you show that you are upset too, then he or she will have you to worry about as well.

If you are both holding back your fears and worries, whom do you each have to turn to? Are you both pushing it all beneath the surface and developing a pattern of not being able to see each other as a source of support during tough times?

> *Diane:* Our husbands had to hold us up and hold up for us—our attention was on the baby. Fathers get pushed

aside unfairly. Everyone focuses on the mother; the mother is the one who had the baby. During that first month when Catherine was in the hospital and I spent most of the time with her, my family said my husband wasn't eating and that he didn't talk. He was trying to put up a strong front, and he had to go to work and keep functioning.

Susie: Six weeks after Betsy was born, we didn't know if she would even survive. I lived each moment in terror, and I could see that Bruce was suffering, but we couldn't talk about it. We had almost always talked, but this was so new, so different, so much out of our control. Then Bruce said to me, "Know this: Whatever caused this doesn't matter. What matters is that whatever happens, whatever Betsy needs, we will do this together." That statement released us both. I was able to let go of all the guilt I was carrying—and some of the fear. I didn't know what was ahead of us, but I knew I would survive.

One of You May Be Confused and Scared

One of you may be confused and scared about what the future holds and keeping it inside, while the other may be saying "Don't worry so much; it will all work out." This is another common reaction couples may have. You may be having a harder time getting through the Surviving stage, while your partner may be moving past those feelings at a faster pace. In some couples, one of the partners may zip through the initial, awful feelings and feel pretty optimistic about handling the future. Who knows why couples can differ so much? Some say "opposites attract," and there certainly are couples in which one is an optimist and the other a pessimist. In some couples, one seems to carry the role of "worrier" or "complainer" or "comedian" or "the practical one." In one sense, when one of you is worrying and the other is saying, "It will all work out," you are both right. There is something to worry about, and there is the probability that you'll find a way for things to work out. The important point is that you are both entitled to your opinions; few issues in life are totally right or wrong or black or white. You each have the right to adapt in different ways, and you need to respect the differences in each other. If these differences are rigid and go on for a long time, couples tend to either ignore what the other says ("That's just the way he is") or get pretty annoyed with each other.

> *Janet:* I loved and accepted Ryan, but I wasn't really a "proud mother" those first couple of years because Ryan was always having life-threatening medical crises. But my husband—it was almost as if nothing was wrong. Chris couldn't wait to take him to his office, while I had tears in my eyes.
>
> I thought, "Oh no, he has a trach and casts on his feet." I knew how people looked at him. I remembered their stares in the market and I remembered people stopping me. But Chris didn't care. He didn't feel that way—"This is my son, I'm really proud of him. People don't care. They just want to see him."
>
> So we went to his office. I got all dressed up. And Ryan looked so cute, but I was a nervous wreck. And Chris was right. They were really supportive, and said, "You guys are really great parents." Chris really helped me to focus on the positive and cut through all the unimportant stuff.

You May Have Different Opinions

Perhaps the two of you disagree about the nature or severity of your child's problems or about the kinds of interventions she needs. One of you may actively participate in an intervention program and the other may not. You may not always agree about how to handle your child's problems at home. One of you may set limits and the other may always give in.

Jane and Bill have a 6-year-old who was recently diagnosed as having mental retardation. Bill's reaction was to seek out resources immediately. He found Special Olympics and volunteered his time. Jane became angry and saw Bill's activity as an admission that their child really did have mental retardation; she was not ready to "give up" and believe the diagnosis.

You May Cope in Different Ways

You may cope in different ways and may feel the same emotions, but at different times. If you're both in the stage of Surviving with unpredictable feelings, one of you may be up when the other is down. One of you may get angry just as the other gets past that feeling. One of you may want to withdraw and avoid talking about it; the other may want to start Searching for answers. One of you may want to have another child right away; the other may say, "Never."

And then you may find yourselves switching positions and, if you don't understand what is going on, you can start to have some major misunderstandings about each other.

> *Janet:* We had a real role reversal. I'm usually the one who's really up and sees the positive in everything. But I was so consumed with fear and helplessness about Ryan and whether he was even going to make it that I couldn't see any light at the end of the tunnel. Chris is usually more objective and neutral about things, but when it came to Ryan, he was the one who was always optimistic.

You May Be Tired and Out of Energy

If one or both of you are so tired you have no energy left over for the other, or you're avoiding time alone together because there is so much preoccupation with the things that need to be done for your child or because you may be so worried about your child that you just don't have fun any more, there may be no time or energy left over for your couple relationship. One or both of you may avoid being alone with the other for these reasons. Or one of you may want to talk about it and the other may not. Making time to be together can be really depressing if all you do is complain or worry out loud.

Your Sex Life May Have Changed

You may find your sex life has changed in a way that is not okay for one or both of you. If you are tired, tense, depressed, or preoccupied, you may find it hard to be intimate. If you are concerned about another pregnancy, there may be a tendency to avoid sex entirely.

One or both of you may be feeling that sex is the one good thing you can count on to help you forget all the other stuff you're dealing with. If you *both* feel that way, that's great; if one of you doesn't feel that way, it can be one more area in which you feel depressed and inadequate. Some couples report that their sexual relationships improved greatly as the tension and uncertainty they were sharing about their child brought them closer together and bonded them in a stronger, more intimate way.

Partners may use sex against each other in a relationship. If, for instance, one of you feels that the other is not being emotionally supportive and is working longer hours than ever before, and if the two of you are not dealing with these issues directly, you may genuinely lose interest in being intimate or may feel that pulling back from sex is the only way to really get your mate's attention.

You May Be Reluctant To Leave Your Child

One or both of you may be reluctant to leave your child in someone else's care. You may think, "I'm the only one who can take care of our child." There's often guilt about leaving your child with someone else and fear there will be an emergency. You know that no one can care for your child as well as you can. (But you usually learn that you aren't indispensable and your child can get along with someone else for a while.)

> *Diane:*   This first time we left Catherine overnight was to go to a local hotel for our anniversary—more than a year after she was born. We hadn't had any problem leaving Sara with someone, but we were just afraid to be away from Catherine. Not because she had a prob-

lem. It was us. My sister was the one who finally said, "You guys have to get away. I'll stay with the girls."

You May Be Feeling Guilty

One or both of you may feel some guilt about your child's problem. You may feel that you disappointed your partner by having a child with so many problems. You may be blaming—or feeling blamed by—your partner. You may then feel you need to carry the bulk of the responsibility for your child's care in order to feel less guilty or to "make up" for "causing" the problem. You may feel if you work hard enough you can make your child "normal"—or better than anyone expected.

You May Be Overwhelmed by the Work

One or both of you may find that this is a lot of work. As one or both of you realizes that there is a lot of work involved in raising a child with special needs, you may feel like the work is not being shared enough or that you're not getting enough understanding and support. If one of you is home and the other is working long hours, the parent at home may feel like he or she is carrying the brunt of the child care. But the working parent may feel responsible for working harder to provide financial security and may have no energy to share the care at the end of the day.

You May Be Wondering About Having More Children

For some couples, having another child is out of the question for any of a variety of reasons; others attempt to have another child as soon as possible. The issues may include a genetic risk for another child having the same problem, severe complications from the earlier pregnancy, the moth-

er's age, fear of having another child with a disabling condition even if there is no genetic risk, or fear of not being
able to care for another child because of the time and energy your child with special needs requires.

> *Janet:*   I wanted to have another baby. Chris was afraid we
> couldn't handle it—Ryan needed our undivided atten-
> tion, we had just moved, and we couldn't afford it. As
> much as I loved Ryan, I wanted to see what it was like
> to have a baby drink a bottle or cry. I saw my friends
> doing it, and it looked so peaceful. And I guess a part
> of me wanted to show them that those weren't things
> to bitch about. The instant Erin was born, all of Chris's
> concerns evaporated.
>
> *Stephanie:*   Paul and I both wanted to have another baby
> right away. We had a sense of having been struck by
> lightning and it couldn't happen again. But being in an
> early intervention program and seeing so many other
> kinds of problems that can happen definitely made it
> more scary.

EXTRA PARENTING RESPONSIBILITIES

Stresses Versus Joys

*You have all of the stresses of typical parenting, but not as
many of the joys.* Like all parents, you experience a change
in lifestyle, loss of privacy, loss of spontaneity in your social life, fatigue, irritation from not enough sleep and from
the baby crying every night, and extra expenses for diapers,
equipment, clothes, toys. *Plus you don't always get all of
the joys of typical parenting.* Your child may miss the typical milestones for sitting, walking, or talking; you don't
know if this is a temporary delay and he will catch up, if
he will never do these things, or if he ever does these things

whether he will catch up then. And what control do you have over it? If you and your child spend much of his early childhood in the hospital, in intervention programs, inserting tubes, and waiting for any small sign of progress, you have constant reminders that this was not in the baby books.

However, when a delayed milestone is eventually reached, the joy you feel has a special quality and depth. To see your child struggle to be mobile or to communicate, for example, and then to achieve that goal is an affirmation of your work and patience and your child's efforts and persistence. Your child's progress and achievements may not come naturally or easily and because of that, they have an added dimension of achievement and joy.

More Patience

You need more patience than you do in typical parenting. Things may take longer to do than with typical children. These things include eating; communicating; getting to and into the car; moving around the house; taking a bath; getting ready for bed; getting dressed; daily grooming such as brushing teeth, combing hair, and washing hands; playing with toys; and doing special exercises. *Plus extra parenting can be intense and prolonged.* Parents seem to have a biological time of readiness for their children to walk independently, play on their own, and develop adaptive skills. For a child who is delayed or has physical limitations, all of these developmental milestones are delayed—perhaps for months and sometimes for years. If you think you're tired, you probably are. Your body is at risk for strains, sprains, and chronic pains as your child gets bigger and you are moving, lifting, and shifting her from one position to another.

Extra Skills and Knowledge

You need all of the skills of typical parenting and extra parenting skills and knowledge. Should I pick him up when he cries? Should I ignore her tantrums? Is it okay for him to sleep with us? Do I give in to her too much? What do I do if he won't wear his seatbelt? He's such a picky eater . . . You have all of these "normal" questions to deal with, *plus you need extra parenting skills and knowledge.* You need to know if, when, and how to adapt regular parenting skills to fit your child's special needs. When your child has a problem, like throwing tantrums or refusing to eat, is it a normal problem for her age, is she having a major emotional problem, or is it related to her disability?

Some children with cognitive and social delays, for example, enter their "terrible 2s" when they are 3 or 4 years old, often catching parents by surprise and making it difficult to determine if these are "normal" developmental surges of independence that should be greeted with enthusiasm or whether the tantrums are expressions of frustration related to learning problems. Sometimes problems need to be handled in the same way regardless of their "reason," but sometimes it's hard to decide what to do. Some children with physical disabilities, who have limited ways to have any control over their environment, often use eating or toilet training as the ultimate ways to have *some* control over *something* in their lives. Sometimes parents need to "wait it out," or give their child other ways to make decisions and feel independent.

Scheduling and Services Nightmares

You have all the schlepping and scheduling problems of typical parenting. You have to deal with car-pools, scout meetings, soccer practice, and three kids needing to be in three places at the same time. One may be sick and need to be in bed; the others may need to go to swimming lessons. There may be no sitters for miles around. *Plus you have extra parenting scheduling nightmares.* This is one job where you get to have your office at home. You have to cope with feeding and medications; use of special medical or therapeutic equipment; hours on the telephone finding programs and services; making sure the other children in the family have their "fair share" of your time and attention and get to their music lessons, ball games, and tutors; finding babysitters and training them to meet your child's needs; and modifying your environment to keep your child safe at home and to be more mobile. *Plus you need to be a professional team leader in getting services for your child.* To do that well, you have to assign roles, know your limits, and be able to ask for help when you need it. So you take your work with you (usually in a large appointment book) wherever you go: appointments with doctors, therapists, and specialists for emergencies; evaluations, ongoing checkups, or weekly meetings; your child's school or extracurricular program; car-pooling, fundraising, parents' meetings. (And you usually have to do a lot of these things more than once! Your child outgrows a program, funding runs out, programs close, you move. . . .)

SPECIAL ISSUES RELATED TO SINGLE PARENTS, DIVIDED FAMILIES, AND STEP-FAMILIES

While the "traditional" mother–father family is still with us, many families are now headed by single parents or unmarried couples. Other families are "blended"—a remarriage for one or both parents in which "your kids, my kids, and our kids" are all mixed in together. Some divided families share custody, with the separated parents equally involved in providing care for their children. And there is a growing number of families who are adopting or providing foster care for children with a range of special needs.

Although many of the issues related to extra parenting, adaptation, and communication occur in all families, these can get even more intense and complicated when parents are not living together. One parent may feel that the other doesn't meet the child's needs as well; the other may feel that the other is overprotective. One parent may not follow through with recommended interventions or necessary medications. If one parent has the majority of time with the child, he or she may not feel understood and supported by the other parent who sees the child only on weekends or occasionally. When extra parenting is necessary and when families are divided, there are extra opportunities for miscommunication. All parties concerned may need more telephone conversations, checklists, and face-to-face discussions that may not always be too comfortable. It is important to keep the parenting issues among the adults, however, and not have your child (or other children) be the carrier of messages, concerns, or plans.

Single parents, whether mothers or fathers, can profit from connecting with a support group because there are so many issues of extra parenting, stress from the constant responsibility of child care, and the difficulty of having to make all decisions alone. When single parents are also working parents, there are added issues of daily child care and back-up child care when the child is ill. Many single parents express concern about issues of dating and remarriage, how those considerations would affect their child, and how their child's special needs would affect a future stepparent.

Step-parents face a special kind of challenge. They join families at a particular point in their spouse's adaptation process, and need to understand the "big picture." A step-parent who enters the family does so by choice and may have a more objective view of family relationships that may interrupt established patterns and attitudes. Frequently, this "interruption" can be very positive, but it definitely affects the overall adjustment of everyone concerned. In addition to going through all of the "typical" issues that come with being a step-parent, there may be extra issues related to the child's special needs, including balancing time for all the children, dealing with the separated parent, and dealing with the family he or she brought along—or left behind.

WHEN EXTRA HELP IS NEEDED

If your relationship is already on shaky ground, having a child who has special needs may exaggerate problems or may move you beyond them. While some problems are magnified, others just don't seem as important as they used to.

Is either of you having prolonged feelings of depression and/or anger that you just can't get past? For whatever reason, if you feel unable to regain a sense of vitality and to move ahead, you might consider counseling with a psychotherapist to help you understand your feelings and to offer you support and guidance during this difficult time.

One couple reported, "We didn't get any outside help for a long time. We just kept redecorating the house. And after 7 years, we finally realized there are just so many rooms you can add on before you get to the root of the problem."

You may want to consider joining a support group, where you can hear how other couples work through communication problems and the issue of sharing extra parenting responsibilities.

STRATEGIES FOR SUCCESS

Communicating with Each Other

Your child's needs will change and your needs and moods will probably change. It is important to plan a regular time to talk about how things are going.

How To Have a Serious Conversation

1. *Listen to each other's point of view.* You may each see a situation differently, which can be good or bad. Before you decide if it is good or bad, listen to what the other has to say. Also remember that a point of view you or your partner has today may change as you get new information or as your child makes progress. Therefore, just because your partner had a certain opinion a month ago doesn't mean it's still the same. Also, maybe something you said in your last discussion really impressed him or her and created a shift in thinking.

2. *Don't interrupt.* That means be quiet. Don't correct or clarify or say, "Get to the point" and shake your head. Let the other talk. If the other says, "Last Tuesday, when we had beef for dinner," don't jump in and say, "it was chicken." You have the right to the same respect when it's your turn.

3. *Don't tell each other what to feel; don't judge or criticize each other's feelings.* You know how awful it feels when you say, "I'm scared" and someone says, "Don't be silly" or "There's nothing to be scared of" or "That's stupid." If you and your partner are going to be able to talk about feelings, you both have to trust that you will not be told your feelings are wrong, silly, crazy, or stupid. You may not like feeling scared, either, but if you are going to work through that feeling you have to feel accepted and be able

to talk about it. A feeling is only a feeling. It's not a personality test or a measure of your worth.

> *Stephanie:* We often see a problem in different ways, and that can be a good and healthy thing. A lot of times when I'm on an emotional roller coaster, Paul will say, "Don't worry. It's going to work out." That helps ground and balance me and feels really supportive. I can get overwhelmed with an issue, and Paul's approach helps me to focus on what is really important.
>
> *Susie:* I know what you mean. I get all hot under the collar and Bruce will say, "Is it worth it?" He has such a great perspective—and makes it sound so easy.

4. *Pay attention. Don't glance through the paper or watch TV.* And sit where you can see and maybe touch each other. Really listen to what your partner is saying; don't think about what you are going to say as soon as you get your turn.

5. *Give advice only if you are asked for it.* We have the tendency, in American society, to give advice whether people ask for it or not. We are "solution-oriented" and often forget that sometimes people like to just say what they are feeling, complain, or express their frustration. They just want to be listened to and understood. Everything doesn't need to be "fixed."

Realizing that You May Express Feelings Differently than Your Partner

In spite of many changes in American society about the issue of expressing feelings, many men are not able to talk about their feelings, especially feelings like sadness and helplessness. Usually women have more opportunities to meet other women, share their feelings, cry, ask for help, and appear vulnerable. Fewer opportunities for this kind of interaction are available for fathers, and this may add to the discomfort men often feel. It also seems that there are fewer chances for men to repair their shattered feelings and address their fears. They may feel they can't "let down." Sometimes mothers want them to be "strong" but sometimes mothers wonder what private feelings, questions, and fears their partners aren't talking about.

Or you may just be two different types of personalities. One of you may "let it all hang out" and the other may be the silent type. One of you may see the glass as half full, the other as half empty.

Repairing Breaks in Communication

Perfect communication, total understanding, and superior empathy (with a little mind reading thrown in) are ideals that few relationships ever achieve. There will always be breaks in communication. The real strength in a relationship is being able to recognize breaks and repair them.

1. *Remember that breaks in communication occur in almost every relationship.* One mother complained that her husband would come home at night and say, "Let's go to a movie" like she could just drop everything, or he'd plop in front of the television and not help with the kids. Shortly after that, the father's side was heard. He said he would come home at night, knowing his wife had had a really hard day. He wanted to give her a break, so he'd offer to take her to a movie, but she complained she was too tired to go out and she couldn't get a sitter at the last minute. He said he gave up trying to help with their child at night because his wife kept telling him he was doing everything wrong. She said it was true—he didn't make the kids brush their teeth, and they got too rowdy going to bed.

2. *A break in communication means that you (or the*

*other person) feel you have not been understood or heard,
or that you are engaged in a power struggle* in which winning or losing is more important that what you are trying
to talk about.

3. *You need to decide which is more important—
winning* an argument or *ending* an argument.

4. *It only takes one person to make a break, but it
takes two to repair one.* You can create a break in your
relationship by saying something hurtful, being rigid and
stubborn, not listening to the other's point of view, or
withdrawing and refusing to discuss an issue.

5. *Repairing breaks involves some risk* because
sometimes it may involve admitting you were wrong (at
least a little—maybe); asking for something from the other
person; or giving something to the other person.

BALANCING YOUR EXTRA PARENTING RESPONSIBILITIES

When one parent is the primary "searcher" for information
(usually the mother), the other parent (usually the father)
often gets information about their child secondhand and
must rely on the searcher to make and keep appointments,
therapy visits, and so forth.

> *Diane:* I used to resent the fact that I was the one who
> made all of the appointments and went to all of the ap-
> pointments and was the one to hear any bad news. I
> had to deal with it alone until I could reach Ray on the
> telephone or until he got home. If it was really bad,
> he'd drop everything, no hesitating, and come home
> immediately. If we knew ahead of time it was going to
> be a really important appointment, like a decision
> about surgery, he would take time off work to go. But
> we didn't always know, and there were so many he
> couldn't go to all of them.

What can easily happen in a subtle way is that one parent (usually the mother) becomes the "expert"; she learns the system and has the contacts, and the other parent (usually the father) feels more distanced. In some families this works well, and many mothers have reported they learn skills of management, advocacy, and assertion and feel in control and competent. In some couples, a gradual pattern emerges in which the mother feels like the burden is all on her and she resents her husband's lack of participation. But there can come a point when some mothers don't want participation—it's more trouble than it's worth to get their partners involved, and by the time they explain how to do something, they could have done it themselves. Or they don't trust that their partner is capable of doing what needs to be done with their child (e.g., working with speech-language lessons, foreseeing problems by bringing extra clothes) or knowing what to do in an emergency. These problems can develop when families are intact, but may need special attention when families are divided, custody is shared, and communication between households may be strained.

Questions To Ask Yourselves
About Your Parenting Partnership

Do you feel like you are really working together in raising your child, in understanding what your child needs, and in seeking the help you need? (That doesn't necessarily mean the work is split evenly down the middle. It means, *are you both satisfied* with the division of responsibility, and can you talk about it if you're not?)

> *Stephanie:* Sometimes it's our own fault because we don't ask for help. We need it and we want it, but we get resentful if they don't offer or take the initiative and figure out what has to be done.
> *Diane:* And sometimes you feel like—they work all day

and they already have enough to worry about. I should be able to handle this.

Janet: I know. I felt that way sometimes even when we were both working full-time jobs. It's still the message we get—that mothers are basically responsible for the home and kids.

If one of you carries all the responsibility, you also get a lot of the blame—or you blame yourself—when something fails or goes wrong. When things go well, you get and feel a lot of credit, but then having something not go right can be devastating. When you are both involved, decisions are made jointly, and interventions carried out with a clear balance of responsibilities, it eases the burden of work and responsibility.

Stephanie: In the beginning, I was in charge of all the medical stuff and schools. Paul's been able to have a more flexible schedule and has been more involved with going to school meetings and doctor appointments. It makes such a difference in the quality of our decisions.

Do you agree about discipline, setting limits, and encouraging independence? Is one of you too overprotective to the displeasure of the other? It's okay to disagree—as long as you agree about how you will disagree. All parents of all children have some areas of disagreement about discipline, and children can learn the difference between what Mom and Dad will encourage and what they won't tolerate. Sometimes the little differences between parents aren't really very important. What is important is that your opinions about limits and risk-taking are based on what your child needs *as a child* and what *extra* precautions or experiences you introduce for his special needs. Sometimes our discipline is based on our own experiences as children, or on what works with our other children, or on what seems like a good idea at the moment because *you* are tired and cranky.

Are you in agreement about who does what and when, and can you both be flexible about it? Each of you has expectations about what moms do and what dads do. These are based on how your parents raised you (or how they didn't raise you and your determination not to make the same mistakes they did); the roles you have already established if you have other children; and all of those parenting books you've read.

Make some time to make a list. Some families need to sit down weekly, maybe including all of the children, to plan household chores, extra household projects, things to be taken to be repaired or videotapes to be returned, things to pick up from the cleaners or the pharmacy, telephone calls for information or appointments, car-pooling, soccer games, and so forth. You may have regular assignments, or they may need to change because of work schedules, illness, or emergencies and other unexpected events. The key is planning ahead, knowing that things can change, and being flexible.

1.   Make a list of what has to be done.
2.   Decide who will do what and when.
3.   Make a back-up plan.
4.   Consider all of your resources.
5.   Make a plan for emergencies.

YOU GOTTA DO WHAT WORKS FOR YOU

It doesn't matter "who does what, when."
What matters is agreeing with each other
about who does what, when.

What matters is that if one of you says,
"I need you to share this with me,"
the other will be there.
What matters is that you can trust that you want
to be there for each other.

HELPING YOUR RELATIONSHIP GROW

With all of your parenting and extra parenting responsibilities, you may lose sight of your couple relationship. This may be especially true during the Surviving and Searching stages, as you need to focus a lot of time and energy on understanding and finding interventions for your child's special needs. But neglecting your relationship with each other can have negative effects both on your partner and on your children. One of the best things you can give your children is the experience of living with parents who are committed to each other, love and like each other, and have fun and laugh together. Your romance, your friendship, and your working toward the future together is the model of your children's expectations for their own adult relationships.

Even if you are separated or divorced, you can present a united front for your children to see that you have successful separate lives, even perhaps with new partners. It may take extra effort (maybe a lot of it) to work together on the issues concerning your child, but if at all possible, try to keep your feelings about each other (if they are uncomfortable or negative) separate. There are successful divorces that can provide children with positive role models, effective communication and problem-solving skills, and a sense of safety and stability.

Keep the Romance

What happened to the relationship that made you want to spend the rest of your lives together? Do you do spontaneous, thoughtful things for each other? Do you remember birthdays, anniversaries, and other occasions? How often do you laugh together and have conversations that are *not* about your child and related issues? If you are tired, tense, depressed, or preoccupied, you may find your sex life suffering, especially if there is pressure or concern about another pregnancy.

Does it feel like your relationship is okay, but that you never really tell each other how much you love each other and how much you appreciate the support and understanding you receive? Is there still a sense of romance in your relationship? Do you do thoughtful things for each other? Do you ever go out for a romantic dinner or a moonlight walk? Do you ever give or receive little gifts that mean, "I thought of you today"? Do you miss each other when you're apart, but also enjoy your separateness? Do you feel like your partner really respects and recognizes the hard work you are doing? There are a lot of ways to re-affirm your love and commitment. Try some.

Nurture Your Friendship

Relationships are at risk when any kind of trauma is imposed. There are conflicting reports about the divorce rate among parents of children with special needs; some say the rate is higher and some say it is lower and some say it's no different from the national average.

There is always the possibility that a steady, reliable relationship may not make it through the challenges of raising a child who has special needs. One of the partners may simply not be able to deal with the changes that are required, or the couple may find that they are not able to work together in this new direction. However, the likelihood is that if your relationship was strong and secure before your child was born, you will probably find yourselves sharing even greater intimacy, companionship, and support after the birth of your child with special needs.

If your relationship was shaky before your child was born, it may deteriorate even more. If your relationship is strained, your child may serve as a point of focus for unhappiness so that other problems between the two of you are shoved under the rug, or your relationship may be stressed to the breaking point.

Many relationships in typical families go along for years with issues of life goals and personal values never tested. Many couples never share the depth of feelings, the giving and taking of support, and the problem-solving that you must deal with. These can enrich a strong relationship or exaggerate the problems of a weak relationship. The child may be blamed as "the cause," but this is simply not true. A child with a disability does not cause divorce.

The friendship you and your child's other parent have is a vital connection that transcends your roles and responsibilities as parents. Your friendship enables you to share interests and to support and encourage your individual goals and interests. Your parenting roles will change as your children grow up and away from you, and the relationship with each other that began before you had children will again be your focus. Raising a child with special needs will probably change each of you in ways that you may not have expected. The strength and support you have given to, and desire from, each other can create a bond of friendship and respect that no other can equal.

Look to the Future

When you are both Surviving, you are heavily focused on coping and reacting one day at a time. Your thoughts about the future are fearful ones—wondering how your child and your relationship will weather uncertainties. When you are focused on Searching, your views of the future may still be clouded with confusion and uncertainty, and much of your energy is spent on the immediacy of finding services.

During times of feeling more Settled In and as Separating issues come into the foreground, you become more aware of future possibilities and challenges for your child. You may be more able to see and plan for your future as individuals, as a couple, and as a family. As you work to balance your life, to look ahead instead of needing to focus on the "now," you have more energy, more hope, and a greater sense of choice about where you are going together. You will find your parenting experience to be both more and less of what you expected, but the truth is *all* parenting experiences are like that.

9

Brothers and Sisters

*It's amazing how many different kinds of people
can be found in one family.*

Like most parents, you are undoubtedly concerned about
the impact your child's special needs will have on your other
children. Children don't have problems just because their
brother or sister has a disability. They may develop problems if their own special relationships with their parents
are interrupted, if their lives are affected by stresses in the
family, or if their own childhood is impinged upon too
greatly. They will all react in different ways depending on
their ages, how their lives are affected right now, their own
personality styles, and how you behave around them.

1. Your relationships with your children may be influenced by where you are in the adaptation process.
2. Brother–sister relationships in typical families aren't
   perfect, so you shouldn't expect they will be perfect in
   your family, either.

3. Your other children go through their own stages of adaptation, too, but in some different ways than you do.
4. Your child with special needs may have both positive and negative reactions to having brothers and sisters who do not have disabilities.
5. No matter how much you want to be a perfect parent, you won't be. There are strategies to prevent problems and build better sibling relationships (but not without pitfalls).

STAGES OF ADAPTATION IN YOUR FAMILY

When you are dealing with Surviving emotions, you may feel preoccupied and you may have less time and energy available for your children. You may be uncertain what to tell your other children. If you are feeling the confusion of Surviving, your children may sense what is wrong. If you share your parental fears with your children, and they see you falling apart, they may feel unsafe and confused.

During your Searching struggles, you may find that the needs and wants of your other children get less of your attention if you are involved with the many tasks of finding interventions; you may be busy on the telephone or taking your child to appointments. And depending on the ages of your other children and the availability of child care, they may get to spend a lot of time in the car and in waiting rooms.

When you are Settled In, and your emotional life is more predictable, life for your other children may, if you're lucky, continue as it did before you had to focus on surviving. Separating issues may involve brothers and sisters as you encourage increasing independence in your child with special needs. You may be thinking about future care and responsibility and how your other children will be involved in lifelong decision-making about your child with special needs. In their own ways, depending on their ages and personalities, your other children will go through their own stages of Surviving and Inner Searching, and eventually, they will have their own issues and feelings about Separating.

SOME REMINDERS ABOUT TYPICAL SIBLING RELATIONSHIPS

Every family and every child is different. There are so many combinations of factors—family size, number of children, age spacing, boys versus girls, and so forth. There are no precise predictions that can be made about how each of your children will react to his or her sibling's special needs. There are some general things we know about brother–sister relationships (which should ease your mind considerably) and about risk factors in families like yours.

All Children Have To Give Up a Part of Their Parents When a New Child Is Born

When a new child is born, all children have to give up a part of their parents. Your children who "got there first" will have mixed feelings about any new arrival. They may feel excitement about a new playmate as well as resentment at being dethroned. Older sisters may be especially prone to becoming "little mothers" and may take this role very seriously. The youngest (or only other) loses his special role as the baby. He's now a big brother. He may see that as a big deal or a big pain. Boys and girls may react differently. A middle child may feel differently than the other children. Those who arrive after your child with special needs may react differently, too. Your family patterns with your child who has a disability are already established, and

a new child doesn't know that things were ever any different and just joins right in.

Children Are Naturally Self-Centered

Children interpret the world based on how events affect their lives. The fact that their brother or sister has a disability does not in itself mean that they will develop problems. The issues are how you behave toward them, how the child's special needs impinge on their lives, and how your attitudes and attention toward your child with special needs affects them. Brothers and sisters may develop problems because they receive less attention from one or both parents, because their parents are tried and irritable, because of financial limitations that may restrict their educational or social choices, or because of attitudes about restrictions placed on family activities because of their sister's or brother's special needs or problems.

Children grow up adapting to what they know. Many families have crises or ongoing struggles—divorce, illness, poverty, moving, and so forth. Children adapt according to how things affect them directly. If they feel safe and secure, and their childhood is protected from adult strains and problems, they'll adjust—some better than others, to be sure, but that seems to be true for many children for many reasons.

> *Diane:* I realized in looking back through family albums that there were no pictures of me when I was young because my brother, a year younger, had heart problems. That must have been so consuming, so stressful that there was no time for me. I remember getting angry with my brother because he took so much of my mother's time. I didn't know they were just trying to keep the poor kid alive. She had three other kids to take care of, and she probably didn't even have time to feel bad.

Children React to Changes and Inconsistencies in Roles and Expectations

Having a child with special needs in the family usually places different demands on the other children than a typical baby would. Children react when their status changes by the birth of a new child. Children react if they are suddenly and prematurely expected to be "little adults," to be extra responsible, or if their own needs are ignored.

In Most Families, Children Help Take Care of Each Other

In most families, the children help to care for each other. In fact, in many other societies, older children in families do most of the caregiving of the younger children. American society is one of the few that has the view that child caregiving is the responsibility of the parents (primarily the mother) and that "sibling caregiving" deprives older children of having their own needs met and deprives younger children of parental nurturance and influence.

In many families, older children seem to naturally imitate the parenting role with their younger brothers or sisters and often delight in being "Mommy's helper." Bigger kids help the smaller kids in all kinds of activities, and this can be a source of pride and competence for the older children.

Siblings Go Through Phases of
Not Getting Along with Each Other

It isn't unusual for children to go through times when they "don't like" their brothers and sisters. They may not want to spend time with one or more of their brothers or sisters. They may be jealous of another's looks or accomplishments; they may feel one of their siblings is smarter or more athletic or gets more positive attention from a certain relative. Brother–sister relationships change over time. They may be best friends for years, then enemies and then move in together.

"Life Isn't Fair"

Most children complain at some time that something just isn't fair, which is also known as "You love her more than me." Most children complain when they think they get the short end of something. Someone got to stay up later, got to sit in the front seat again, had more time with the video-game, or used all the hot water. Children seldom report when they get the biggest piece of pie. You think you treat all your children pretty much the same, but they all come out different and they even have different memories and interpretations of identical events.

POSSIBLE REACTIONS OF BROTHERS AND SISTERS TO A DISABILITY IN THE FAMILY

Brothers and sisters may experience any of a number of reactions upon learning that their sibling has a disability. The following reactions may or may not apply to any or all of your children. Even if one or more of your children have any of these reactions, they may not be a signal that they have a serious adjustment problem. Children go through phases. What makes them angry today may no longer be an issue a month from now. You may never know what started or stopped some feelings. In a family, children sometimes seem to take turns at being cooperative and easy to live with, while another is being impossible. Their ages, their personal issues outside the family (such as with friends or at school) affect how they may appear to be reacting to your child with special needs.

Most brothers and sisters have mixed reactions to their sibling's "special needs," and that's the way it should be. The meaning of "special needs" is very different for them than it is for you, and for many children, their lives do not need to be greatly affected. When you combine all of the factors in your own situation, you will know that, first of all, every family is different. The size of your family, the birth order of your children, the extent of disruption created by "special needs," the quality of the support you have, your own emotional reactions, and your religious and cultural beliefs affect the reactions of your other children.

Most brothers and sisters have many "positive" reactions—excitement about a new brother or sister, "optimistic concern" about problems the sibling has, and tender caregiving and nurturing. And many brothers and sisters don't give much consideration to the special needs at all. It just doesn't matter, and they don't see them as any big deal.

> *Diane:*   Does Sara think of Catherine as having a disability? No way. Not at all. And I don't think she ever did. She's just Catherine. In fact, she often tells me that I let Catherine get away with too much. She tells me, "She's perfectly capable of doing it herself, Mom." And she's usually right.

The following "negative" emotions are not really negative at all, but are a normal part of childhood and a normal part of the adaptation process—just like when you experienced Surviving and Searching issues. Be patient, optimistic, and observant. When you see one of these reactions in any of your children, you may tend to overreact and to wonder if your child's anger or worry is about to develop into a serious problem that will last into adulthood. Remember, most feelings come and go, and children usually work things out. Your own fears often exaggerate a simple childhood exchange. For example, your typical child, Billy, just hit and screamed, "I hate you" to Susan, your child with special needs. Did that happen because Susan knocked over Billy's Legos? Or was it because Billy resents all of the time you spend taking care of Susan because of her special needs? It's probably a Lego issue, and if *overall* you think Billy and Susan are doing fine together, let them work it out. However, if problems persist, you may want to talk to some other parents or get professional advice. The following are some normal reactions brothers and sisters may have that usually come and go, but could be potential problems if they persist:

- *Anger* that you are not as available to them as you were before; anger toward the child who has taken you away

from them, or anger that they have to give up some of
their own time, freedom or activities

- *Worry* that they may also develop a disability; worry that
  their brother's or sister's problem will become worse; or
  worry that they will be responsible for their sibling's future
- *Fear* that they somehow caused the disability; or fear
  that they will make you unhappy if they don't excel
- *Guilt* for feeling angry or for wishing their brother or
  sister would just disappear
- *Confusion* about what the problem is; or confusion about
  whether everything is going to be okay
- *Anxiety* about sadness, tension, increased activity in the
  home, and your preoccupation with taking care of your
  other child's special needs (Children who are anxious
  don't always know why they are anxious; sometimes they
  show their anxiety in other ways such as bedwetting,
  nervous mannerisms, fear in other areas, withdrawal, or
  behavior problems.)

Children have their own Inner Searching issues, too.
These are not the big "Why" questions of adults, but they
do have questions about why their brother or sister has a
disability. They have to develop their relationships with the
child with special needs as it affects their daily lives. Their
Searching will be more focused on how this turn of events
affects their own relationship with you. They may become
extra clingy; be too good, too compliant, and too unde-
manding; or place high expectations on themselves because
they perceive that you need them to be the outstanding
child and become afraid to fail or let you down. They may
begin to feel that you love them because of their accomplishments, and that failure, or even "averageness," may
result in loss of love.

They may enter a caregiving role and become so "adultified" that it's hard for them—and you—to remember they are still children. They may become "little mothers" to the point where they actually do feel responsible for their brother or sister. It is difficult to know at what point this issue becomes a problem because there are many wonderful aspects to brothers and sisters learning to care for each other, especially when one of the children has extra needs for daily care. This can become a problem when the older sister or brother is deprived of her or his childhood needs.

POSSIBLE REACTIONS OF YOUR CHILD WITH SPECIAL NEEDS

What about the reactions of children with special needs to having brothers and sisters? They may see their younger brothers or sisters surpass them—walking, talking, going to school, going outside to play, and perhaps having more responsibilities and more privileges. Your child with special needs may have reactions to being dependent on a brother or sister for basic self-help skills, such as being fed or for assistance with play.

Your child with special needs may be quite sensitive to your joy and praise of the accomplishments of his brothers and sisters for many things he can't do and may never do. There may be a resulting feeling of shame and of anger toward his brothers and sisters. His own accomplishments may be viewed as small by comparison (either by himself or others), and they may be overlooked or not given as much value or importance. However, your child with special needs may get a lot *more* attention for his efforts than his siblings do because you are much more focused on his development. Finding the right balance can sometimes seem impossible!

Janet: Sometimes it's hard to remember to praise your typical children. We're so used to praising every tiny step of progress with Ryan, that when his sister does something that comes easy for her and I know it would take Ryan 10 times the effort, it's easy to forget that she is just as proud of her effort as he is.

In some families, the child with special needs has "privileged child" status. Because he can't do certain things, he always gets to go first or have the most. He may be so indulged that he develops an attitude of being entitled to special privileges and expects others—even those outside the family—to make exceptions for him and to give him special treatment. This frequently does not go over well with peers or brothers and sisters.

Whenever possible, you need to have the same standards of behavior for all of your children, based on age and ability. Exceptions may not always be seen as "fair" and may need explanation. Some standards, such as respect for personal space and property, need to be the same regardless of age or ability.

Brothers and sisters inspire and motivate each other. Younger children—whether in age or development—observe and want to copy the advanced achievements of their older brothers and sisters. All of your children will learn valuable lessons about human differences—that everyone has things they do faster or slower than other people and that some people have legs that don't work, others have a harder time talking, and others can't see or hear very well. They will be learning that when you can do something another person can't, you can help out and you can find ways to communicate, play, and live together.

Janet: Ryan's sister and brother have always seemed to know to be more careful with Ryan. I've never told them to; they just seem to instinctively know he's not as physically strong.

PARENTING PITFALLS

*I could be a perfect parent . . . if it weren't for
my children.*

No matter how hard you try, how sensitive you are, and
how well intentioned you are, you will find yourself saying
or doing the very thing you know is absolutely wrong (you
and every other parent). Here are a few of the most common pitfalls of parenting:

1. *You may find yourself expecting more from your other
    children because of the time and energy your child with
    special needs requires.* You may want or need them to
    be more self-sufficient, quiet, and patient; to wait longer;
    to spend long hours going to clinics and doctor appoint-
    ments; to not "make waves"; or to figure things out for
    themselves. You may expect them to do better in school,
    sports, or music.
2. *You may indulge your typical children or give in to
    their impulses and demands* to make up for what you
    think they may be missing out on or for expecting so
    much from them. Making up is an impossible task. In
    order to attempt it, you have to keep a "list" of all the
    time, activities, and energy your typical child doesn't
    get and decide which gifts, privileges, and activities have
    equal value. It's mentally exhausting to even contem-
    plate, and the fact is that "list makers" are motivated
    by guilt, so the list never comes out even anyway.
3. *You may try to tell them how to feel*—that they should
    always love their brother or sister and never feel angry.
    They need to have their feelings heard and respected
    without criticism or judgment. Or you may ignore their
    signals of problems because you can't handle any more
    frustrations or disappointments in your children.

4. *You may find yourself repeatedly interrupting the activities* of your other children to take care of your child with special needs, or you may insist they always include the child with a disability in their play or other activities. Be aware if you have a tendency to overdo this. It can create resentment in your typical children that their needs always seem secondary. Or it may make them feel guilty because they feel resentful when they think they should be *willing* to have their needs come in second.

When Extra Help Is Needed

Sometimes your other children may develop problems in areas that may or may not be related to their brother's or sister's problems. Some problems may be in trying too hard to be the "perfect" child, fears of leaving you, extreme persistent resentment or anger, withdrawal, behavior problems at school, or physical complaints. If too much attention is focused on the child with special needs, your other children may feel the only way to get your attention is to become ill or develop a problem that will be sure to get attention.

Many problems you may see in your children may be phases; children go through them. When you are concerned about a problem you see in one of your children, evaluate what is going on in the whole family and what your relationship is like with that child right now.

There are family therapists and child therapists who can help you evaluate the nature and severity of a problem any of your children or your family may be having. And sometimes, but probably not often enough, you may be able to find a sibling support group for your children—or maybe you can help start one.

STRATEGIES FOR SUCCESS

You want, of course, for your other children to be affected in only positive ways: to be generous, tolerant, patient, good-humored, understanding, and loving toward their brother or sister with a disability. And if you, as their most important role model, consistently portray all these traits, perhaps they will, too.

Set the Tone and Stay in Charge

Set the Tone

Your task is to provide a positive, optimistic, happy, loving, stable, and balanced environment in which all of your children can be admired as individuals whether they are smart or not, agile or not, strong and healthy or not. Your children look to you for the important messages: Is this a tragedy or does life go on? Is this a happy family that has fun and laughs together? Are responsibilities shared?

> *Susie:*   Our families are not balanced, and we're always striving to compensate for this. Betsy doesn't get yelled at; Andy does. Andy has chores; Betsy doesn't. But Betsy doesn't have everything Andy does. I hate having to say, "Andy, you have to come with me because of whatever for Betsy." But you know what? In other families kids have to do that, too. We're three people taking care of Betsy, and there's no way around it.

Stay in Charge

Your children need to feel that you have the situation in hand, that they do not need to worry about the disability, their brother or sister, or you. Even if there are problems that don't have answers, your other children need to know that you are looking for answers, and the experts are looking for answers. They need to hear your feelings of concern and worry—but to a limited degree and in a way that they can understand and still feel safe. They do not need to think that Mom or Dad is falling apart (and that they must then take care of you!).

Communicate

Talk to Them

Encourage your children to express their own concerns. Some of the most common needs and feelings brothers and sisters may have are fear (that their brother may die or that they may catch the disability), worry (that there won't be enough money or she won't have any friends), and anger (that she breaks their toys, goes in their rooms, says dumb things in front of their friends). Feelings don't get worse by talking about them. They do get worse if they're "not allowed." There is a tendency to think that we can help brothers and sisters "adjust" by telling them how they feel ("I know you love your brother") or how we wish they would feel ("You shouldn't get mad at him; he can't help it.").

> *Diane:* Never say, "I know how you feel." You probably don't know how they feel.

Listen to Them

When your children express feelings, ask questions, or say something you really don't want them to feel or wonder about, try not to overreact, change the subject, or preach at them. Listening to your kids is listening to a lot of stuff that doesn't seem very important and may not even be very interesting (to you). That kind of listening is the important kind, though. It leads to a sense of trust that you care enough about the person, that you're available and you know how to listen. Listening to the "little" stuff is basic training for the "big stuff."

Give Information

Give your children information they can understand, and encourage them to ask questions. There is often a tendency to tell brothers and sisters too much about the process of medical treatment or about ambiguous diagnoses and of letting them think they are part of the decision-making process regarding their brother or sister. Children often overhear parents talking, fretting, and pondering, and think something awful is about to happen.

There are a number of books written for children about all kinds of disabilities. There are information books and picture books for young children, and junior high and young adult fiction. Check with your children's librarian and in children's bookstores. Many general bookstores also carry children's books and many have new "special needs" collections.

> *Diane:*   Ask the kids what they want to know, and you'll be surprised how little information often needs to be given.

The main thing your children will be reacting to is how you are dealing with them. If your child had a problem from birth, and there was a flurry of activity related to medical crises or a diagnosis or if urgent decisions had to be made, the joy and expectancy your other children had about the new baby was interrupted. You need to decide how much information to give and then give it in a way that will not scare or upset the other children.

> *Stephanie:*   Even though Emma is 2 years older than Teddy, there are a lot of things he can now do more easily or quickly than she can. When something like that comes up I tell him that some things don't come as easy to her, or she needs a little extra time to do something because everybody has a different pace or a different way of learning and doing things. It's not

about what is "better"; it's about differences, not defi-
ciencies.

Reassure Them

There are some things he can't do, and that means he needs
a little extra help. Focus on what he can do and how he can
learn to do other things in new ways. When they ask what
is going to happen and will he ever walk or talk, don't give
false promises and don't lie. Stay optimistic. Say things like,
"No, he won't ever walk. But he will ride—in his own
wheelchair," or "We don't have all the answers yet. Some
answers are hard to find, but we're still looking."

Have Weekly Family Meetings

You can hold weekly family meetings to air complaints,
solve problems, review and assign family responsibilities,
plan family activities, and decide who gets to choose des-
sert for family dinner that week and who needs extra time
or money for the coming week. When you have a child with
special needs who requires extra parenting and that means
extra brothering and sistering, too, then you need to convey
the message that *everyone helps, but everyone gets their
needs met, too.*

PREVENTING PROBLEMS WITH EACH OF YOUR CHILDREN

Like many parents, you may be concerned about whether
your typical children will develop problems because of the
special needs required by their brother or sister. Many of
your concerns probably began when you were feeling confused and overwhelmed—usually during your Surviving time.
As you move forward and feel more self-confident as a parent and have more information about your situation, your
general concerns will lessen. As you adapt and Settle In,

your total family will benefit from your greater feelings of competence and control. Meanwhile, here are a few reminders about what all of your children may be needing from you:

Protect Their Childhoods

All of your children need their own time for friends and activities and for just "hanging out" and being alone. They need their own space for privacy and possessions—even if it's only a drawer or a box in the closet. They need their own time with you for special individual attention. They need to have their time, privacy, and possessions respected.

Give Them Some Control Over Their Own Lives

Give them freedom from feeling in charge of raising themselves or their brother or sister who has a disability. Balance family responsibilities. In any family, there are chores to be done. Every family is different. In some, the kids don't do any chores; in others, all of the chores are divided equally. A common complaint heard from brothers and sisters is: "She never has to help; I have to pick up her toys." Include the child with special needs in appropriate ways and talk to your other children about it.

> Janet: Ryan, at 10, hated to watch his sister play soccer, and I'm sure it's because he's not real athletic and he's not interested. I used to take him along to soccer practice because I just didn't think about it and one day he said, "Hey, how about you drop me off at the library (it was right across the street) and pick me up when it's over." I was so proud of him for solving the problem instead of just complaining, and he was proud of himself.

Remember that All of Your Children Have Special Needs

All of your children have special needs. Be available and make sure they have individual time with each of you and know you are there for the "little" things. Keep in touch with their lives, interests, feelings, and activities. They need more than the leftovers of you.

> *Susie:* I said to Andy, "Do you know how easy so much comes to you?" He had had a frustrating day with his tennis lesson. It was on the tip of my tongue to say, "Look at Betsy. She can't even hold a racket," but thank goodness I didn't say a word about her.

BUILDING BETTER RELATIONSHIPS AMONG BROTHERS AND SISTERS

Raising children involves a lot more than just preventing problems! You want your children to develop positive, caring relationships with each other. To increase your chances of success, you want to model the traits that you want them to imitate. Treat them each with respect for their individual needs and also demonstrate ways they can work together. A few suggestions for involving your typical children with your child with special needs are given below. The ideas need to be modified in ways appropriate to the ages and needs of all of your children.

> *Stephanie:* Kids seem to develop a sense of what others can do and can't and accommodate each other in a very natural way.

Planned Playtime

Brother–sister relationships develop through giving and taking, working and playing, and fighting and making up.

In typical families, playing together can be spontaneous; it can stop and start; and it can be mobile. Disputes over toys or rules can be worked out. But when one child has special needs, some interactions can't happen naturally. They may need to be planned for or adapted. If your child has a short attention span, he may want to sit at storytime but gets distracted and disrupts the reading; if your child has a problem holding toys, he may need assistance in being able to play make-believe.

Many times you might like your other children to include your child with special needs in their play, but they aren't in the mood, have homework, or are just "busy." Planned Playtime was developed for a number of families with children with developmental delays who had older brothers and sisters. A specific time of day was selected (around the dinner hour is usually a good time). Each brother and sister selected a 10- to 15-minute time period to play one-to-one with the child with the disability. Their mom set a kitchen timer to measure the time. They could play longer if they wanted. During Planned Playtime, the two children played whatever they wanted, but there was no watching TV, and none of the other kids could interrupt. This was their special time together.

Planned Playtime accomplished several goals. In families with several children, the special time gave the parents a predictable break from supervising some of the children; it gave the child with special needs some concentrated, individual playtime with each brother or sister that seldom happened before; and it gave the typical brothers and sisters a chance to have a successful play experience. The success came from its brevity, its predictability, and the sense of cooperation and fun arranged by the parents.

Scheduled Sitting

Carl was a 10-year-old with autism. He had two older brothers and an older sister. All were in high school and none were at home very much anymore. They considered Carl pretty much of a pain. Carl's dad worked long hours, and his mom was exhausted. She was always trying to get the older kids to help with Carl, but they had basketball and dates, and other places to go. Every week there was tension about who could help take care of Carl.

Scheduled Sitting was created. The parents announced that henceforth a schedule would be made each week. The three siblings would each choose one weeknight to be home. He or she had to be available to help Carl get ready for bed, read to him, and watch TV with him. Each had to sign up for one weekend night a month so the parents could go out. (The more kids you have, the more nights you get to go out.) In return, their mother agreed to not bug them endlessly about helping out and they would not be asked to give up important activities. It worked. The older kids quit complaining, and actually began to enjoy their individual time with Carl; Carl loved the special attention three nights a week; and Mom got a well-deserved break and stopped nagging.

Free Time

All of your children need their own time and the right to decide how they want to use it. They may want to be alone, with friends, with you, or with one or all of their brothers and sisters. They need time to play with each other as they choose, have arguments and resolve them, to just hang out together watching television, rolling on the floor, or coloring a picture. They need to learn each other's pace and establish their own bond without structure or pressure.

> *Diane:* I guess the moral is that everybody's got something. And unless we're an only child, we'll always have some memories of "life isn't fair." Hopefully, somewhere along the way, we give each of our children the experience of being an "only child"—the chance to feel special, to have undivided attention, and to not have to share anything for a few hours.

10

Friends, Relatives, and Other People You Know

You experience so many emotions while you are Surviving that it may be hard to understand how your parents and other family members feel. We all have hopes and expectations about our families, and when we are struggling with a problem, we may find ourselves setting up expectations and discovering that our families are more supportive than we could have imagined or not as available as we would like them to be. In some families, a major event such as the birth of a child with a disability or the diagnosis of a chronic illness will bring out the best. In others, it won't. As you are going through the process of adaptation, it is important to keep the following ideas in mind:

1. Your reactions to your friends and relatives will differ depending on where you are in your adaptation process.
2. Your family and friends will react to your situation in

different ways. Some will be highly supportive and involved, and others may distance themselves. Some of your friendships may change.

3. You may have to be clear about what you need and take the initiative in enlisting the support of your friends and relatives.

YOUR REACTIONS TO FRIENDS AND RELATIVES

When you are feeling the intense emotions of Surviving, friends may not always come around the way you need them on any given day. You may feel extra needy for your family and friends, or you may want to be left alone. You will probably have different moods at different times. For some parents, this may be a lonely or confusing time as they and their friends and family redefine their connections to each other.

While you are in the throes of Searching, you may get impatient with your friends who may not be interested in details of your frustrating experiences with professionals. You may be extra sensitive to any signs of prejudice toward people with disabilities. In your Inner Search you may find yourself criticizing your friends and relatives from your new perspective. You may try to change them or decide to avoid them, and they in turn may see you as "touchy" or "pushy." Although they may be uncomfortable talking about their typical children, you may also find yourself resenting their complaints about a child throwing food off the table.

When you are Settled In, you may feel more competent and more relaxed with your child around friends and relatives. You may find it easier to put your child's needs first and to be more assertive with your relatives, telling them what you need and how they can best help your child. And you may see a new arrangement of friendships. If your child has been in an intervention program and/or you've attended a parent support group, you may find you have a new circle of friends—other parents of children with special needs.

When you are dealing with the issues of Separating, you may find your alliance of friendships changing in another way. If your child has a major behavior, learning, or social problem that makes daily living a non-stop challenge, or if anyone else in your family has problems or is suffering under the strain of care required for your child, the question of out-of-home living may come up. Your family and friends probably have opinions about what you should or shouldn't do. You may find yourself getting advice or comments of concern from others that you may interpret as well meaning, intrusive, or rejecting. Many won't say anything because they respect your ability and your need to make your own decision, and they see their role as supporting you, whatever you decide.

1. *You may feel totally safe and comfortable with your family and friends, knowing they are there for you however you are feeling.*

   Susie: My neighbor may say, "How's Betsy" and I may say, "I can't talk about her today." And then she'll say, "Fine, you know there's a sale at the nursery on those begonias you like?"

2. *You may have a hard time accepting or asking for help from your friends and relatives.* You may not even know what kind of help you need. You may think you're supposed to be able to handle everything on your own. And you know that other people have busy lives, too, and you don't want to add to their responsibilities.

3. *You may feel like you want to protect some of your relatives or friends from what you are dealing with.* Maybe you're concerned about their age or their health,

or they live far away and they would just worry about you.

> *Susie:* My mom would ask, "How's our granddaughter?" "Well, her new teacher is terrific," I would answer and move on to another topic. If I told my mom too much, her concern turned to worry, and I didn't want her to worry. You learn to edit what you tell. The problem, though, is in trying to remember what you told and what you kept back.

4. *You may feel you have "let everyone down."* Maybe your child has a symbolic place in the family—first grandchild or first boy in five generations—or maybe some of your family members have a hard time dealing with the idea that any of *their* relatives should have any kind of "problem." Some families can go to great lengths to deny there is anything wrong or can make you feel like it's your fault and, therefore, your burden.

5. *You may find yourself feeling disappointed and angry at some relatives and friends* who don't rally around and offer you help and support. And you may at times feel resentment toward those who seem to be getting on with their own lives just fine. This is one of those subjects that can make you feel very confused. You don't want other people feeling sorry for you or worrying about you, but you do want them to be interested and concerned. And with some friends and relatives, it's not *what* they say (or don't say) but the *way* that they do it that makes you feel supported or disappointed.

6. *You will have different reactions at different times.* Sometimes your child's special needs are not at all in the foreground, and you don't want to talk about them at all. Other times you may want some advice or a shoulder to lean on. Other times you know you are handling it all very well and feeling quite competent, and you'd like someone to notice and acknowledge that.

7. *You may have a variety of uncomfortable feelings with different friends and relatives.* You may feel embarrassed about your child's behavior or like your parenting is being judged. You may feel defensive, hurt, or angry when a relative says something that is inappropriate—or that you just take the wrong way.

> *Susie:* You know what's sad? Not living close to my family. They don't really know my child. They ask about her all the time, but they don't know her and they don't know me with her. We go back and visit, but it's not the same. You're out of your daily rhythm, your child's out of her environment, and everything is busy. My family, who meant so much to me growing up, are strangers to my child.

8. *You realize you are changing, and your relationships may feel temporarily awkward.* You find you are "growing up" in ways that are new to you and you want to talk about different, sometimes more serious things than you used to. You are in a transition time with your life, and you need time to sort out all your new feelings and expectations about relationships.

POSSIBLE REACTIONS FROM FRIENDS AND RELATIVES

You will have different reactions to your friends and relatives depending on your general stage of adaptation and your mood or needs at a particular time. Your friends and relatives have their own moods and needs, too, and may react to your situation in ways that may please or frustrate you.

1. *Some friends and relatives are supportive, understanding, and nonjudgmental, and are right there to help.* They ask questions and want to know what your course of action is. They don't judge your decisions or

give advice unless you ask for it. They may call to find out how a doctor's visit went or drop by with treats for your other kids. They always seem ready to listen, and they jump in to help when they can.

Susie: Our cousin the physical therapist would come by and visit, and I knew she did little tests when I was out of the room. I didn't like her to visit very much because she might figure something out that I didn't want to know. She knew all along, and I knew she knew, and she knew I knew she knew, and yet she just let me go with it and that was wonderful. And even now I know that she knows a lot more than I know, but we have a wonderful relationship and if I want to explore various parts of the future with her I can, but I don't have to and I choose not to most of the time.

Diane: In the first month after Catherine was born, two of my friends went to the library to look up those unknown words for us—words like *spina bifida* and *hy-*

drocephalus—and then they called the March of Dimes and all of the organizations. They had brochures sent to them and looked through them first to make sure I could handle them.

Janet: One day, my mom called and said, "Starting next Wednesday, Aunt Millie and I are coming over 1 day a week to take care of Ryan, and you're going out." They called themselves *The Wednesday Ladies*. I was so happy just to have someone there that it took several visits for me to even leave. And when I finally went out alone, I didn't know what to do with myself. Finally, I went to a department store and stood there and said, "What do I do now?" I'd leave for an hour and then 2, and each time it got a lot easier. A whole lot easier.

2.   *Some friends and relatives are "background" supporters.* "Background" supporters are friends and relatives you know are there if you need them, but they wait for you to set the pace of contact.

Janet: All I needed to say was "I need . . ." and my family was there.

Stephanie: My mother was so proud of Emma, her first grandchild, and so loving with her that it always made me feel great just to see them together.

3.   *Some friends and relatives are really interested and curious.* Some of your friends and relatives would love to talk about your child's special needs and what you are doing. They may be reluctant to ask you because they are afraid you will think they are "nosy," so they hold back. You, meanwhile, may think they're not saying anything because they aren't interested. These family members and friends may be your greatest untapped resource for understanding and support.

4. *Some friends and relatives are simply uncomfortable.* Some of your friends and relatives don't seem to know what to say to you or how to interact with your child. They may treat your child as if she were ill or fragile; they may not know how to talk to your child. They may be afraid they will say too much or not say enough. They, too, are interested and curious, but they are also uncomfortable. It may take some time, information, demonstration, and lots of encouragement to get beyond their discomfort, but they, too, want to be your support.

5. *Some people may feel intense grief for you.* Some people you know may be grieving for you. They don't know what to say or do. They may want to comfort you but may be afraid they will break down or seem clumsy. They may stay away because they think that is easier for you or because they just can't deal with their feelings.

6. *Some people seem to feel pity for you.* Some people may assume you feel burdened and that you live in chronic sorrow. They may tend to talk about "these children" and be unable to see beyond your child's disability. One mother tells of hating family gatherings because the "elephant aunts," as she called them, were always there. They'd sit in a corner, watch her child, shake their heads, and go "Tsk, tsk."

7. *Some people may feel uncomfortable because their kids are doing well (or absolutely fantastically), and they aren't sure if it's okay to talk about that.* They may be afraid it will sound like bragging or make you feel bad or envious.

8. *Some people may think you are seeing a bigger problem than really exists.* Some people may say things like, "He'll grow out of it," "She just needs to put on a little weight," "He'll be fine. Einstein didn't talk until he was 5," or "You always did worry too much."

9. *Some people will think you're "in denial" and not doing enough.* They may say things like, "Have you seen any specialists for his behavior problems?", "Do you think she should be eating all that sugar?", and "What does the dentist say about Sally's crooked teeth?"

10. *Some people are intrusive and "should" all over you.* Some people are constantly telling you what you "should" do:

    "You should take him to another doctor" or "You shouldn't listen to what all those doctors tell you."

    "You should let her be more independent" or "You should help her more. I can see that's too hard for her."

    "You shouldn't be so strict. Let him have a little fun" or "He really needs more limits. You let him get away with murder."

11. *Some relatives undermine what you must do for your child.* Suppose your child needs constant structure, lots of rules, and consistency. But Grandpa says, "What harm is there in letting him stay up late, just while we're visiting?" Or, maybe it takes your child 10 minutes to get up the stairs, but he can do it. But Aunt Emily can't stand to see the poor little guy work so hard, so she swoops him up and carries him. Events like these can undermine what you need to do for your child.

12. *Some family relationships are just plain difficult.* Regardless of what you say or don't say, some family relationships are difficult. Some relatives think what they think, and it may make you sad or mad but you probably can't do anything to change them. You may need to be able to say, "That's the way Uncle Harry is," and get on with your life. Maybe your situation will bring everyone closer together, old hurts will be healed, and past injuries will be put to rest. But maybe it won't do any of those things.

13. *Some friendships may change.* Some acquaintances, co-workers, or neighbors may pleasantly surprise you with the depth of their sensitivity and availability. Casual friends may become very close ones as they rally around and provide you with support and caring. Meanwhile, some people you know may grow more distant; some may assume you're not available; some may be afraid of intruding or that you may be feeling bad and may consider them "in the way"; some may not want to be involved in hearing about your problems because it makes them too uncomfortable or depressed; and some may feel guilty because their kids are doing just great. Some friends may drop out of your life because they see that you are changing and they aren't, and the "old" relationship just doesn't exist any more. You may also find that new and deeper friendships develop, and old friendships become alive again.

14. *Some family relationships may change, too.* If you are lucky, the changes will be for the better, but sometimes the changes are for the worse. Some families just can't deal with added stresses. As folk wisdom states, "You can choose your friends but you can't choose your relatives." So, if you can't change your relatives, change how you deal with them.

STRATEGIES FOR SUCCESS

TEN TIPS FOR INVOLVING FRIENDS AND RELATIVES

1. *Be forgiving and patient with your friends and relatives.* Just like you, they're new at this and learning how to deal with this. They may be clumsy, shy, or uncomfortable; they may hurt your feelings with in-

sensitive remarks. Give them the benefit of the doubt; they have to go through their own Surviving and Searching issues, too.

2. *Set the tone.* Your friends and relatives will take their cues from you. If you talk comfortably about your child, have a positive attitude, and a sense of humor, they will sense that you are "okay," and that allows them to feel comfortable with you. Relatives look to you for information, direction, and "show and tell." Don't expect them to understand the problem unless they have adequate information about it. Don't expect them to ask for information. Don't expect them to feel comfortable without some direction.

3. *Put yourself in their places.* What if this had happened to someone else in the family instead of you? What would have helped you to understand and to reach out to them? Many people who see a child with a disability don't know how to act or how to talk to him. Many people assume a child with a disability can't hear or understand or that he will do something "odd" and they won't know how to react.

4. *Take the initiative.* Let them know what is going on and what you need. Friends may not want to intrude, and you may interpret this as disinterest. When friends or relatives ask about your child (or you), you need to decide what and how much you want to tell them. They won't know how to behave without some guidelines.

5. *Give information.* Explain what the problem is, how to act, what it's like for you, and what you are and will be doing about it. Tell them what you need, and what helps. Need special toys or equipment? Tell them. Maybe they know someone who can get it for you wholesale or help build it. Tell them how much

you need an evening out or a weekend away. Give them brochures and newspaper articles. And most of all, help them know your child as a total child and understand your child's needs for special relationships with relatives and friends.

6. *Have a family meeting.* Explain your child's problem, what you have done about it, and what the future holds. If you can't get them all together for a family meeting, send a letter that fills them in. You might be surprised at the size of your support network.

Diane: We had a group meeting at my house—all our family and close friends. We wanted them to know we appreciated everything they did and said and all the ways they tried to help, but to please not treat us any differently and to do the same things. I had Catherine on my lap. The whole room was crying. It was really hard but I wanted them to know we were going to do everything we could, that the doctors told us she'd probably at least be in a wheelchair and maybe walk with braces. I told them, "Don't be afraid to have us over or to come see us or call. Treat her like you do her sister." My dad said, "Don't sell her short." Grandparents can hold out so much hope.

7. *Get them involved.* If you're planning to write a letter to a congressperson, ask them to write one, too. Take them to visit your child's programs and to meet other children with disabilities. Encourage them to donate money or buy raffle tickets for your child's school.

8. *Whenever anyone offers help, accept it.*

9. *Include them on your support team.* Invite them to visit your child's school and other programs to meet and talk with the professionals who are working with your child. As your child's grandparents or other relatives learn directly what your child needs

(and doesn't need), they may be able to take a more active role in helping you in your extra parenting, and they may feel more competent in providing child care. You will also increase the size of your support network as you have more informed, caring people to talk to, to weigh decisions about interventions, to validate your parenting, and to appreciate your child's efforts and progress.

Janet: My sister, Jenny, joined our team in the best possibly way. She was 18, in her first year of college, and ready to leave home, but couldn't afford a place of her own. Ryan was 2. Chris was working days, and I was working nights. There was a crucial hour in between when we didn't have any coverage for Ryan. So, Jenny moved in, helped take care of Ryan, and in the 18 months she was there taught Ryan and us sign language.

10. *Send them notes*—"thank you's" for something nice they've done for you lately, or photos and news about your family. Let them know you appreciate them for thinking of you.

HOLIDAYS AND OTHER HAPPY OCCASIONS

Holidays involve rituals that evoke memories of holidays past. They may be nostalgic memories from childhood; cheerful repetitions of traditional family rituals; or feelings of loneliness, sadness, and loss. Holiday celebrations change their form as friends and relatives move away, grow up, grow old, and die, but many holiday traditions and feelings remain inside of us. You have expectations, and you may have disappointments. Holidays may be anticipated with enthusiasm or dread.

Susie: Our worst get-together was the Memorial Day
          picnic. It was the first outside activity of the year. Betsy
          was exposed on a grand scale as she disrupted the play
          of her cousins, grabbing handfuls of potato salad, and
          continually wandered off. I can't say it really bothered
          anyone else, but I sure didn't have a good time.

There are other occasions that mark the beginnings and
endings of expected paths through life. They may include
graduations, first communions, bar mitzvahs, and mar-
riages. They can also be reminders of important rituals that
you and your child may never experience. They can bring
a rush of feelings to the surface that you thought you were
already done with. The feelings may be fleeting, but they
may punch you in the stomach as they rush by.

For many parents, birthdays are the hardest; they're
markers for how far their child has come—or hasn't. The
third birthday is one of the hardest of all. If your child isn't
walking or talking, and she's in a stroller in diapers, and
you can say, "She's 2," well, no one thinks twice about that.
But turning 3 is a whole different matter. "What, she's still
in diapers?" Three is no longer a toddler; at 3 she's a child,
and expectations change. One father said, "For years I felt
sad after my child's birthday. The birthday itself was a joy-
ous occasion. We made another year. We'd gone so much
farther than the year before . . . but the next day was hard.
It was a reminder of where we weren't."

For most children, birthdays are cake, ice cream, bal-
loons, presents. For many parents, birthdays are milestones
on their journey through parenthood—a marking post of
growth and progress.

Janet: When Ryan was 1 year old, we were so ecstatic. We
          didn't think he would still be alive. So I invited a
          hundred people and made lasagne for everyone. He
          was still sick, and it was still touch and go, but this first
          birthday was definitely going to be celebrated!

VISITING FRIENDS AND RELATIVES

When you have a child who has physical, cognitive, or emotional limitations, the feelings you have about holidays and other occasions may be exaggerated when you go to visit relatives or friends. The most important thing you can do to have the best time possible and to prevent problems is to Be Prepared.

Anticipate and Make a Plan

Take the time to think through any possible problems and make a plan so that you will have as much control and as many choices as possible. And ask yourself: What's the worst thing that can possibly happen? How will I deal with it? And what's at stake if I don't handle it perfectly?

Where Is the Event?

Consider where the event is being held. You need to prepare differently for a quiet weekend at your parents' house than you do to stay in a hotel. If you're going home for the holidays and it's always been assumed you'll stay at your sister's but it's getting uncomfortable for your family or hers, maybe it's time to break tradition and stay somewhere else. If relatives are coming to stay with you, you need to think about what part of your family schedule needs to be maintained and how you can incorporate visitors into your daily living.

What Is Going To Be Happening?

A quiet, unscheduled weekend visiting family can be a relaxing change from your usual routine. If you are visiting for a holiday celebration, there may be more people, looser schedules, and a lot of excitement and stimulation. Any of these may affect your child's need for a familiar routine, and your anxiety level may rise if you have extra concerns about your child's ability to cope or about the reactions of others.

If the occasion involves a large, tightly scheduled event such as a wedding or a funeral, you must consider your child's needs and ability to handle situations like sitting quietly through a long ceremony, meeting many people, and having his schedule thrown off.

How Will You Get There?

How are you going to get to the event? If you are driving, you can make rest stops as needed, and your child can have easy access to snacks. If she acts up, you don't have to worry about other people's reactions. You can probably carry a lot more equipment, toys, and changes of clothing. If you need to fly or take a train, your options are much more limited, and you may have to plan much more carefully.

What Will You Need at the Other End?

Will you need equipment for your child that needs to be borrowed or rented? Will you need to know about medical resources, such as a physician or hospital emergency room? Will you need to have prescription medications refilled? Do you need a hotel room with a refrigerator for special foods or medications? If you travel frequently, keep a checklist handy.

How Long Will You Stay?

Depending on your child's (and your own) special needs when you are visiting relatives, you need to consider the expected plans people have for you and what is realistic. You may need to go early to let your child get settled in, or go late to increase the chances that you will be able to stay later.

Sometimes during an extended visit, everyone needs a break, so you may want to plan a side trip or suggest some different combinations of relationships for a day. For example, if everyone is together all of the time, you might want an afternoon at the mall with your brother or to go bike riding with your dad.

Prepare Yourself

If you will be with any relatives who you know will probably say something that will send you into a tailspin, you need to decide if this is the time to deal with them. If your tendency is to get defensive, hurt, or angry, plan what you want to say. No matter how prepared you are, something may hit you between the eyes during the event when you least expect it.

> *Susie:* One Father's Day sticks out in my mind. My sister-in-law had a new baby who was 6 months old. Everyone came for a family picnic, and they were all admiring the baby who had already surpassed our child who was over a year old. Bruce was trying to feed Betsy and keep her happy while everyone was playing with the new baby, who was adorable. I wasn't prepared for it and that's when I decided I'd have to say to myself over and over: "You don't know who's going to be there and how you will feel about the other children. Something may set you off." Sometimes nothing happened, but you could never predict.

One mother tells of a Christmas at her parents. Her son, Jimmy, was 5 years old, but his play and social skills were like those of a 2-year-old. Her sister was there with her bright 4-year-old daughter. Grandma gave each child a jigsaw puzzle. Jimmy's puzzle had six big pieces; his cousin's had 50. The mom was crushed. To her, it was a blatant reminder of her child's retardation, and she knew her sister was uncomfortable. She told her mother how she felt and then her mother was crushed—she had spent a whole afternoon choosing puzzles to make sure they would be right for the children's developmental levels.

Can you allow yourself to modify the plans to make the experience more enjoyable and successful for you and for your child? Even if someone gets their feelings hurt? Think about what you learned from previous problems and try not to make the same mistakes again. It may be a lot of extra hassle and you have to consider if it's worth it for everyone. Family events may feel like a test of how well you're doing or how well your child is doing. You are probably your own worst critic and may have super-high expectations.

Protect Your Child

Does your child have problems with behavior or attention span? Does your child get easily overstimulated, frustrated, or tired? Can your child handle an onslaught of well-meaning relatives? You may need to take an aide or hire a cousin, or you and your partner may need to have a plan for who's in charge when. Forget what other people expect or want from your child. You must think of your child's needs first. If your child needs a nap and it's too noisy, make a graceful escape.

> *Susie:*   It's hard with the cousins. They sit and build with blocks or whatever and basically get along. Then Betsy walks into the room and you can feel the tension. The parents say, "Let her play with you," and everyone tries to include her as a regular family member, but she just messes up whatever they're doing. On the other hand, one can argue that those kids are learning about differences, and this is good for them; but it hurts so much.

If possible, try to maintain regular routines as much as possible. This provides a sense of safety and predictability for your child, and it also gives you a sense of control in a setting where you don't have your familiar schedule. It also gives you an excuse for a break from the family happenings, if you need it. It can also serve as a positive way to involve grandparents, cousins, and others by including them in storytime or snacktime.

Bring along some familiar objects for your child. Anything that brings familiarity also brings security. Take toys, a cup, bath toys, books, or a box of cereal so your child will have feelings of home.

THINK POSITIVELY AND PLAN FOR SUCCESS!

As you become more comfortable and more in control,
your reactions change—
even if your relatives don't.
If you want your family and friends to be optimistic,
you have to lead the way
If you want them to see your child as a total child,
you have to be their guide
If you want them to focus on your child's progress,
so must you
And remember, nobody's perfect—
not even your family and friends

11

Working with Professionals

When you are the parent of a child who has special needs, you quickly learn that many of those special needs require the participation of a variety of professionals in your child's life. Depending on the nature of your child's needs, you will meet professionals from a range of disciplines who will advise and guide you about your child's medical, educational, physical, social, and emotional development.

You will have many interesting experiences with professionals along the way. You will learn that professionals aren't perfect, but that most of them are committed to working with you to provide the best possible interventions for your child.

1. Your attitudes toward professionals may change according to your stage of adaptation and your satisfaction and frustration levels in getting services for your child.
2. Finding and evaluating professional help presents some

major challenges, and you will find yourself becoming a "professional parent."

3. Your role as a professional parent in building your professional support team is to advocate for your child, coordinate services, and reduce fragmentation of care.

YOUR REACTIONS TO PROFESSIONALS

When you are dealing with the new emotions of Surviving, you may feel confused and overwhelmed about which professionals to seek, what to ask for, and how to respond to recommendations. You may hold professionals in awe, not questioning their authority or power, and you may assume that they have the ability to heal and make your child's problems go away.

During the Surviving stage, you may be passive and insecure in the presence of many professionals. You may be afraid to disagree, to ask questions, to ask for clarification of answers, and to ask why or why not. You may wait for hours in crowded waiting rooms, let yourself be rushed through appointments, and allow yourself to be judged or talked down to. Sometimes, in your frustrations, you probably get angry and may refuse to ever go back to that professional, but that doesn't lead to a lot of progress. It also puts all of the blame on the professional instead of taking some of the responsibility yourself. However, if you consider your child's problems to be outside the scope of professional care—if you believe he will outgrow it or that other people are exaggerating the need for intervention—you may avoid seeking professional advice or may reject it when given.

When you have a greater sense of control and direction, your Outer Searching may show more focused energy. You become more competent in dealing with "the system" and often want everything it has to offer. You may also be more demanding and assertive and sometimes downright difficult to deal with. You are now aware that professionals of many types are going to be a part of your child's life for a long time, so you know the need for building effective working relationships. You gain a more realistic view of what professionals can and cannot do, and as you Settle In, you become more selective and objective about your relationships with professionals.

When Separating issues are in the foreground for you, there may be a resurgence of your feelings of urgency for finding resources that will encourage independence for your child. By this time, you probably have finely honed skills for working with professionals but you may also carry some feelings of disillusionment. Some old Surviving feelings of fear, helplessness, and anger may resurface.

THE PROFESSIONAL RELATIONSHIPS YOU WANT

The professionals you admire and trust are the ones who sit down, listen to you, make good eye contact, respect your knowledge about your child, see the positives about your child, are willing to admit when they don't know, and are willing to find out about something or send you to someone who knows more. When you are going to have long-term relationships with any professionals, you need to feel that that person knows your child, likes working with your child, is accessible when necessary, and does not take away your hope.

> *Stephanie:* Early intervention programs should be re-
> quired for every family, whether their child has special
> needs or not. They make you feel so good about your
> child and about your parenting. They always stroke
> you.
> *Susie:* But sometimes it was confusing because I'd leave

thinking maybe nothing was wrong with her. I knew
she couldn't walk or talk or do anything.

Janet: They took your child's one strong point and made
it big and made you feel so good about your child.
That kept you together when you got home.

Diane: Every parent should have someone saying, "You're
doing a good job and it's okay to set limits."

Janet: Ryan's first pediatrician was such a grandpa; he
talked right to your eyes. He gave us his home number
and told the nurses, "This lady has a special situation
and when she comes, don't make her wait."

I clung to everything positive he said about Ryan.
He always asked how my husband was doing. "I just
want you to know that when a child like this comes
into a family, you're at a high risk for marriage problems. I don't know if that applies to you, but if it does,
I have some professionals I can recommend." I felt of-
fended at the time, but later on I thought that was
really important.

Diane: All our doctors knew each other and worked together. And they talked about the financial part on a
really practical level. Every time I went for a visit they
found something else wrong with Catherine, and one
day our pediatrician said, "And how's the mom doing?"
He touched my arm, and I just went to pieces. He
closed the door, sat down, and said, "Tell me what it's
like. Help me understand."

Stephanie: The skill of my pediatrician made all the difference in our ability to care for Emma. He directed us to
the best possible program in our area after he had
screened all of them.

Susie: Technicians in the hospital make you feel for the
moment that you have the most wonderful child in the
world. They have a special touch, and you get the
sense they deal with these kids because they really
want to.

Diane: Yes, but first you have to convince a lot of them

that you have the need and the right to be in there.
You have to fight through a lot of people who try to
separate you from your child because it's "policy."
Susie: A lot of the most qualified people are in the public
school programs. The therapists and the teachers have
so much experience with so many kids, and they seem
to be on top of the latest information.

CHALLENGES IN SEEKING PROFESSIONAL HELP

As you find yourself seeking services for your child, you
will experience and hear some pretty amazing stories. You'll
hear everything from the special education administrator
who asked a mother if her child had Down syndrome because of a birth injury, to the orthopedic surgeon who left
a 2-inch rod in a 4-year-old's foot.

Finding Services for Your Child

You may not know what kinds of services exist for your
child. In many areas, services are not coordinated and you
have to seek help one program at a time. If you are in a
program now or have contact with even one professional—
your child's teacher or your pediatrician—ask what other
interventions may benefit your child and whom you could
call. Ask for names of other parents with similar issues you
can talk to. You may need to make a lot of telephone calls.
Try not to get discouraged.

Dealing with the Expenses

Professional services, equipment, and other needed interventions can be extremely expensive. Insurance policies have

become increasingly restrictive, if you have insurance at all. There are publicly funded programs and community service organizations that may sponsor activities, but there are many therapies, equipment, program fees, and other financial issues, such as transportation and child care, that can make your expenses high.

Choosing Which Professionals You See

You may not always be able to control whom you see for professional help. Depending on where you live and what kind of insurance you have, you may have few choices of physicians, school programs, or speech-language therapists. You may live in a large urban area where you are able to choose from a variety of resources and that may bring up a whole other set of problems.

Educating the Professionals

You may need to educate the professionals you work with on behalf of your child. When you know you will be working with a specific professional, you may want to give them a written summary of your child's *total* history (not just the particular "special need" that the professional will be working with). Give them a list of other professionals in your child's life.

Finding Time and Energy

Seeking professional help can be time consuming and complicated. If you live in a small town with one school, one doctor, and one speech-language therapist and they all are just a mile away, life may be relatively simple (if that's all

your child needs). But many parents have to work their way through a maze of services, spend hours on the telephone trying to find programs, fill out endless forms, and wait in clinics, often feeling that the care they are getting is impersonal.

Insurance issues are extremely complicated. American society is now undergoing major changes in its health care system, and as the changes take place, there will undoubtedly be confusion for a while. You may find that you end up with improved coverage or more limitations than you have now.

EVALUATING PROFESSIONAL SERVICES

There may be times when you have to see a certain professional—regardless of whether you like him or her. But sometimes we don't question the professional care we, or our children, are getting just because it never occurred to us that we have the right to evaluate the service and maybe make some different choices. You have the right—and the responsibility—to ask yourself the following questions:

Is the Intervention Working?

You may not be sure an intervention is working, but you're not sure enough to stop. We are often so used to quick results that it's often hard to keep a program going when you don't see observable gains. You may need closer contact with the professional so that you can really understand the goals and procedures.

Do the Professionals Support You and Your Child?

Some professionals do not seem to take a really personal interest in the parents and/or the child. Parents want support, caring, and patience from professionals and are consistently surprised, angry, and saddened when they are rushed through evaluations and appointments. Some professionals only see the part of your child they are trained to remediate. Sometimes that's good enough because your primary goal with some professionals is to focus on one problem area, and you will get support and caring somewhere else.

> *Janet:*   I took Ryan in for a 3-minute check for one of his problems. We waited 3 hours and 17 minutes. It's a whole hour drive from home, and I had to take him out of school to go there. I had both babies with me as well. Finally the doctor came in and I said, "Do you know how long I've waited?" I got another one of those famous lines, "No, how long? We're really busy."
> "Well so am I," I countered. "I was here on time,

and the receptionist was rude." (I decided that as long as I had the floor I might as well throw it all in.)

"Well, you have to understand we never know how long a case is going to take."

I said, "You're talking to the wrong person."

He said he was sorry. I'm sure he's not going to change, and nothing was accomplished. But what are my choices? It's a special problem and a special clinic, and sometimes you don't have a choice.

Are the Professionals Too Pessimistic?

Some professionals take a negative stance regarding the problem and are pessimistic about the future. Many make definite statements about the prognosis: "Your 3-year-old may be able to walk and talk, but of course she'll never be able to get married and hold a job."

Are the Professionals Too Optimistic?

Some professionals are overly optimistic or minimize the problem: "She'll grow out of it; you worry too much." Or, "Surgery will definitely correct her problem."

Are You Overwhelmed by Titles and Information?

You can get overwhelmed by titles and information and recommendations when you see a lot of professionals. We often expect a magical healing ability, especially from those in the medical field. They have the power (or so we believe) to heal, cure, and fix. The higher we put professionals on pedestals, the farther they fall when we are disappointed at their genuine limitations.

Stephanie: Overall, you learn professionals are human. They're not godlike, and modern medicine does not necessarily work magic.

You will hear conflicting philosophies, and they may all make sense to you. For example, if your child has a hearing impairment, you are likely to hear about different methods for communicating: sign language, total communication, oral communication, aural-oral communication, auditory verbalization, and cued speech. As your child enters the school system, you will hear different philosophies about special education classes: resource centers, integrated classes, mainstreaming, and inclusion. Many people who work with children with special needs theories and methodologies have their own biases about what works best.

You will begin to have to make hard decisions as soon as you begin services for your child. If your child has developmental delays, you must decide if you want him to be in a regular nursery school where he may lag behind his peers in terms of coordination, language, or play skills. However, a regular nursery school may give him the opportunity to observe and play with kids who may motivate him. The ideal may be a mixed class, with lots of kids at different levels; but these may be hard to find. Some parents report that they want different things for their kids at different ages. At some points, they want them to have more specialized and individualized instruction. At other times, inclusion in a "real-world" setting is the priority for the parents and for the child.

Has Your Child Been Tested Enough?

Some professionals get carried away because there are always more tests they can do. You have to set limits, and sometimes they try to make you feel like you're not doing everything. Or they may be unable to talk without using professional jargon, and you may think you'll sound stupid if you ask what the heck they're talking about.

Janet: Ryan was 2 years old, and we were doing great. We went in for a routine, quickie update to a specialist who was following him. The doctor went over him from top to bottom.

"He has micrognathia; we're going to have to work on that jaw to build it up. We don't want him looking unusual. That forehead is jutting out; it may stop, but if it continues in that direction, we may have to sand down those lobes on his head." I had never heard these things before. I knew he had a protruding forehead, but come on!

"His mouth is a mess; those teeth are going to be coming in one on top of the other. His upper palate is too short. We have to get that trach out, but right now it'll come in handy for all the surgeries he's going to need. And we've got to keep an eye on that scoliosis. If it gets real bad, he may develop a hump and maybe be a hunchback."

Well, I came out of there and all I could think was I've got an Elephant Man. He'll have to wear a mask; everyone will laugh at him. And Ryan had heard it all! I don't know how much he understood, but he knew this wasn't a "Look, Mom, no cavities" meeting.

I called Diane and fell apart. She did a number on me like I always did on her. After I had spilled it all out, in her calm voice, she said, "And how soon do they want to do all this?"

That made me laugh. I realized I had let them take control of me. I hadn't been able to ask any questions, or get any other information. I just reacted in a helpless way. That was an important lesson for me—be prepared.

PARENT ASSERTION WITH PROFESSIONALS TEST

Rate how effective you are in the following situations:

3 = Very   2 = Okay sometimes
1 = Need help or practice

_____ 1. Appearing self-confident and comfortable in meetings with professionals

_____ 2. Asking a professional to clarify terms or procedures you do not understand

_____ 3. Telling a professional if you do not agree with a diagnosis or recommendations

_____ 4. Questioning an intervention you think is unnecessary or undesirable

_____ 5. Calling a professional and talking about a question or problem by telephone

_____ 6. Telling a professional you would like a second opinion

_____ 7. Asking professionals for copies of their reports for your files

_____ 8. Letting a professional know when you are pleased with the service

_____ 9. Taking notes while meeting with a professional and feeling comfortable doing so

_____ 10. Remaining calm and keeping your focus when a professional becomes annoyed or impatient with you or is being condescending and not taking you seriously

_____ 11. Negotiating with a professional for reducing or increasing an intervention plan (e.g., therapy visits, treatment costs, wearing braces)

_____ 12. Bringing an advocate with you to a meeting concerning your child

_____13. Handling your irritation or anger toward a professional calmly and assertively

_____14. Asking a professional for more time or a follow-up telephone call if you feel there is unfinished business

_____15. Leaving a meeting and feeling you have effectively requested clear, specific information and have had all your questions and concerns addressed

STRATEGIES FOR SUCCESS

You, the Professional Parent

If you present yourself as informed, decisive, and confident, you are going to find that most professionals take you very seriously and will acknowledge what you already know—that you are the expert about your child. Professionals are consultants to you. You pay them for their knowledge, their experience, and their skills.

You are your child's advocate and the leader of your child's team. You need to know your strengths and your limitations, what situations you can already handle assertively, and where you need to improve.

Your Professional Responsibilities

In the beginning, you naturally look to professionals to diagnose and treat your child and to educate you. As you learn more about your child's special needs—and about your child's total needs, likes, and personality, there is a shift in your relationships with professionals. You become an equal member of your child's team and you are the pivotal person on that team. You know your child best; you know the nature and extent of interventions your child and your family can manage; and you know how much money and insurance are available. Your role is to establish the balance and the limits.

1. *Keep an ongoing file of your child's history with professionals.* Document your contacts with doctors, therapists, and schools. You will be amazed by how many times you will be asked to "fill out your child's medical history." Have copies of everything, and save yourself unnecessary work. Some parents keep everything in a notebook with divided sections; others need a filing cabinet.

2. *Get a medical coordinator.* If your child is going to be seeing a number of medical specialists, select one—perhaps your pediatrician—to serve as medical coordinator. Have copies of all reports and tests sent to this person and keep the doctor up to date on decisions pending or made, problems in getting adequate service, and so forth. Doing this can often facilitate getting to the right person sooner, and many specialists are glad to know there is a physician who is tracking the total medical care of your child.

3. *Document your child's progress and problems at home.* If you have access to a video camera, record vignettes of your child playing, eating, and moving in her own environment. This can be useful for those meetings or evaluations when your child is having an "off" day and simply won't—or can't—show her best skills and behavior.

4. *Remember that decisions about your child are ultimately yours.* You want the best information, you want to know your options, you want to know the opinions

of other parents, of professionals, you want to know the risks as well as any promised benefits.

Susie: It doesn't matter how hysterical you are, how intellectual you are, or how cool you are, you're the parent and if you're conscientious and love your kid, you're the one who knows. You have to be the smartest one. You need to take from everyone you can in learning about your child, but the final, ultimate decisions, have to be yours.

Planning for Appointments and Meetings

Don't just go. Go prepared! Anticipate as many potential problems as you can. Each step you make to plan ahead gives you a greater sense of self confidence and control. Then you are better able to relax and keep your mind open to deal with unexpected problems (e.g., being late because of traffic, being given upsetting information). You want to get the most out of every appointment you have with or on behalf of your child. You want to have your relationships with the professionals be as positive, productive, and equal as possible. Plan ahead.

1. *Know what to expect and not to expect.* Expect professionals to be competent in the specific area in which they are trained, but know that your neurologist may not have been trained in counseling anxious, angry, frightened parents and your child's teacher can't prescribe medications. Don't expect all your professionals to be Marcus Welby, Florence Nightingale, or Mr. Chips.
2. *Whenever possible and appropriate, send information to professionals ahead of time.* Then call the day before your appointment to remind them that you sent it.
3. *Whenever you think you might need it, bring a support person to meetings with you.* It is helpful if your part-

ner or another parent of a child with special needs is there with you. Tell them what role you want them to play. Do you want them to participate and to feel free to ask questions, or do you want them to just be there? Do professionals take more time and answer questions more thoroughly when both parents are there? You decide. Maybe it's strength in numbers; perhaps there are remnants of sexism still at large in our society. It definitely takes the pressure off you to have to remember everything if someone else attends the meeting.

Stephanie: I always feel like we make better decisions when Paul and I both go. Sometimes we hear things differently, or we think of different questions to ask. My husband can't go to everything because of his work schedule, so we've had to learn to choose the most important ones.

Diane: The spina bifida team is so regular, and I see so many doctors that they really treat me with respect. A lot of other professionals we've seen, though, will talk more seriously to your husband. One doctor talked to me like I had the mentality of a goldfish. But now I don't leave the room unless all of my questions are answered. When your husband can't be at any of the meetings, then you also have to ask questions that you know he would ask.

Janet: The more support you bring with you the better. Our speech-language therapist goes with us to our IEPs, and she's made such a difference in how the IEP goes. She cuts through a lot of the jargon for me. Sometimes it all gets thrown out there too fast for me to even interrupt.

4.   *Prepare a list of questions.* Discuss them with your partner, your child's teacher, and whoever may be important in your child's life. If you want to make sure you have time to talk with the professional, let the per-

son doing the scheduling know you need a half hour or whatever. Schedule a double appointment if necessary. You may also want to send the list of questions to the professional ahead of time or leave a message on the answering machine about the topics you will want to cover.

5. *Schedule the first appointment of the day,* especially with physicians, whenever you can. That lessens the probability of getting caught in the inevitable back-up of patients. Call before leaving home to find out if the professional is on schedule or is behind. And if you *ever* have to wait more than 45 minutes, complain. Complain to the professional, not just the office staff. If it's a clinic or institution, complain to the administrator. You have held your end of the agreement for the appointment time, and your unpaid time is as valuable as the professional whom you are paying.

6. *How you look can make a difference.* If you want to be taken seriously, present yourself as competent and in charge. Don't just throw some clothes on; "get dressed."

7. *Plan child care.* If your meeting is one in which your child will be involved, but you also want to talk with the professional privately, ask if any arrangement for brief child care is available at the office. (If you go to a professional regularly where your child is known, this is often possible if you ask ahead of time.) Otherwise, you may need to have both parents go or take a relative or friend to be with your child.

During Your Appointment or Meeting

You don't have to personally like all of the professionals you see with or on behalf or your child, but it doesn't hurt to try—especially if you will be having an ongoing relationship. You attitude will probably be influenced by where you are in your adaptation process, the purpose of the meeting, the attitude of the professionals, and how well prepared you are.

1. *If it looks like you are going to have to wait* in spite of your best preventive efforts, ask how long it will be and then either leave and go for a walk or settle in (if you can't fight it, you might as well make the most of it). Fretting and feeling uptight won't get you in any sooner. You might want to take a Walkman and headset. Update your address book; address Christmas cards; read; or write a letter. If your child will be with you, plan ahead and bring activities for her or for the two of you to play together.

2. *Don't go in with a chip on your shoulder.* Sometimes you may have leftover anger or frustration about other professionals, and you assume you're going to have another bad experience. Leave your anger in the elevator.

3. *Give a quick verbal review of why you're there*, no matter how often a professional sees your child. Ask for clarification of anything you do not understand. Many times, professional jargon is used for convenience and out of habit; often, jargon is not very specific and can be misleading. State your desires and expectations clearly and ask how they might be accomplished. Make sure there is agreement on both sides about goals and plans for follow-up.

4. *Be informed.* Be armed with questions. For example, if a physician wants to put your child on medication, you have the right and the responsibility to find out all you can about it. What's it for? How long will it be necessary—and how do they know? What are side effects, both long- and short-term? How will a medication react with ones he is already taking? What other choices are there?

Ask a lot of questions; don't let anything slide. Don't leave the room unless all of your questions are answered. If your partner won't be at most of the appointments, you have to be the advocate and report back. Take notes. Better yet, take a small, portable tape recorder. But ask permission to use it. Don't assume it's okay.

5. *Ask for written information whenever that might be indicated.* For example, ask for information about your child's problem and community resources (or least the name of someone who can give you more information). If you're inclined toward reading medical research literature, ask the doctor for references or copies of articles if they are available. When dealing with the school system or an agency regarding your rights to services, ask for written copies of laws and guidelines. Ask for parenting articles and books about raising children with special needs. Ask for names of other parents or other professionals who might know more about your needs.

6. *Leave the door open for calling back* with those inevitable questions you will think of as soon as you reach the parking lot or when you review the meeting with your partner or another professional involved in your child's overall care.

7. *Get to know the back-up people in the office*—the nurses and secretaries—by name. If you will be having an ongoing relationship with the professional, it always comes in handy. There are inevitable telephone calls when you have to change your appointment because your child is ill, you have a billing question, or you want to know if the professional is running late today.

After an Appointment or Meeting

You hope you will leave feeling positive, informed, and competent. Even if you didn't handle everything perfectly, don't be too hard on yourself. Nobody's perfect, and that's one reason you need to "leave the door open" to call back with unfinished business. If you forget to "leave the door open," call anyway if you need to.

1. *Send thank you notes* to the professionals who have given you quality time and care. Add a tiny summary of why you had been there for the meeting. They frequently only hear from people with complaints. Tell the professional how helpful the back-up people have been, in getting you into, through, or out of the appointment.

2. *Professionals aren't perfect.* Some are highly competent in their chosen field, but could have used a few more classes in compassion. If you are really unhappy with a professional's style or philosophy, and especially if you need to have an ongoing relationship, shop around. Or, you might consider talking to the professional about it. Most professionals really appreciate feedback about their manner of relating to parents if you present it in a positive, constructive manner or if you write a specific, positive letter.

> *Susie:* Don't you love it when people say,"He's the best. You have to take your child to the best"? Does that mean I have to wait for 2 hours? Maybe some other doctor is going to be the best; let's give him a chance. I weigh a lot of things. I used to sit in one doctor's office for hours on end because he was "the best." If you ask around, you can get some new wonderful doctor. The Best are out there, but they're not always the ones you expected.

YOUR CHILD'S SUPPORT TEAM

If professionals are going to have positive attitudes about you, as parents of a child with special needs, then it is up to you to make sure they have positive experiences with you. You are professionals with your children, and you deserve equal status with all the other professionals who are helping you raise your child. You earn equal status by performing your roles effectively.

Your child may need professional services for a very long time. Some professionals you will see only briefly. Some of the services and professionals will be around for a while, perhaps for a school year. Others, such as your pediatrician, a therapist, or in-home aides, may be around for years.

So much care is fragmented; professionals don't see where you have been, what you have done, or how your child has progressed. New professionals are coming in "in the middle of the movie" and don't know many of the plot developments of your life story.

Fragmented services and a series of care providers can be hard for your child. You want your child to have as much continuity as possible, and it is often difficult because you move on to new programs, new therapists, and new specialists, and there frequently is little or no contact with the ones you have left.

Your child may have a number of caregivers in her life who don't have contact with each other. Whenever possible, arrange occasional team meetings with all of your child's caregivers—therapists, teachers, and babysitters—to reinforce the fact that your child is a total child. It can also help your child to know that her caregivers know each other and are in contact about her.

You are also affected by your child's fragmented care. You get tired of telling your story over and over and of getting your child used to new people and new offices. New professionals don't know what you've been through, how hard you have worked, or how much you loved and honored your child through her many challenges. You may have had disappointments with professionals you saw previously, and you aren't expecting new ones to be much better. Or you may have *loved* the person you saw before and are convinced a new one can't live up to the same standards.

Fragmentation of care and "serial care" is also hard on professionals. Too often, a therapist, teacher, or physician sees a child at a given point in time about a specific problem. By not knowing the child and the parents and by not seeing how things turned out, professionals have a view of only one slice of life. Again, it is like going into a theater in the middle of a movie, watching 10 minutes, walking out, and trying to figure out the entire plot. Professionals who see families only in distress, with no larger context of their life, may eventually assume that most families who have a child with special needs live a large part of their lives in distress.

Most professionals, in every discipline, are devoted and committed to providing the best possible service to your child. And most professionals recognize that you are a necessary member of your child's intervention team because you carry your child's history and you are the expert about your child's abilities, personality, and special needs.

> *Janet:*   Our insurance company knows us so well that our agent has Ryan's picture on her desk.

12

Going out in Public

> *In nature there is no blemish, but the mind*
> *None can be called deform'd but the unkind.*
> Shakespeare

People have all kinds of attitudes about disabilities. Some people think disabilities are tragedies. Others think they are gifts from God. Some think they are a punishment for sins; some believe they are the result of a random twist of fate; and others believe they are meant to be. Some people believe that parents of children with disabilities were chosen because they could handle it; others believe it's a test of faith. Some people think parents who have children with disabilities are exceptionally strong and courageous; others think they are to be pitied. Some people believe that people with disabilities should be totally included in society; others think ramps for people with disabilities are a waste of taxpayer money. Some think people with disabilities should be hidden from view—either taken care of at home forever or sent to institutions. Some believe in mainstreaming or inclusion and believe that all children should be educated together; others think it will harm the progress of the typical child to have to wait for or slow down for a child with a slower pace of movement or learning.

We live in a confusing, contradictory world. Nobody's perfect, but some kinds of "imperfections" have more (or less) social value than others. Wouldn't it be great if "Nobody's perfect" really meant "Everybody's different—but equal"?

Many people, many attitudes. You are going to meet a lot of them. As you move out into the world with your child, you will often be taken by surprise at the kinds of interactions you will have with strangers.

1. *Strangers will react to your child in different ways.* Some people will be interested, positive, and supportive; others curious, but uncertain what to do or say; and others will be rude and insensitive.
2. *You will react to their reactions differently depending on where you are in the adaptation process* and what your mood is at the time.
3. *You may need specific strategies for dealing with other people who make comments* or react in ways that make you or your child feel uncomfortable.

HOW OTHER PEOPLE MAY REACT TO YOUR CHILD AND YOU

Genuine Interest

Some people you run into out in the world are genuinely interested in your child and/or your situation. Many people are simply nice, sincerely caring folks who want to offer support and encouragement. Others reach out to you because they have or know of a similar situation and are able to empathize with your experience. Some people are fascinated or just plain curious. This is a learning experience for them, and it can be highly rewarding for you and your child, as well as an expansion of knowledge and sensitivity for one more person in the world.

Diane: The last time were were at Disneyland, we sat down to have a frozen banana, and a grandparent couple came over. The woman said, "Do you mind if I ask what your daughter's condition is?" She was so polite, and respectful.

"It's okay," I said. "She has spina bifida."

"I thought so. Our granddaughter has spina bifida. And I was just wondering, is she having problems with her shunt?" She wanted to know about crutches and wheelchairs. As she left, she said, "It's real hard for my daughter, but it's really good to see you guys are out and having fun. Have a good day."

Susie: We were at a really nice restaurant at Yosemite. We took Betsy, and I was so proud of myself for doing it. She never disturbed anyone. She was great. Near the end of the meal, a couple stopped by our table. They were older and sophisticated; he was graying at the temples. They had big smiles and looked like they didn't have a problem in the world. You just knew they had four kids at Yale and that the mother sold real estate and did brain surgery.

The woman leaned over, "We have a child just like yours. Your daughter's doing such a good job. Enjoy your meal." She became my inspiration. And the best part was that she praised Betsy for the good job she was doing.

Looks or Stares

If your child looks "different," people may look (or stare) because they are surprised, impressed, curious, frightened, or rude. People often react to glasses, hearing aids, braces, wheelchairs, unusual facial or bodily features, the way your child talks, or if your child doesn't talk.

Diane: Some people look at us with pity in their eyes. I wish more people would think, "Isn't it terrific that they're out and getting around and not letting their disability keep them from doing things?

Janet: It used to be a lot harder to go places, too, because so many places were inaccessible. Kids today will grow up accepting it as natural, but think what is must be like for older people who grew up during a time when most people with disabilities were institutionalized.

Discomfort or Anxiety

If your child behaves in "inappropriate" ways, many people react. Other people may not know what to do or say when they observe acting-out or aggressive behavior, unusual mannerisms, or unpredictable actions. These behaviors make many people uncomfortable, anxious, or even frightened. Therefore, they may back off, smile nervously, offer polite reassurance, or show distaste or fear.

Susie: It used to disturb me to see kids with mental retardation in the supermarket, and now here I am. I make it a point to take Betsy because it's important she learn how to behave in the market and to have that experience. But I can understand how others feel. A lot of people are afraid of people with mental retardation because sometimes they look a little different or have unpredictable behavior. We're not taught how to deal with that, and we fear what we don't know.

Sharing Their "Solutions"

Some people have the solution to your problem and are eager to give you the benefit of their wisdom, even if you don't ask for it. And some people are just rude and insensitive.

> *Diane:* We were at the beach that has access for wheelchairs enjoying a beautiful day. A man came over and said, "You speak English?" I said, "Yeah . . . ." You have to be careful with strangers at the beach these days.
>
> He said, "Do you know there's a heaven where everybody's perfect, and there's no sorrow?" I looked up at him. "Do we look unhappy here?" He looked at Catherine. "Do you know that in heaven you will be perfect?"
>
> I could have said a lot of things at that point but all I wanted was to end this. So, I said, "You are intruding on our nice day. Goodbye." The man walked away, and Catherine said, "Hey, Mom, you handled that really well." "That jerk must think there's something wrong with you," I said.

YOUR REACTIONS TO THE REACTIONS OF OTHER PEOPLE

Do you let people affect you with their remarks? Do you get angry or let a comment affect your feelings of competence? Do you let people who don't matter in your life make or break your day?

It's hard *not* to react when people say hurtful, insensitive things. Part of it is the surprise factor. The comments and looks you hope to get as a parent are positive, affirming, and uplifting ones, not "What's wrong with your child?" When will society get to the point at which "different" doesn't mean "wrong"?

There was a time when you may have reacted to a person who looked or acted in a way that was not "typical." And so you can probably understand how other people feel, even if their behavior is not acceptable. You probably have good days and bad days about all this; in some situations you may let looks and comments pass right by, and in others you may magnify the slightest comment to feeling totally incompetent.

When you're Surviving, if you're on the downhill curve of an emotional roller coaster, you may allow the looks and remarks of other people to get to you. When you feel vulnerable, you can interpret the slightest remark as a judgment or criticism. If you are in a stage of uncertainty and discomfort about your child's disability, you may feel embarrassed, apologetic, or anxious about dealing with your child and other people.

> *Janet:*   I always planned to be part of a Mommy and Me group. I was really nervous, but I got dressed up, took Ryan, and away we went. The teacher was really nice, and Ryan could transfer a rattle and she used him as an example. But no one could overlook his suction ma-

chine and his trach. The other moms asked a few polite questions, and I said, "Yeah, we had a few problems with his birth." And they complained because
their kids would follow them into the bathroom, and I
would think, "Gee, I'd love my kid to be able to do
that." But it was the looks on their faces that drove me
away. They were uncomfortable looking at Ryan; they
didn't see him, they saw his equipment. I couldn't bear
for him to see them looking at him like that.

When you're in a Searching mode, there may be days
you charge into the world ready to educate every stranger
who glances your way. You may feel like you have to be
the Representative of All Parents of Children with Special
Needs and you must look informed, calm, organized, well
adjusted, brave, strong, happy, and in control of your situation.

Some days, especially when you're feeling Settled In,
none of this is a hassle, and even as you read this you may
think, "What's the big deal?" Then there are those other
days: it's raining, you're late, you're in a bad mood, or your
child is hungry, tired, or sick; the stores are crowded, and
if someone says something, you may get thrown back into
a feeling of vulnerability and defensiveness, if only for a
few moments.

Diane: I was in the store with Catherine after one of her
surgeries and the checker said, right in front of her, in
a really abrupt way, "Why is she wearing that bar between her feet?" It was not a good day to ask, and I
decided to cool her jets. "She's paralyzed," I whis-
pered.

Throughout it all, there are some days you get impatient with other people and you absolutely cannot believe

their ignorance. On other days you are sensitive to their feelings, and on other days you try to change their attitudes. Some days you just don't care. You accept that there are all kinds of people in the world. So you deal with them calmly and matter-of-factly and go about your business.

> *Susie:* I have a shoe store story.
>
> *Janet:* I think everyone has a shoe store story.
>
> *Susie:* Betsy and I are in the shoe store, about to be waited on. "Betsy," I say, "come over here." That's her signal to roll on the floor and laugh. That's fine. I know she's going to do that, so I have to get her in a kind of grip, whispering and singing a little song in her ear, and I get her to move with heels dragging. It's part of the game; that's how we operate.
>
> The salesman stares, "Doesn't she talk?"
>
> "No, she has her own set of problems." I don't care to elaborate, so I say it nicely but firmly so the guy won't ask any more questions. Three years ago I would have told him my whole life history. I felt compelled to tell the whole world. I thought the world cared, but they really don't.

You don't owe everyone an explanation and your mission isn't to change the world. (Well, it may be, but it doesn't have to be your goal every time you go out.) Sometimes you need to say something to protect your child and to make you feel better and in control.

> *Susie:* When Betsy enters a room, a lot of people look uncomfortable and frightened. She's out of the norm; she disrupts the flow. I used to feel like I had to take care of the other people, but eventually I realized that Betsy is my first priority. She's usually uncomfortable and frightened, too, and my goal is to make it the best experience for her.

One mom said that when she's having a hard day, she puts hats and sunglasses on herself and her son. She puts him in his wheelchair and off they go. She says people still stare, but they think they're celebrities.

Strategies for Success

Have a Successful Outing

Assess Your Outing Success

Many parents, especially those of young children (and especially when the parents are still struggling with their own Surviving and Searching issues) can tell some real horror stories about trying to buy a pair of shoes, eat at a restaurant, or go to the zoo.

There are some places you go where you and your child have no problems; others are disasters from the moment you hit the parking lot. If you have a problem managing your child in public places because of behavior problems, reactions to being overtired or overstimulated, access problems, or your own discomfort, try these suggestions for increasing your outing success.

Anticipate and Make a Plan

To increase your success rate, you need to practice. Begin by selecting one troublesome spot you go. Select something easy where you can go for a brief time and leave quickly if you need to.

Your goal for each outing is *success* for your child and for you. So keep it brief and make it fun.

1. *Where are you going?* A local park, a fast-food restaurant, the shoe store?
2. *How long do you have to spend in the car to get there and back?* Allow for your child's attention span, reaction to being restrained in the carseat, behavior in the car, and your level of patience for being in the car and

driving in traffic. If necessary, plan a rest stop and break along the way.

3. *How long will you be there?* Ten minutes? Three hours? The shorter the better when you are practicing "how to behave in public" for your child and "how to react in public" for you.

4. *What are the stimulation factors to consider?* Number of people? Noise level? Music? Bright lights? Movement? Crowding? Will any of these stimulants make your child irritable, nervous, frightened, or hyperactive? How much can *you* handle?

5. *What is the purpose of the outing?* Are you going to a fast-food restaurant to practice eating in public? Or are you going to rent a video, to get a haircut, or to do grocery shopping? The reason for the outing may affect your child's motivation, mood, and cooperation.

6. *Are the place and people new or familiar?* If your child is uncomfortable in new situations, you would handle that with more caution and preparation than going into Sunday School with all of his friends.

7. *How much help do you need?* Are you going somewhere that requires other people to carry, lift, or supervise? Are they people your child is comfortable with and will cooperate with? Are they people you trust?

8. *Is the location accessible for wheelchairs and parking?* Can you park and can you get in where you want to go? And after you get in, are the bathrooms accessible?

9. *Do you have a quick escape plan?* If your child has a problem—if she gets upset, has a tantrum, gets out of control—or if you want to get out of there, have a plan for how you will be able to leave.

> *Diane:*   I always had to make sure Catherine was aware of her surroundings and be careful of things on the ground that might make her slip and fall. If we went to an amusement park, I needed to find out about rules

for wheelchairs and what was expected of us. I always had to be prepared.

Prepare Yourself

Be aware of your state of mind and your ability to handle surprises. You may be surprised by something your child does, by something someone says to you, or by the lack of access where you thought there would be no problem. Stay loose and try to not let anything be too important.

> *Diane:*   A really positive situation was at the Symphonies for Youth. On the brochure, it said, "Special Needs call this number." I said my daughter used a wheelchair. "She can be right in front." "No," I said, "we don't need to be right in front. We have another daughter. But we would like to be on an aisle for the wheelchair." Fine, she got us orchestra seats on the aisle for the whole series. But the last time we went the elevator to the parking garage was broken, so we had to take her out of the wheelchair, carry the wheelchair, and assist her down the stairs. Handicapped parking really makes life easier.

Protect Your Child

As you consider all of the above factors in planning an outing, be sure to take into account your child's mood and state at the time of the outing. All the best advance planning can fail if your child has a bad day. You must be alert to his energy level, attention span, flexibility, attitude toward this outing, tolerance for new situations or people, health, and the time of day. Be aware of your state of mind and body as well.

What To Say to Other People

Somewhere, someday, when you least expect it, someone is going to walk up to you and say, "What's wrong with your child?" Your goal is to have a *choice* about how to handle this. You want to deal with people in a way that shows: 1) your self-respect, 2) your concern for your child's dignity, and 3) your ability to take charge of a situation and either end it or continue it.

The question may make you feel angry, embarrassed, or defensive. Or you may just be aware of hot cheeks, trembling hands, or a few rapid breaths. As soon as you are aware that this might be difficult, take a deep breath. (The more experience you have with dealing with people out in public, the sooner you become aware when you need to take some action.) What are your choices?

You could ignore the person and continue about your business. If that is your choice, pretend you didn't hear or make eye contact, smile, and keep on going.

You could get defensive or angry and say something negative. You can show your tension, anger, or lack of control, but a lot of times you'll regret it later. And why spoil your day by getting angry or defensive? Being rude and insensitive with rude, insensitive people probably does not change their lives, and it wastes your energy.

You could ask a question back. For example, you could ask, "What is it you want to know?"or "Why do you ask?" or "What do you mean?" That opens up the possibility of a continuing conversation, if that's what you want.

You could answer the question and move on:

"His bones are still growing."
"She has spina bifida."
"He was born that way."
"She's small for her age."
"His legs don't work yet."
"She has Down syndrome."

You could give a more detailed response, especially if the person was respectful and you want to encourage that attitude. You might say something like:

"He has cerebral palsy. Do you know what that is?"
"She has a muscle problem, but she's fine. Thank you for
asking."
"He has a hearing impairment. Thanks to him, the whole
neighborhood has learned sign language."

If your child is right there and not invisible (as many
people seem to think children are), you might consider a
response like, "Why don't you ask her?" or "Billy, this
woman is interested in your wheelchair. Would you like to
show her how it works?"

You could keep it light and brief, by saying something
like, "It's a long story . . . ." (No wants to hear someone
else's long story) or "You buying lunch?"

Answers that are brief and positive tend to result in
your leaving the situation feeling competent, in control, and
better able to handle future situations. They also increase
the possibility that the person who asked the question will
learn more sensitivity and respect for people with special
needs and their families.

Many people who ask questions or make comments
about your child are really checking *you* out to see how
you're handling this or to reassure themselves that you are
doing okay. Other people look to you for cues about how
to behave. If you are calm, confident, and matter-of-fact, it
frequently relaxes the situation and often turns it into
something quite positive.

> *Stephanie:* It's really amazing how sometimes a total
> stranger can walk into your life and say something that
> you treasure for the rest of your life.

A TRIP TO THE PLAYGROUND

You take your child to the playground and you see other
parents and their children staring at you and your child.
There are a few types of thoughts you may have.

You may have *negative* thoughts. Perhaps, you'll feel angry or think, "Why can't they mind their own business?" You also might feel embarrassed and uncomfortable and think, "They feel sorry for my child or for me."

Your thoughts may be *neutral*, such as, "They're curious about my child.", "They're surprised; they've never seen a child like Ben." or "They're wondering how I'm feeling."

Or you may have *positive* thoughts, such as, "They think I'm a really together mom. I'm glad I lost those 6 pounds." or "They think Kathy is really cute."

There are a number of possibilities for how you'll behave, too. You may take your child and leave because your negative feelings won or ignore them because you feel uncomfortable and anxious or because they aren't part of your life, and it doesn't really matter what they are thinking.

Other options are to smile and say, "Hello" as you pass by them or to approach them. If you approach, you can do so with a neutral topic (e.g., "Is there a drinking fountain nearby?"), a statement about their children ("Your son is so adorable."), or a statement about your child. If you decide to say something about your child, you may want to focus on the disability since that's what they seem to be staring at (e.g., "Vicky needs exercise for her leg muscles and she loves the park."). Another choice is to approach them with a statement about what you have in common—your children. You could say, "Our kids look about the same age.", or "We love this playground; do you come here a lot?"

In general, it helps to remember:

Be Brief
Be Kind
Be On Your Way

13

Support Groups

HOW THE MOMS MET

Diane: Catherine was 9 months old when we came to the
UCLA Intervention program. I felt so sad and afraid of
what was to come, and I really wanted to meet other
moms in the same situation. The mothers' group was
like therapy for me—I always cried, telling my story,
and had everyone else crying, too. But it got easier
each time. I loved it that all the children had different
disabilities. When I was upset because Catherine had
two surgeries in a month, another mom told about her
son who had six and I thought, "Why am I crying?"

It was so helpful to bring in a problem, like "Do
you all think we should have the third operation?" and
gets lots of different suggestions. Then Ray and I
would weigh them all and decide what to do. We were
worse off than some, but a lot better off than others;
there was always a balance. I learned a lot about the
importance of humor.

Susie: Betsy was 20 months old when we came, and I was
scared to go into that group, but I went because everyone else did. I expected the group to be heavy and se-

rious and was both surprised and relieved to find out they talked about absolutely everything. The main message in that room was that life does go on. I started wearing make-up again. I'd go home from the group and arrange for a babysitter so Bruce and I could go out. I went to the library, just for me—the ultimate extravagance. I started exercising again.

Janet: I came in when Ryan was about 14 months old. I went to the group because I thought it was sort of required. I was expecting lectures and a lot of depressed moms, but it was neither. The group went by the mood of the day. If someone was in a crisis, that's what we dealt with. If Susie needed vegetables cut up for an event she was catering that night, that's what we did. Actually, we were really good at doing both at the same time. There was a lot of goofing off, a lot of tears, some anger, and lots of questions about our lives and our futures with our children. It felt so safe; I got a lot of advice and opinions but I never felt judged.

Stephanie: I joined the group when Emma was 14 months old. I didn't want to go to the mothers' group because I didn't feel I needed to. Emma had a little delay—so far so good, take the future a day at a time. I didn't want to admit my child had a disability. I finally agreed to go to a meeting because another mother didn't want to go alone. I was really daunted by you all at first. You were so cohesive. It was like being the new kid in school. You had all been together for a year and you were so familiar with each other and told outrageous jokes, and I was very prim and proper.

After a couple of meetings I started getting things out of the group that had nothing to do with Emma. I learned so much compassion and respect for the other women and for their children.

Susie: I don't think anyone used the group as intensely as I did.

Stephanie: Susie, nobody does anything as intensely as
you do.

Susie: True. Do you know how I thought I had to carry
this thing around my whole life? I didn't know from
groups. I was never exposed to people with disabilities. Talk about being hit by lightning. After joining
that group I decided that there might be a God because I had honestly believed there would be no help
for me and no place for Betsy.

Two meetings and I was hooked; I wanted to get
every ounce out of them and wouldn't have missed
them for anything. Even with heavy discussions, we always laughed. That's why I'd sit in traffic to get there—
for myself as well as for Betsy.

Diane: You know what I remember when Susie started?
She brought platters of cookies to every meeting—not
a bag of Oreos, but lemon bars and chocolate tempta-
tions. We said, "This lady is not going to fit in. No one
who takes the time to do this is going to fit."

Janet: We could deal with anything as long as we had
lemon bars and Kleenex on the table.

Susie: Part of what the group did was to allow us to develop as women separate from being the mothers of
children with disabilities. When you came into the
group it was with the heavy load of being this child's
mother and not able to express any other part of your
identity, because that took 110% of your energy. And
think how different we were from each other.

Diane: I called it "the handicapped mothers' group."

Stephanie: I called it "the women's group."

Janet: I said I meet with some women from UCLA. I was
impressed with that.

Stephanie: I found it enthralling, listening to other people's stories, hearing about how other people's mar-
riages work. These were women's issues, not just
handicapped child issues.

Susie: I loved the alumni days each month, hearing how

the moms with older kids could sniff out networks and how they reacted when their kids weren't invited to birthday parties, and how they learned to take risks. I loved the thought that a mom would call up a hotel and make a reservation and go away for the night. I thought she must have so much respect for herself to do that.

Ryan stayed in the program for 2 more years in a new class for 3- to 5-year-olds with normal cognitive development who needed to develop communication skills. (Ryan had his tracheostomy until he was 5 and, therefore, had no verbal language.)

Catherine went to a local church nursery school when she turned 3, as the school's first child with a disability. She was walking with braces and crutches.

Betsy left the program at 3 to attend a public special education school in a preschool "noncategorical" class.

Emma went to a community nursery school. At the same time, her brother, Teddy, turned 18 months old and was enrolled as a "typical kid" role model in the toddler program. After a year, he was ready for a community preschool, so Teddy left but Stephanie didn't want to leave, so she stayed for another year as a volunteer.

Stephanie: When I went back and volunteered, it was like coming full circle. From my first reaction of "Oh, those poor things . . ." I had learned to look at people differently. And now I had a detachment I didn't have with Emma or Teddy there. I had actually felt embarrassed when Teddy was there because he could do so much. I was prouder of Emma in a way because of all she was able to do in spite of her disability. But my hope was that this experience would teach Teddy to reach out and feel compassion and respect for people, not like I did when I walked in there the first day.

One of the major symptoms of depression and low self-esteem is feeling alone—not having a sense of social support. But support is different for everyone. There are some people who live very much alone, don't need other people, and avoid social contact whenever possible. Some people need to know there is one person who is there for them—perhaps a spouse, parent, sibling, friend, or therapist. Others like a whole gang of folks around.

Support groups have become very popular as a means for people who are sharing similar struggles to come together and find encouragement for their efforts and acceptance for their problems. Support groups are available for many different issues and may take several different forms.

This chapter is for people who may be new to the idea of going to a support group and for those who are thinking about starting a group and would like some suggestions for how to get organized and begin.

IF YOU THINK YOU WANT TO GO TO A SUPPORT GROUP MEETING . . .

Taking the first step to attend a support group meeting is usually the hardest part of becoming a member. You may assume that everyone else there will be relaxed and comfortable, and you won't know what to do or say. It may help you to know that most parents who go to a support group the first time:

- Have never been to a support group and don't know what to expect
- Are uncomfortable because they may not know anyone else who will be there (or maybe they will know only one person)
- Are confused, saddened, angry, or fearful about their situation

- Are afraid no one else will really understand how they feel

CONCERNS YOU MAY HAVE ABOUT SUPPORT GROUPS

Some parents, especially during their Surviving time, aren't at all sure if going to a group is a good idea.

- You may be afraid you will feel pressured to talk about your private feelings.
- You don't know if you're able to hear the problems and pain of other families.
- You may feel so fragile you are afraid you may appear weak or "crazy."
- You may believe everyone else in the group has "got it together."
- You may feel that going to a group is a reminder you need help, and it's hard for you to ask for help.
- You may be very shy or uncomfortable in a group and may not like being the center of attention.
- You may feel you will be put "on the spot" and have to talk a lot.
- You may be afraid you will break down and cry and feel foolish.
- You may feel that talking about your problems will make them seem worse.
- You may believe that your personal life is nobody else's business, and problems should be kept at home.

SOME PARENTS TRY OUT A GROUP AND DECIDE IT'S NOT FOR THEM

After the first meeting or after a couple of meetings, you may decide not to go back to the group. You may want to seek individual therapy or marital counseling in a setting that feels safer and allows you to focus only on your own issues. Or you may want to attend a group, but this one didn't seem like the right group for you for a variety of reasons—group membership, the focus of the group, or practical issues, such as the day or time of the meeting, transportation, or cost problems, or child care difficulties.

Parents who are in different stages of adaptation from the majority of the group members may not feel that their needs will be met. For example, if you are just Surviving and feeling pretty vulnerable, and you find yourself in a group of parents who have resolved many of those issues and are focusing on Searching or Separating issues, you may feel pretty overwhelmed with their competence and focus. However, you may also see them as fabulous role models and want to soak up their expertise and self-confidence.

Similarly, if you are Searching for whatever connections you can make, and you visit a group of parents who are new Survivors and are feeling generally confused and sad, you may feel like you don't want to deal with some of those issues again right now.

Parents of older children will be dealing with Separating issues, such as emerging puberty, socialization opportunities, and different kinds of behavior problems than parents of preschoolers, who are often awed by the energy and skills of more experienced parents. Sometimes parents of very young children love to hear the "success stories" of parents who are Settled In, who represent the "ideal" of what they hope to achieve if they can just get past their roller coaster of emotions.

But sometimes parents who have a lot of uncertainty and fear about their young child's future can feel overwhelmed and depressed when they hear about new or continuing problems some older children may have. For example, hearing about a lightweight, motorized wheelchair may be met with enthusiasm by parents of older children, but be viewed with terror and despair by parents who are still uncertain about their children's future, but are holding on to hope that their young children will walk.

Sometimes one parent may want to return to the group but the partner cannot attend or chooses not to attend. That can happen; there may be a lot of reasons people don't come back.

How Support Groups Can Help

What you get from a group is others who listen; what you give is listening to others. There's also a wonderful feeling of accomplishment to know that you have made it possible for someone to open themselves up. *A support group is a place to rant and rave and not be judged or told to cheer up.*

Every group is different. Some are busy and move at a fast pace; others are quiet and move at a slower pace. The mood and pace of the group often depend on who's at the meeting, what the agenda is, and the kind of crisis someone is dealing with. There's often a different atmosphere when everyone knows each other or when people are just getting acquainted. A group may even differ from meeting to meeting.

The main benefits you get from belonging to a support group come from being with other people like yourself and struggling through a common hardship together. Being in a support group is:

- Finding noncritical acceptance that is free from the emotions and opinions of close family or friends

- Being in an environment of hope that will give you strength
- Keeping a sense of humor about your life, your situation, and the world
- Discovering that you can feel weak and helpless and not be abandoned or rejected for expressing those feelings
- Being in a room where your problems are put in perspective as you hear the problems of others.
- Talking honestly about your feelings, your hopes, and your fears
- Practicing tolerance and gaining understanding for other parents who may feel bitter, angry, or victimized
- Learning new solutions to your problems by helping solve problems for others
- Sharing resources and identifying the gaps in resources in your community
- Working together to influence existing programs or to develop new ones

When you need something for your child and you never talk to other parents, it's easy to assume you are the only one with that need. When you hear that other parents need afterschool activities or Saturday programs for their child, you can join your efforts by identifying a community need and deciding if you want to take some form of group action.

> *Susie:* A group works because of giving. You have to show your vulnerability and share your feelings, and you have to listen. You have to listen to others and for others. That's the giving. If you only listen for yourself and only think about what you can get from a group, it doesn't work.
>
> *Diane:* One of the advantages of a group is being able to hear a lot of opinions.

Susie: You can pinch off the parts that work for you and put together your own ideas.

How To Be a Good Group Member

1. *Realize that you don't have to like everyone in the group,* and you don't have to share the same philosophy of life. You don't have to have the same level of education or income.
2. *Ask people if they want advice or a suggestion before you give it.* Many people have a tendency, as soon as they hear a problem, to start thinking about how to "fix it." Sometimes people just need to say how they feel and aren't ready to "fix it." And one person's "solution" may not work for someone else.
3. *Understand that people in the group will be in different stages.* For those busy Surviving, remember when you were there (if you aren't there now). Survivors need to feel listened to and understood. They often feel worse when someone says, "Cheer up." Some Searchers may impress you or intimidate you with their energy and exhaustive schedules.
4. *Know that some parents can be very intense and goal-directed.* You may want to criticize or disagree with treatments or services other parents are seeking for their children. But remember, everyone's gotta do what they gotta do. No one has the right to judge for another parent what kind of program or intervention they need to pursue. If there is a question of any abuse, neglect, or malpractice, however, it should be brought up as a question for discussion or with the parent privately after the meeting.
5. *Expect that you may not always get a chance to talk as much as you want.* Sometimes, if you want to talk about a problem or raise an issue, you just have to get

very assertive and announce that you need a few minutes to talk about a problem. If you tend to be a quiet person, you may feel uncomfortable about speaking out at first.

6. *Realize that support groups cannot solve all personal problems,* but sometimes they can help you to recognize what some other problems are and where to get further help. And many problems about your child can't be solved in the group. For instance, if your child has a severe behavior problem, the group leader or other members may be able to offer a few suggestions or offer you support and sympathy, but specific techniques may have to be handled by someone else.

FINDING A SUPPORT GROUP

Many support groups are organized around a specific diagnosis, such as Down syndrome, autism, learning disabilities, or hearing impairments. Others may be organized by age level, such as preschoolers or adolescents. You might want to ask your pediatrician, your child's teacher, or another professional who works with you and your child to help you find a contact person. Your local hospital, through the pediatrics department or the staff social worker, may be able to provide a lead. You may be able to find information through your local chapters of United Way or March of Dimes, or a local family service agency.

HOW TO START A NEW SUPPORT GROUP

If you can't find a group or if you know there are other parents around who would like a group but no one has one organized, you might decide that it's up to you to get the ball rolling. You might begin with an informal meeting with one or two other parents and make some plans for inviting more people. It may take a while to develop something really solid and self-sufficient, but some of the strongest, most successful organizations began with a cup of coffee at someone's kitchen table.

Listed here are some issues to consider. (Don't let them overwhelm you. They're intended to help you organize your efforts.) A few possibilities are given for each. You need to discover what is needed and what will work for your group.

Naming Your Group

Give your new venture an identity! You may want to call it something that identifies the school or program that is sponsoring the group, such as The Main Street Children's Center Mothers' Support Group. You may want to focus on location, such as The West County Parent Support Group. Perhaps your child's age is the key—for example, Support for Parents of Infants with Special Needs. It's a fun challenge to come up with a name that you can make into an acronym, like S'PORT for Support for Parents Of Rude Teenagers.

Group Membership

Some groups are based in programs and serve the parents whose children are enrolled in that particular program. Other groups are based on a problem area or disability—such as Down syndrome.

Your group may be for mothers only, fathers only, couples only, or open to whichever parent combination can come. You may also want to consider opening the group to grandparents, friends of parents of children with special needs, and parents without a child with special needs. One mother got a ride to a meeting with a friend; the group said to the friend, "Come on in for coffee." Three years later, she was still attending.

Group Leadership

Some support groups are organized and led by mental health professionals (e.g., social worker, psychologist, family counselor) who may be paid by a program, the parents who attend, or by several programs pooling their resources. Some groups are entirely organized and run by parents, with mental health professionals serving as occasional guest speakers or consultants.

You may want to assign leadership roles for your group if you need specific tasks done (e.g., chairperson to lead meetings, secretary to take notes and send letters or flyers, treasurer). Some groups rotate the assignments every few months so that everyone shares the work; others find it's easier to change assignments once a year.

Some people in your group will have real leadership talent, while others shy away from formal involvement. And some parents may be dealing with so many stresses in their families that they don't have the time and energy to commit themselves to regular responsibilities.

Many parents report that being actively involved in a group's efforts (e.g., fundraising, outreach), is a welcome distraction from the stresses they have to deal with. Some parents get a feeling of being able to do something productive and a sense of confidence that they might not always have with their child.

Confidentiality

A major concern for members is that they have their privacy respected. You need to decide clearly at the beginning and review for new members as they join what the agreement is about confidentiality. What goes on in a meeting should stay in the room. Members must not be talked about in any identifiable way outside of the group.

Meeting Place

Some groups meet at a program site in a conference room or classroom; some meet at whatever community place they can find that is convenient, free (or cheap), and comfortable (e.g., a school, church, community center). Some groups meet in the homes of members, perhaps rotating for each meeting, depending on child care issues.

Meeting Time

Your target population will help determine the best times to hold meetings. A morning time may be best for parents who are not employed during the day and who have children in a program. This may work especially well for a group whose children all attend the same school or program.

Evening meetings may draw working parents and have an increased chance of attracting fathers. This may be affected by the location of the group; if it is to be held in an area where long driving distances are involved, people may have a more difficult time coming at night. Working parents can sometimes take long lunch hours if meetings can be held in the middle of the day.

Conducting a Meeting

Have name tags if the group is new or if you have new members. The leader of the group will need to be assertive to get the group started. Some groups begin with general announcements from anyone who has information to share about future meetings and other topics of general interest.

Some groups, especially when there is a new member, have each person in turn briefly describe their child with special needs, current issues or questions they are concerned about, and maybe something about themselves and the rest of their family. A lot of important networking occurs during these times as families discover that they share orthopedists or that someone knows someone in another city whose child has a similar disability.

At some meetings, everyone's life may be fairly calm and the discussion may move lightly around the room. At times, one or more families may be in crisis and need to talk a lot and to hear the ideas and support of the group members. Sometimes, everyone is having a crisis and can lean on each other from comfort, reassurance, and reminders that "this, too, shall pass" and meanwhile, "we're all in it together."

Have several boxes of Kleenex available. Some groups like to sit around a table (because it's easy to reach the Kleenex and cookies); others prefer a circle; and some sit on the floor. You may have to adapt to the size of your room and the furniture that's already there.

Group Size

The minimum number of group members is two. The maximum depends on what you want to accomplish in the group and what is comfortable. For example, if the group is meeting for a specific number of sessions with a set goal and the purpose is for each family to have individual attention paid to their issues, then 8–10 people (4–5 families) may be the optimal number. Some groups have dozens of parents; others have three or four people.

Frequency of Meetings

Some groups meet weekly, especially when they are program-based or when they are organized around a particular topic. (For instance, a group that ordinarily meets once a month may decide to hire a professional for four or six weekly meetings to discuss parenting techniques or personal stress reduction or for planning a conference or fundraising activity.)

If weekly meetings are not possible or desired, once a month is often enough for people to remember and to feel like it's an ongoing commitment. It's usually helpful to select a particular day, like the first Monday. Another option may be a morning or evening meeting each month to reach parents who work or have schedule conflicts. And you may want to consider other ideas—perhaps a discussion group on the first Thursday, a "Mom's Night Out" on the third Thursday, a "Dad's Night Out" or a "Couples' Night" on another evening. One toddler intervention program had a Fathers' Group that met monthly on a Saturday morning in the classroom where the children and their dads went through a "typical day" with the teachers and therapists.

Length of Meetings

The length of your meetings may be influenced by the time of day or location. Usually 1½–2 hours is a good length of time. It is important to begin and end on schedule. If you decide to allow a 10-minute "traffic delay" starting time, that's fine; but try not to let it drag out. People will just keep coming later. As for ending, it is often hard to draw a meeting to a close if everyone is involved in an active discussion. Someone must be in charge, and the group must know that is that person's job. You may want to give a 10-minute warning or stop a discussion at a specified time in order to handle any other business or questions that may arise.

Child Care

Will you provide child care during the group meeting? This can be a major obstacle for some parents who may not have access to child care. However, bringing young children or children with complex medical needs out at night may be overly disruptive for the child's sleeping routine. The child care issue is more easily taken care of, of course, if the group meets while children are attending school or a program.

Transportation

Transportation can be a major issue in rural areas where people live far apart and in cities where public transportation must be used. Can you arrange transportation or carpooling? The easiest solution is often to use a van owned by a program if you can get permission and a driver. In many situations like this, however, there are insurance liability issue to be considered. (Nothing is ever simple, it seems sometimes!)

Advertising and Announcements

Depending on the people you want to attract, you may want to make flyers to post in schools or put in parents' mailboxes, or you may get an article published in the local newspaper, do a telephone calling tree, or mail a letter. (Sometimes it's hard to get mailing lists from programs and schools who keep their family names confidential—for good reason—but they may be willing to send flyers home with the children.)

Refreshments

If the group is sponsored by a program with funds, refreshments may be provided for the meetings at no cost to the members. Some groups provide refreshments at the first meeting and then let the group decide. Group members may decide to take turns bringing refreshments (this usually results in the best quality!), or you may ask everyone to contribute a one-time fee or pay each time.

You want refreshments that are easy to handle, eat, and clean up afterwards. If you meet during the day, you might consider a lunch meeting, with people bringing their brown bag lunches. Sometimes people who can't get away from work can take a long lunch hour.

A pot of hot water with instant coffee, tea, and hot chocolate is usually easy if you want hot drinks. For cold drinks, you may want to consider fruit juice, lemonade, or bottled water. These are usually less expensive and more nutritious than colas. Again, each group will be different.

Some groups may see this as their one chance to indulge themselves and want something chocolate every meeting.

Let it be a group decision whenever possible. One of the reasons people like group meetings is to feel nurtured, and what better way to feel cared for than to provide healthy and interesting foods.

Group Format

There are several kinds of group formats. Once you decide you want to start a group, you can mix and match formats according to the interests of the group members and re-sources available.

Fees

You may want to charge a fee to cover the cost of refreshments, to order books for a parent library, to rent video-tapes, to pay for speakers and to provide child care if it is necessary.

Suggested Group Activities

You may want to invite speakers to talk about or lead discussions on a variety of topics. Topics vary according to the interests of the group and the availability of speakers. Some suggestions are listed here:

- Parenting techniques
- Child development and self-esteem
- IEPs and working with the schools
- Legal issues, such as wills and guardianship planning
- Advocacy legislation and public policy
- Experiences of other parents

Other events your support group could hold include:

- Field trips to other programs or the park
- Mom's Day (or Night) Out

- Couples' Night
- Dad's Day (or Night) Out
- Meetings for sisters and brothers or grandparents
- Potluck dinners
- Holiday parties
- Weekend retreats for mothers, fathers, or couples
- Brainstorming sessions about advocacy, legislation or public policy
- Fundraising events

As Your Group Changes

As your group becomes established, some of the membership will change. Children grow older, parents move or go to work, new babies are born, or priorities change and members don't need the group as before. It can be helpful for new members to have occasional visits from alumni who can share the benefit of some of their experiences and give information about resources. Alumni members may want to have their own time to get back together, keep in touch, and maintain that important bond they shared in the group.

Evaluation of Group

You may want to plan a group evaluation once or twice a year to discuss whether the group is "on track" with the current members' needs and interests. Sometimes a group loses its energy and sense of purpose and members may drift away as their needs and priorities change. By setting new goals or adjusting the old ones, a group can redefine its purpose and move forward.

SOME GROUPS NEVER END

Your group may evolve from a support group to a political action group, advocacy group, or outreach group. Or it may remain a support group, perhaps not meeting as often, but as a touchpoint for parents—a holiday potluck dinner or a summer picnic. You may want to accept new members or you may want to limit the group to the people who have shared many intimate feelings and experiences together.

There is no one right way to organize a group. There are lots of right ways, limited only by your time, energy, and creativity and the size of your committee. So whatever you do, get others to help.

A SPECIAL KIND OF FRIENDSHIP

The friendships you develop from support group experiences are forged by a shared openness of feelings as you progress through—and cycle back through—each stage of adaptation together. There is so much identification with the sorrows and the joys that a bond may form that goes beyond the connections you feel with most of your other friends. It is a sense of safety—you have exposed your deepest and most honest feelings and they have been heard and honored. You have not been judged; you have felt the empathy and sympathy of others who know how you feel, and there is an acceptance of your child that transcends the disability. These friends are a reflection of yourself, especially as you would like to be, as they not only truly understand but they have a degree of objectivity for your situation—as you do about theirs—that makes their advice, suggestions, and questions especially valuable and important.

THE MOTHERS' FINAL WORDS

> *Dr. Miller:* If you could go back now, 12 years later, and talk to parents who are just beginning this journey, what would you want to tell them?

Stephanie: I really know how you feel and what you're going through. There's some really hard stuff, and you've got a lot of work ahead.

Susie: And if you work at it, you're not going to just survive. You'll do better than survive.

Stephanie: It's how you survive that makes the difference. And what made that possible was the support. From all the early intervention people and from the other parents we've met. It's knowing everyone is behind you, saying, "You're doing the right thing."

Janet: The most important point I'd make is: If you don't have support, get it. Make it happen. Susie, you didn't have your family close, and even though they were supportive, they were far away and you pulled support from as many people as you could.

Susie: I had my friends here. But they didn't know what to do or what this was like for me. The UCLA program gave me a family, a place to be. Everybody needs a family. Everybody needs to belong, and that's how the four of us came to be. We had a common bond.

Diane: The bond develops when you know someone else is hurting as much as you are, and you don't have to talk about it all the time—you just know it's there.

Stephanie: It takes you out of you and gives you some perspective.

Susie: And it helps you look for the good in yourself, in your child, and in the world. We looked for the good just by the fact that we walked into the group the first time. "Oh, there's a little ray of light; I don't know what it is, but I want to grab on to it."

Epilogue

The Moms and Their Children Today

DIANE AND CATHERINE

During her first 7 years, Catherine was hospitalized 10 times and had 7 surgeries for hip dysplasia and shunt revisions. She was in a full body cast three times for 10 weeks, each time followed by a prone brace from her chest to her feet for 3 months that seemed like forever. She could only lie on her stomach or her back the whole time.

Catherine is 13 years old. She is in the eighth grade in a junior high gifted magnet program and sings in the chorus. She manages the multilevel school quite well with leg braces and uses her wheelchair when we go to an amusement park or a mall. She attended our neighborhood public school for all of her elementary education. The only special education service she used (briefly) was adaptive physical education.

Catherine's paralysis is from the waist down, although she occasionally has some unbalanced sensation in her legs and can move her legs. She is incontinent and is totally independent in managing her hygiene.

She's a typical teenager in almost every way. She needs to be reminded to clean up her room and to allow other family members use of the telephone. Catherine began swimming when she was 3 years old, is now on the swim team at the YMCA, and works out three times a week. Her favorite hobby is flowers. Ever since she was little, we'd go to a market or a mall and while other kids would go searching for toys, she always went to find the flowers. She'll use her allowance to buy fresh flowers or a new plant for her room. She would probably turn her bedroom into a greenhouse if she could.

Sara is 16 and goes to a Humanities high school. She has been an enthusiastic soccer player for 6 years and is an active member of Junior Statesmen of America.

Until a year ago, I worked as a teacher's assistant at the elementary school the girls attended. Ray is still employed at the aircraft company where we first met and has become the avionics manager.

We do a lot together as a family—going to movies and out to dinner. Catherine's disability has not prevented us from living the everyday routine of family life. It is an inconvenience at times—when there is limited access to places we want to go—but I rarely think of her disability as a handicap. The neurosurgeon was right—Catherine is living a normal and fulfilling life.

When Catherine was first born, Ray thought life was going to be really hard, but recently he said it hasn't been so tough. Looking back, I think the hardest part was worrying about the future. I learned not to try to look too far ahead, but to take care of problems along the way. I think I've done really well in providing care for Catherine and for all of us. The reward for me is when I see how my girls are around other people and I hear them talking. They think about how other people feel, treat others with respect and kindness, and are so careful not to hurt other people. The greatest compliment is when my family and others tell me how great they think my girls are.

SUSIE AND BETSY

Three years ago, when Betsy was 11, a wonderful teacher's aide from her school moved in with us to work with Betsy on her self-help skills. Lori was truly an addition to our family; she adored Betsy and devoted incredible energy to helping Betsy reach for new levels of skill. One unexpected bonus of Lori's stay was the friendship she and Andy developed, the kind of relationship he has never been able to have with Betsy. After 18 months, Lori left to move on with her own life, but she has continued to be an active part of our lives and, most importantly, a part of Betsy's life. This was a difficult time for us, because it made us painfully, yet absolutely, aware of the fact that we were no longer equipped, physically or emotionally, to care for Betsy at home.

In August 1991, Betsy moved to a group home where she resides with five other teenagers who have autism. We see her weekly and are able to enjoy her without all of the frustration, guilt, and anger that can drain the family of a child with autism. Betsy has adapted well to her home and her friends; she is developing her own social group in an environment that is geared to the adaptive levels of all of the teenagers who live there.

Our lives continue. Bruce is still involved in the production of television shows, and Andy is preparing for his first year of college, playing his guitar, and composing music. He is well on his way to an independent adult life. Most of my time, talents, and energies are devoted to Absolute Necessities, Inc., a gourmet cookie business I started several years ago. Our speciality is the Logo Cookie—a prod-

uct I invented that involves imprinting cookies with company logos and special messages. It has become a thriving
business in California, and we are now printing and ship-
ping 20 varieties of cookies nationwide. I wish my grandmother were alive to see what I've done. She would have
loved it!

Our lives have not been all sunshine and roses. Having
a child with autism has defined a large part of our lives. We
are different people because of Betsy. As her mother, I can
truly say that I can't imagine what my life would have been
without her. She has pushed me to untold heights of sensitivity, understanding, and accomplishment.

Parts of my personality are fine-tuned because of
Betsy. My intensity has served me well in searching out
and developing programs to get the services Betsy has
needed, and my optimism and tenacity have helped keep
me hanging in there when Betsy made little progress for
many years.

I am Betsy's advocate and will always have to be.
Sometimes, I am drained of the ability to care for any more
people. When I lose that capacity, I have to stop and re-
group because I see the effort Betsy exhibits in controlling
her behavior and then Betsy becomes a lesson to me, instead of a trial.

STEPHANIE AND EMMA ROSE

Emma Rose has experienced considerable delays in most
aspects of her development and has required intervention
in the form of various therapies, medical treatments, and
tutoring. The biggest challenge for us in raising her has been
to maintain our vision of her as a whole child. There is a
fine line between the importance of addressing special needs

and simply allowing a child to develop in her own way and at her own speed.

Emma has needed treatments for a number of physical problems, such as strabismus ("lazy eye"), hearing difficulties, scoliosis, and orthodontic problems. Because she is very short and actually stopped growing for a couple of years, she underwent extensive evaluation for human growth hormone deficiency. Although she was deemed eligible for hormone treatment, we decided to give it more time. Shortly after that, she started growing again.

We enrolled Emma in the UCLA Intervention Program when she was 4 months old, and she continued there until she was 3 years old. Since then, her mainstream education has been augmented by speech-language therapy, sensory integration therapy, equestrian therapy, and tutoring. For most of her primary education, she has attended a Waldorf school, which provides a very nurturing atmosphere and a balanced curriculum designed to educate the whole child. As she gets older, it is becoming more of a struggle for her to keep up with her class academically, particularly in the more abstract fields of study. However, because a Waldorf education also places equal value in subjects like handwork, Eurythmy (a dance form), singing, drama, gardening, and art, all of which she enjoys and does relatively well, Emma is very happy at school. She also enjoys taking ballet lessons and has performed in a community production of *The Nutcracker.* We hope that she will be able to keep up sufficiently to complete eighth grade at Waldorf. Now we need to look ahead and explore the options for her education through high school and beyond.

Emma brings many wonderful qualities to our home life. She has always been a happy, friendly, and easy-going child whose inner strength and gentle ways have endeared her not only to her family but to all who have worked with her over the years. Watching her develop and unfold continues to be a source of great inspiration and satisfaction to us as her parents.

JANET AND RYAN

Nearly 15 years ago I never could have predicted the unbelievable positive turns that have occurred in our lives since Ryan's birth. The struggles have been numerous, mostly for Ryan. By his fifth birthday, he had had pneumonia 24 times and monthly dilations under anesthesia for his tracheostomy. He has had eight other surgeries thus far and another four scheduled (there may be more) for his feet and jaw. He has been hospitalized about 57 times.

As difficult and complicated as our situation was, I knew I desperately wanted to experience the birth of a healthy child. Five years after Ryan was born, this would prove to be the medicine for healing my soul. Today, Ryan has a beautiful 9-year-old sister, Erin, and an adorable brother, Kevin, who is 7. Their addition to our family was the balance we needed.

Ryan's biggest gift in life was having his trachea reconstructed. It allowed him to speak and show us that he had been participating in our world all along. Until this point, the prognosis for Ryan's life was dim at best. Against all odds, he continues to amaze us.

Shortly after the removal of his trach when he was 5 years old, we discovered to our amazement and the astonishment of Ryan's educators that he had taught himself to read. Before long, he was competing in the regular education spelling bees. Today, in eighth grade, his reading and comprehension are at college level.

In 1992, Ryan was diagnosed with attention deficit hyperactivity disorder (ADHD), which helped explain his problems focusing on his work in school and his high level of distractibility. We are currently working with a therapist to help Ryan learn to handle his anger and frustration by talking about it instead of kicking or banging something.

Ryan continues to demonstrate an increasing level of maturity and responsibility. He rides his bike to school every day instead of taking the school bus. He has a keen interest in medicine and computers and hopes he will work in a hospital someday. With the experiences he has had, a hospital environment is, remarkably, like a "second home." He feels totally comfortable and at ease in a medical environment and loves talking to doctors.

In spite of his advanced reading skills, Ryan has a learning disability and was enrolled in a learning disability class in our local public school from first through sixth grade. He was mainstreamed in English and science classes last year. He is now in junior high school and is still in a learning disabilities class. We are working to have Ryan fully included into the regular academic program. He doesn't want to be in a special class anymore. He recognizes his differences and is working through that, and it's hard for him sometimes. The special class is a constant reminder.

Ryan is definitely the "big brother" in the family. Both his sister and brother defer to him and have always been instinctively careful and protective toward him. They seem to know, without anything being said, that Ryan doesn't have their physical strength. They just knew not to jump on him or play rough. Ryan has some speech difficulties, and other people often have problems understanding him, but Erin and Kevin have always understood everything he says. His differences are not a problem for them.

During these years, I am proud to say I resumed my education and have graduated from college. It wasn't easy, but I learned that by taping my classes, I could put on my Walkman and re-listen to the lectures late at night while I was catching up on household chores or while commuting to school. It was hard to get back into school study habits after so many years, but the life experiences I have had in between have enriched my learning. I feel like my education is just beginning. I am taking piano lessons again and am finding more time for my drawing and cartooning. We have had some rough times, but today my life is in balance, and I feel that I have many choices ahead of me.

Ryan has taught Chris and me many things about life and brings more to our family than we can ever express in words. He has heightened our sensitivity to people with disabilities and taught us to take nothing for granted. And he has taught us that nothing is impossible. One important thing I've learned is never to make assumptions about people because you never know what kind of disabilities they may have hidden away inside. Ryan's just happen to be observable. All people deserve a chance at achieving and living among everyone else.

Having a child with special needs certainly can take its toll on a marriage and family, but consistent networking with our family and good friends kept us focused on the important things—that Ryan was alive, that our lives would go on, that there was hope, and that you never forget your child needs to celebrate life in a way as close to normal as possible.

For all those incredible individuals who listened when I needed an ear, who said a prayer during the most critical hours, and who allowed us to lean on them when it seemed hopeless, I thank you profusely.

Now, the journey feels more comfortable than I ever dreamed possible. Participating in this book is my way of returning the favor, and I hope that sharing our experiences will offer the same kind of support to other parents.

Readings
and Resources

This book may be one of many you have read in your search for information, understanding, inspiration, and techniques. Or maybe *Nobody's Perfect* is the first book you have read on the topic of special needs and you would like to read more, but you're not sure what is available or where to look. This section was written to be a guide to finding more information that will be helpful to you.

There are so many books, magazines, newsletters, videotapes, and organizations that it is impossible to try to include them all here. Instead, I have created a brief list to get you started and to recommend some personal favorites. I am sure there are many terrific books; important organizations at local, regional, state, and national levels; and high-quality newsletters, magazines, and other materials I don't know about. I sincerely regret the omission of any resource that should be here.

As you begin your personal resource search, go one step at a time. Try not to get overwhelmed or discouraged. You may want to focus on one or two specific areas and find links from one resource to another. (The bibliographies in each book you read will often lead you to other resources.) Each step you take leads you to several more, and you end up building your own custom-designed resource collection. It may take some time, postage, and telephone calls, and possibly even some dues or subscription fees.

WAYS TO GATHER RESOURCES

Libraries

Whether you are in a small town or a large city, one of your best resources is your library. Call or visit, and tell the librarian what you are looking for. Maybe you want books specifically about your child's condition, magazines about disabilities, personal stories about disabilities, or children's books about special needs. You can look for magazine articles in the Periodical Index, browse the bookshelves, and search the card catalog. If you think your library is "too small," the staff can get books from any library in your state. And most of the library's resources are yours to use for free. There might be a small charge to get interlibrary loan materials.

If you want to explore some of the professional books and journals and you are able to get to a university library, there is a wealth of information waiting for you. You may find information of interest in all kinds of fields—medicine, social work, education, psychology, and others.

Bookstores

There are small, independent booksellers and large chain bookstores. Most bookstores have sections on self-help, child care, and parenting. Barnes & Noble, Bookstar, and B. Dalton Bookseller have special needs sections, and many other bookstores are adding these sections. (If your favorite bookstore doesn't have one, you may want to suggest that they consider one.) If you don't see a book you've heard about, ask the store to order it. Sometimes the smaller, independent bookstores are better able to order books that are hard to find.

Computer On-Line Services

If you have one of the on-line services with your computer and modem, you have access to a rapidly growing network of users who "talk" to each other. It's a great new way to share resources and support through your computer. With a computer modem, you also may be able to have access to your library's card catalog.

Sharing Resources

If you belong to a support group or have regular contact with a group of other parents or professionals, you might suggest that you each buy and donate a book on a rotating basis and keep them in a central place or pass them around. One way to celebrate your child's birthday is to give a book, or money for a book or magazine subscription, to your child's classroom or other program. Stocking a library is often not in the budgets of many programs, and it is a way of sharing resources with other parents and with the staff.

If your child is enrolled in a program, you and other parents may want to consider donating a book (or about $20 for the program to buy a book) to the program when your child graduates or leaves. If each parent gives one book each year, a sizable library can be developed!

If you attend a group and know of other parent or professional groups in your community, you may want to form a committee (one member from each group) to pool your resources of books, magazines, videotapes, and newsletters.

GENERAL RESOURCE GUIDES

Exceptional Parent magazine. Published nine times a year, subscriptions are available from Post Office Box 3000, Department EP, Denville, New York 07834 (1-800-247-8080). Regular features include the Family Support column for parent readers who are looking for other families whose children share similar disabilities; the Family Life column, which focuses on specific family issues; book and media reviews; and feature articles. Each issue includes a specialized feature (e.g., toys, computers, equipment, schools, camps).

Batshaw, M.L., & Perret, Y.P. (1992). *Children with disabilities: A medical primer* (3rd ed.). Baltimore: Paul H. Brookes Publishing Co. A comprehensive guide to a number of specific disabilities and issues that pertain to them.

Moore, C. (1990). *A reader's guide: For parents of children with mental, physical, or emotional disabilities* (3rd ed.). Rockville, MD: Woodbine House. An annotated bibliography of more than 1,000 books, journals, newsletters, and directories.

Pueschel, S.M., Bernier, J.C., & Weideman, L.E. (1988). *The special child: A source book for parents of children with developmental disabilities*. Baltimore: Paul H. Brookes Publishing Co. I describe this book as "Everything you've wanted to know about disabilities (and what to do about them), but didn't know what to ask." Written in a direct, comfortable style for parents and professionals.

Schoenberg, J., & Stichman, J. (1990). *Heart family handbook*. Philadelphia: Hanley and Belfus. Although this book was written as a "complete guide for the entire family of anyone with any heart condition," it offers outstanding suggestions for working with professionals,* for taking care of the needs of everyone in the family, and for coping with the necessary life changes that occur with any major medical problem.

STORIES OF PERSONAL EXPERIENCE

Beisser, A. (1988). *Flying without wings: Personal reflections on loss, disability, and healing.* New York: Bantam. A candid, moving story of a doctor who develops polio and is paralyzed from the neck down. His struggles, his victories, and his reflections on life are inspiring for parents and professionals.

Burke, C., & McDaniel, J. (1993). *A special kind of hero: The star of "Life Goes On" tells his remarkable story.* New York: Doubleday. Inspiring. Times are changing.

Callanan, C.R. (1990). *Since Owen: A parent-to-parent guide for care of the disabled child.* Baltimore: Johns Hopkins University Press. A father's challenges in raising a son with mental retardation resulted in this practical and realistic guide for other parents.

Dorris, M. (1989). *The broken cord: A family's ongoing struggle with fetal alcohol syndrome.* New York: Harper and Row. A moving account of a father's challenges in trying to understand and find help for his adopted son.

Featherstone, H. (1981). *A difference in the family: Living with a disabled child.* New York: Penguin. The author, a parent and a professional, provides a thoughtful and extremely articulate portrayal of the ways families adapt when a child has a disability.

Gaul, G.M. (1993). *Giant steps: The story of one boy's struggle to walk.* New York: St. Martin's Press. This wonderfully written, personal story of raising a son with spina bifida reflects the feelings and experiences of many families.

Kaufman, S.Z. (1988). _Retarded isn't stupid, Mom!_ Baltimore: Paul H. Brookes Publishing Co. The dramatic story of a family growing through the challenges of raising a daughter who has been diagnosed with mental retardation but who is determined to live a life like everybody else.

Krementz, J. (1992). _How it feels to live with a physical disability._ New York: Simon and Schuster. Photos and self-reflections of 12 children, ages 6–16, who have a variety of physical impairments.

Weiss, E. (1989). _Mothers talk about learning disabilities: Personal feelings, practical advice._ New York: Prentice-Hall. A collection of anecdotes and thoughtful reflections by experts.

RAISING A CHILD WITH SPECIAL NEEDS

The resources listed below are a tiny sample of what is available. I have selected more "generic" resources; you may want to search for books related to your child's unique needs. (The list of publishers later in this section may be helpful.)

Atkins, D. (Ed.). (1987). Families and their hearing impaired children. _Volta Review, 89_(5). A comprehensive collection of articles by parents and professionals that describe the experiences of families who include a child with a hearing impairment.

Dickman, I. (1993). _One miracle at a time: Getting help for a child with a disability_ (rev. ed.). New York: Simon and Schuster. A collection of articulate, practical parent responses to a nationwide questionnaire on a range of topics related to raising a child with special needs.

Lindemann, J., & Lindemann, S. (1988). *Growing up proud: A parent's guide to the psychological care of children with disabilities.* New York: Warner Books. A wonderfully positive and practical guide for parents from their child's infancy to adulthood.

Nowicki, S., & Duke, M. (1992). *Helping the child who doesn't fit in.* Atlanta: Peachtree Publishers. An extremely useful guide for teaching children socially appropriate language and nonverbal communication skills such as observing interpersonal distance, touching, and dressing.

Perske, R. (1981). *Hope for families: New directions for parents of persons with retardation or other disabilities.* Nashville: Abingdon Press. Every child with a disability should have their parents read this book and see the drawings by M. Perske.

Taylor, J. (1990). *Helping your hyperactive child: From effective treatments and developing discipline and self-esteem to helping your family adjust.* New York: St. Martin's Press. A well-written, comprehensive and balanced view of the problems faced by the child and the challenges of the whole family.

Thompson, C. E. (1986). *Raising a handicapped child: A helpful guide for parents of the physically disabled.* New York: William Morrow. A well-balanced view of the issues for families written by an experienced, sensitive physician.

Turecki, S. (1989). *The difficult child: Understanding and managing hard-to-raise children.* New York: Bantam. A detailed, highly usable presentation of behavior management techniques for parents.

RAISING ANY CHILD

The books listed below are only a few of the multitude that are available. I have included books that deal with a variety of family issues to let you know some of the choices. You may want to use this list as a map to get you to the right shelves of the library or bookstore; then review these or venture out on your own.

Ames, L., Ilg, F., & Haber, C. (1982). *Your one year old.* New York: Delacorte Press. Followed by *Your two year old, Your three year old, Your four year old, Your five year old, Your six year old, Your eight year old,* and *Your nine year old.* Excellent, reassuring, practical paperbacks that describe the range of "typical" child behavior.

Briggs, D. (1975). *Your child's self-esteem. Step-by-step guidelines for raising a responsible, productive, happy child.* New York: Dolphin/Doubleday. A classic. Warm, readable, positive suggestions.

Clark, F., & Clark, C. (1989). *Hassle-free homework. A six-week plan for parents and children to take the pain out of homework.* New York: Doubleday. A very specific guide for parents of children with learning disabilities and also for "typical" children who can't seem to get their homework done. Includes important issues such as learning styles, motivation, and homework concepts.

Faber, A., & Mazlish, E. (1980). *How to talk so kids will listen and how to listen so kids will talk.* New York: Avon. Also available and highly recommended on audiotape. The techniques work with everyone in your life.

Golant, M., & Golant, S. (1992). *Finding time for fathering.* New York: Fawcett Columbine. An interesting overview of fathers' issues, with many appealing suggestions for increasing the quantity and quality of fathering activities.

Kelly, M., & Parsons, E. (1992). *The mother's almanac revised.* New York: Doubleday. "The most complete book ever written on loving and living with small children. Everything from discipline and independence to cooking, crafts, and other adventures." Hundreds of ideas that can be adapted for children with special needs in learning daily living skills.

Sullivan, S. (1992). *The father's almanac revised.* New York: Doubleday. Hundreds of fun ideas for dads to do with their kids.

Wolf, A. (1991). *Get out of my life, but first could you drive me and Cheryl to the mall? A parent's guide to the new teenager.* New York: The Noonday Press. Optimistic, entertaining, and very practical.

Wyckoff, J., & Unell, B. (1991). *How to discipline your six to twelve year old without losing your mind.* New York: Doubleday. There are a lot of "discipline" books. This one and the following one are positive, easy to read, and deal with specific problems. Also by Wyckoff and Unell, *Discipline without shouting or spanking; Practical solutions to the most common preschool behavior problems.* (1984). New York: Meadowbrook Press. Many terrific examples; an approach that thoroughly respects the child's developmental needs.

PERSONAL GROWTH

Everyone travels a path of personal growth that fits with his or her own needs and interests at a given time. The books I have included are personal choices; they may not be the choices you would make. They are intended to provide starting points for several of the areas described in this book.

Alberti, R., & Emmons, M. (1992). *Your perfect right: A guide to assertive behavior* (6th ed.). San Luis Obispo,

CA: Impact Publishers. The oldest and still one of the best.

Bridges, W. (1980). *Transitions: Making sense of life's changes.* Reading, MA: Addison-Wesley. Brief, powerful, and positive descriptions of the endings, beginnings, and the necessary "neutral zones" that occur when we have life changes.

Burns, D. (1992). *Feeling good: The new mood therapy.* New York: Avon. A best-selling book using cognitive therapy techniques to help you have more control, more choices, and more satisfaction in your life. Good "self-tests" for depression and perfectionism.

Butler, P. (1992). *Self-assertion for women.* New York: HarperCollins. An extremely helpful book that addresses special issues many women have related to setting limits, assertion, and self-esteem in their relationships.

Freeman, A., & DeWolf, R. (1990). *Woulda, coulda, shoulda: Overcoming regrets, mistakes, and missed opportunities.* New York: HarperPerennial. An entertaining, easy-to-read book filled with ways to rethink some of the ways you let guilt control your life.

Kottler, J. (1990). *Private moments, secret selves: Enriching our time alone.* Los Angeles: Jeremy Tarcher. Viewing solitude as a time for renewal and growth.

Kushner, H. (1983). *When bad things happen to good people.* New York: Avon. A rabbi's wisdom on our attempts to answer the *Why* questions of life, based on his personal experience. A classic.

Sanford, L., & Donovan, M. (1984). *Women and self-esteem: Understanding and improving the way we think and feel about ourselves.* New York: Penguin Books. An excellent overview about expectations and roles for women in our society and how to improve self-esteem. A balanced, nonjudgmental view.

Sinetar, M. (1986). *Ordinary people as monks and mystics: Lifestyles for self-discovery.* Mahwah, NJ: Paulist Press. The author's writings about creative adaptation and the roles of solitude and silence in self-discovery have had a major influence in the creation of *Nobody's Perfect.*

Sinetar, M. (1988). *Elegant choices, healing choices: Finding grace and wholeness in everything we choose.* Mahwah, NJ: Paulist Press. Learning how to enhance your personal growth by paying attention to the quality of even the smallest choices you make in your everyday life.

Sinetar, M. (1990). *Living happily ever after: Creating trust, luck, and joy.* New York: Villard Books. Developing your own creative power and self-esteem in your ad aptation to major life crises and change.

PARENTS AS PARTNERS

The books listed here relate to families that may be divided. An increasing number of titles is available every year, and most of them are easily available in bookstores.

Anderson, J. *The single mother's book.* (1990). Atlanta: Peachtree Publishers. Many suggestions and much support for the single parent who has to "do it all."

Cohen, M. (1991). *The joint custody handbook: Creating arrangements that work.* Philadelphia: Running Press. Good, practical advice for preventing and solving problems.

Prilik, P. (1990). *Stepmothering: Another kind of love.* New York: Berkley Books. A caring, common-sense guide to step-family life. This practical, lively, and well-organized book describes the many issues that families must deal with when there is a re-marriage of either (or both) parents. There is a chapter about children with special needs.

Ricci, I. (1980). *Mom's house, Dad's house: Making shared custody work.* New York: Macmillan. An excellent guide to the issues with specific suggestions for making shared custody work (although children with special needs are not addressed).

Scarf, M. (1987). *Intimate partners: Patterns in love and marriage.* New York: Random House. A well-written book about the typical issues couples have in the growth of their relationship.

Tannen, D. (1990). *You just don't understand. Women and men in conversation.* New York: Ballantine Books. An entertaining, easy-to-read book about why men and women sometimes have trouble communicating with each other.

BROTHERS AND SISTERS

A number of books are available in paperback about raising more than one child at a time, and some of them deal with issues around developmental differences in children.

Faber, A., & Mazlish, E. (1987). *Siblings without rivalry. How to help your children live together so you can live too.* New York: W. W. Norton. Practical, humorous suggestions for raising more than one child at a time, and it includes a chapter about children with special needs.

Lobato, D.J. (1990). *Brothers, sisters, and special needs. Information and activities for helping young siblings of children with chronic illnesses and developmental disabilities.* Baltimore: Paul H. Brookes Publishing Co. Includes a thorough review of the professional literature. A major portion of the book describes specific, step-by-step details for planning and carrying out a workshop series for brothers and sisters between 3 and 8 years of age.

Meyer, D., Vadasy, P., & Fewell, R. (1985). *Living with a brother or sister with special needs: A book for sibs.* Seattle: University of Washington Press. Written for children 6–11 years of age, as the result of many workshops with siblings, this guide describes many feelings that are typical and explains different disabilities and interventions.

Powell, T. H., & Gallagher, P. A. (1993). *Brothers and sisters: A special part of exceptional families* (2nd ed.). Baltimore: Paul H. Brookes Publishing Co. This well-organized book summarizes sibling research, explains the unique needs siblings have, and provides excellent descriptions of individual and group counseling and workshops.

Sibling Information Network publishes a quarterly newsletter for $7 a year. It includes articles for parents regarding issues among brothers and sisters, book reviews, upcoming events, and a Sibling Mailbox column. Obtain a subscription by contacting Lisa Glidden, Coordinator; Sibling Information Network; The A. J. Pappanikou Center; 991 Main Street; East Hartford, Connecticut 06108.

FRIENDS AND RELATIVES

Not much is available in this area; the following two books are helpful.

Tada, J. (1987). *Friendship unlimited: How you can help a disabled friend.* Wheaton, IL: Harold Shaw Publisher.

The author, who became quadriplegic as a young adult, offers candid, helpful advice for understanding and reaching out to others who have a disability. Because of the author's personal spiritual ministry, the book has a strong Christian focus.

Wasserman, S. (1990). *The long distance grandmother: How to stay close to distant grandchildren.* Point Roberts, WA: Hartley & Marks. Clever, useful ideas for any "long-distance" relationship with children, with a whole chapter about grandchildren who have special needs.

WORKING WITH PROFESSIONALS

Most of the parenting books listed earlier include good discussions about working with professionals. The following are excellent resource books.

Buscaglia, L. (1983) *The disabled and their parents: A counseling challenge.* Thorofare, NJ: Slack. Written with vitality and respect, this sensitive book balances the points of view of parents, professionals, and people with disabilities.

Cutler, B. C. (1993). *You, your child, and "special" education: A guide to making the system work.* Baltimore: Paul H. Brookes Publishing Co. This dynamic, action-oriented book will tell you what you need to know about your child's educational rights and how to get the school system to meet them.

Leff, P., & Walizer, E. (1992). *Building the healing partnership: Parents, professionals, and children with chronic illnesses and disabilities.* Cambridge, MA: Brookline Books. This is a book for parents and professionals. It is written in a clear, informal style and contains many parent quotes. The authors treat the parent–professional points of view from the time of diagnosis through long-term bonds with sensitivity and respect.

GOING OUT IN PUBLIC: UNDERSTANDING SOCIETY'S ATTITUDES

This is an area that needs more study and understanding; for meaningful program development and inclusion to occur, there must be acceptance in the community. The following books are consciousness-raisers.

Groce, N. (1985). *Everyone here spoke sign language. Hereditary deafness on Martha's Vineyard.* Cambridge, MA: Harvard University Press. An engrossing thought-provoking account of how disabilities are handicaps only if society defines them that way. For more than 200 years, hereditary deafness occurred at such a high rate on Martha's Vineyard that it wasn't considered "deviant." Everyone, hearing and deaf, spoke sign language.

Hatfield, E., & Sprecher, S. (1986). *Mirror, mirror . . . The importance of looks in everyday life.* Albany: SUNY Press. This well-written book helps explain why people have negative or uncomfortable attitudes about people who "look different" and tells many tales of our society's attitudes about beauty, size, aging, and sexuality.

BOOKS FOR CHILDREN ABOUT SPECIAL NEEDS

Many books about many disabilities are being published for children of all ages. Every child is unique, and what "fits" for one child may not work at all for another. Talk to your children's librarian, or visit a children's bookstore. There are some excellent books for and about children with special needs. A very small sample is listed below:

Bernstein, J., & Fireside, B. (1991). *Special parents, special children.* Morton Grove, IL: Albert Whitman & Co. A different kind of book about differences. True stories about children whose parents are "different." Wonderful photos. Informative and sensitive. An excellent book for middle grades and above.

Byars, B. (1970). *The summer of the swans.* New York: Puffin Books. Winner of the Newberry Award. The story of a 14-year-old girl and her relationship with her younger brother, Charlie, who has mental retardation.

Cummings, R., & Fisher, G. (1993). *The survival guide for teenagers with LD* (*learning differences).* Minneapolis: Free Spirit Publishing. A fun, upbeat book that deals with friendships, dating, sex, exercise, school, and learning to be independent. Easy-to-read, inviting format.

Emmert, M. (1989). *I'm the big sister now.* Niles, IL: Albert Whitman & Co. The story of Amy, who has cerebral palsy, as told by her sister Michelle, who was born when Amy was 5 years old. An excellent middle-grade book, with lovely illustrations, that deals with Amy's special needs in a sensitive, compassionate way.

Zelonsky, J. (1991). *I can't always hear you.* Austin, TX: Raintree Steck-Vaughn. A wonderful, middle-grade book about differences and the fact that many kids feel "different" about something.

PUBLISHERS

The publishers listed below specialize in books for professionals and for parents of children with special needs. Some of them only sell through their catalogues; some are available in bookstores. Call or write for their free catalogues, which describe all their books in detail.

Paul H. Brookes Publishing Co.: Post Office Box 10624, Baltimore, MD 21285. Telephone: 1-800-638-3775. An extensive collection of books and some videotapes for family members and service professionals that provide timely and practical information on a range of issues related to children and adults with special needs. Behavior, communication, education, employment, family matters, health, legal rights, medical advances, service delivery, and social opportunities are among the many concerns addressed; books are also available on specific disabilities or conditions. Brookes Publishing has been honored seven times by the President's Committee on Employment of People with Disabilities and twice by the American Library Association (Choice) for its high-quality products.

Cassell Educational Limited: 387 Park Avenue South, 5th Floor, New York, New York 10016 or Artillery House, Artillery Row, London, England SW1P 1RT. Features the "Special Needs in Ordinary Schools" series (available from Paul H. Brookes Publishing Co.). The series is by various authors with titles that include: *Children with Hearing Difficulties, Children with Learning Difficulties, Children with Physical Disabilities, Children with Speech and Language Difficulties,* and *The Visually Handicapped Child in Your Classroom.* Although written for teachers, these books are extremely informative and useful for parents and other professionals.

Research Press: Department G, Post Office Box 9177, Champaign, Illinois 61826. Telephone: 217-352-3273. Books and videotapes in special education, parent training, school psychology, and family counseling.

Singular Publishing Group: 4284 41st Street, San Diego, California 92105. Telephone: 1-800-521-8545. Books and journals about special education, learning disabilities, speech and language pathology, early intervention, rehabilitation, and hearing impairments.

James Stanfield Publishing Company: Drawer G, Post Office Box 41058, Santa Barbara, California 93140. Telephone: 1-800-421-6534. Books, videotapes, and slide programs related to Life Horizons: sex education, social skills, job preparation, and community living skills for adolescents and young adults with learning and developmental disabilities.

Woodbine House Publishers: 5615 Fishers Lane, Rockville, Maryland 20852. Telephone: 1-800-843-7323. The Special Needs Collection features sensitive, informative books for parents about specific conditions such as autism, cerebral palsy, epilepsy, mental retardation, deafness, Tourette syndrome, and visual impairments. Also publishes a new series of publications called Topics in Down Syndrome.

ORGANIZATIONS

There are many organizations for specific diagnoses such as Down syndrome, spina bifida, hearing impairment, and autism, and for general categories of disabilities such as mental retardation, severe disabilities, rare disorders, learning disabilities, and others. Most organizations have a national office, state offices, and local chapters, and most produce informative newsletters and hold annual, and sometimes monthly, meetings. You can find specific information in the resources lists in some of the books mentioned previously, by calling a reference librarian at your local public library, or by asking one of the professionals who works with you and your child.

One excellent resource for finding the organizations you need is the "Annual Directory of National Organizations," which is published in the September issues of *Exceptional Parent* magazine. In addition, the National Information Center for Children and Youth with Disabilities (NICHCY) (Post Office Box 1492, Washington, D.C. 20013; Telephone: 703-893-6061 or 1-800-555-9955) is a federal clearinghouse that provides free information to assist parents, educators, caregivers, advocates, and others in helping children and youth with disabilities to become participating community members.

As examples, here are a few of the national family support groups:

Federation for Children with Special Needs, 95 Berkeley Street, Suite 104, Boston, Massachusetts 02116. Telephone: 617-482-2915. A coalition of parent groups representing children with a variety of disabilities.

National Parent Network on Disabilities, 1600 Prince Street, Suite 115, Alexandria, Virginia 22314. Telephone: 703-684-6763. A coalition of parent organizations and parents that works to influence policy issues concerning the needs of people with disabilities and their families.

Parent to Parent Network, % Betsy Santelli, Beach Center on Families and Disabilities, University of Kansas, Institute for Life Span Studies, 3111 Haworth Hall, Lawrence, Kansas 66045. Telephone: 913-864-7606. State and local chapters that provide one-to-one, parent-to-parent support by matching trained parents to newly referred parents on the basis of their children's disabilities and/or family issues they are encountering or have encountered.

Index

Page numbers followed by "f" indicate figures.